State Violence and Moral Horror

STATE VIOLENCE AND MORAL HORROR

JEREMY ARNOLD

SUNY PRESS

Published by State University of New York Press, Albany

For information, contact State University of New York Press, Albany, NY
www.sunypress.edu

Production, Jenn Bennett
Marketing, Michael Campochiaro

Library of Congress Cataloging-in-Publication Data

Names: Arnold, Jeremy, 1980–
Title: State violence and moral horror / Jeremy Arnold.
Description: Albany : State University of New York Press, 2017. | Includes
    bibliographical references and index.
Identifiers: LCCN 2016051108 (print) | LCCN 2017021167 (ebook) | ISBN
    9781438466774 (e-book) | ISBN 9781438466750 (hardcover : alk. paper)
    | ISBN 9781438466767 (pbk : alk. paper)
Subjects: LCSH: Political violence—Moral and ethical aspects. | State, The—
    Moral and ethical aspects.
Classification: LCC JC328.6 (ebook) | LCC JC328.6 .A76 2017 (print) | DDC
    323/.044—dc23
LC record available at https://lccn.loc.gov/2016051108

10 9 8 7 6 5 4 3 2 1

CONTENTS

ACKNOWLEDGMENTS

THIS BOOK really began some twenty-one years ago in the interdisciplinary humanities program at Cleveland High School in Reseda, California. I want to thank all my teachers there, specifically Richard Coleman, Marty Kravchak, Ray Linn, the late Mike Miller, and Howard Wilf.

My time as an undergraduate at Berkeley was life altering, both in class and with my extended family in and around the HoG: Katy Ansite, Eli Batchelder, Matias Cudich, Katie Feo, Mike Kokorowski, Jeff Neilson, Erin Peacock, John Rauschenberg, Anita Sarrett, Sookoun Song, Jon Stan, and Arjun Varma. A special, genuine debt is owed to Mark Pedretti and Fred Dolan. Mark chastised me for producing work beneath my abilities. After doing better, he told me that if I kept at it, I would be very good someday. I don't know if that is true, but I will never forget the lesson and the encouragement. Fred, in the usually small classes in the Department of Rhetoric at Berkeley, blew me away. He appeared to have read everything and to have something of interest to say about what he had read, and this became a model of what a scholar should be.

I earned my PhD from the Department of Political Science at Johns Hopkins. I cannot imagine a more intellectually diverse, vibrant, supportive, and friendly community of faculty and graduate students across a number of departments. In seminars, epic symposia at Charles Village Pub, and weekly barbecues on Cresmont Avenue, I met some of my best friends and began to think seriously. There are too many names to list, but for their friendship and intelligence I would like to thank in particular Alex Barder, Shlomit Barnea, Adam Culver, Kevin Darrow, Bill Dixon, Tom

Donahue, Christie Ellis, Marc Fishel, Stefanie Fishel, Daniela Ginsburg, Simon Glezos, the late and missed Joshua Gold, Jake Greear, Jairus Grove, Rob Higney, Anatoli Ignatov, Jacqui Ignatov, Suvi Irvine, Alex Lefebvre, Daniel Levine, Jennifer Lin, Noora Lori, Michael McCarthy, Paulina Ochoa, George Oppel, Nobutaka Otobe, Chas Phillips, Luke Plotica, Brighu Singh, Terukazu Morikawa, Mina Suk, Lars Tonder, Joyce Tsai, Ittai Weinryb, Drew Walker, Dylan Weller, and Melanie White.

I need to thank especially Jane Bennett, Jennifer Culbert, William Connolly, Hent de Vries, Richard Flathman, Joel Grossman, and Paola Marratti. What I have learned from each of them cannot be reduced to ideas. Dick was the chair of my dissertation committee, and he remains, even after his recent death, a loud, growling presence in my mind. He is one of the few people to have read a complete draft of this manuscript (despite being ill at the time) and he was, as always, encouraging. Dick, along with my other advisors, Bill Connolly and Jennifer Culbert, are and always will be exemplary.

The University Scholars Programme at the National University of Singapore is happily a very nice place to work. The best part is that I get to talk every day to a diverse group of scholars, from theoretical chemists to biosemioticians, anthropologists, rhetoricians, physicists, and literary critics. Thanks to my colleagues, I always get to feel like a beginner, amazed at what there is to know and reminded of my profound ignorance. In particular, I thank Mark Brantner, Donald Favareau, and Peter Vail for their conversation and friendship.

Thanks to David and Doris Wong, Bennett Wong, and Lynn Sim for all of their love and support during the last several years in Singapore.

I thank my parents, Marci and Gary, and my older brother, Mathew, and younger sister, Jennifer, for, well, everything.

I met my fellow political theorist and wife, Mabel Wong, at Johns Hopkins. For the past twelve years we have helped each other handle dissertations, disease, death, disappointment, and other difficulties. We have had some good times, too. Now, with our son, Isaac, every day brings with it new forms of joy and terror. Neither thanks nor acknowledgment are sufficient, but this is not the place to say more.

INTRODUCTION

LEGITIMACY AND VIOLENCE
IN CONTEMPORARY LIFE
AND POLITICAL THOUGHT

AMID THE PROLIFERATION of already present and emerging catastrophes in the human world and on the Earth we share with other beings, the one to which I feel most compelled to respond is not new at all: the pervasiveness of violence in human life. This has become a pressing issue for me, which is partly a consequence of the usually imperceptible—because so assimilated to the everyday—fact that over the past twelve years or so my country, the United States, has been constantly at war in various parts of the world. Of course, depending on how one defines *war*, the United States has been at war almost constantly for (at least) the past seventy years. But it is not just the United States. I was born in 1980, and in just my lifetime numerous genocides have taken or are taking place in Rwanda and Sudan and in the Balkans and in El Salvador and the Congo; Iraq and Iran engaged in a horrific, deadly war; Israel has been a cause and focal point of regional violence; Syria is not only undergoing a civil war but also apparently seeking to destabilize Lebanon (again); and the list could continue. The presence of violence in our world and our lives is undeniable.

But war is only the most visible manifestation of violence. Nation-states maintain their internal security through legal systems that entrench violence within the homeland. Consistent police brutalization within minority communities; a deeply racialized judicial system, including the uneven (to say the least) use of a (morally dubious) death penalty; the passage of the USA PATRIOT Act and various suspensions of constitutional guarantees and rights; and the extreme violence of jails are features not only of the United States but of many of the "advanced developed" countries of the world (to be sure, not all of these features apply in each country). Then, of course, there are the acts that the legal system aims to prevent and prosecute, violent acts that for Americans seems so peculiarly American, including recent events in Colorado, Texas, and Virginia as well as the long and continuing history of racial, gender, sexual, and other forms of violence.

It is a disturbing realization that we live our lives as we do, as we can, not only amid violence but from it and thanks to it. Of the many conditions of human existence that form our background or lifeworld, perhaps no condition is so invisibly present as violence. Yet few conditions of human life are so potentially damaging to our conception of the human being—of its autonomy, capacity for morality, rationality, prudence, and so on—as violence. For this reason, among others, we hide violence in various ways, physically and intellectually, by confining violence to specific demarcated spaces (even if they never can contain that violence) and by justifying violent acts by calling them legitimate. Many of us may be able to accept that we cannot contain violence or keep it away from us completely. But how many of us would be able or willing to accept that there is no morally justified violence, that is, that all the acts of violence that sustain our lives in common are immoral, unjust, wrong? What would it entail for our lives and politics to accept, if it is indeed the case, that all of our violence, the violence that sustains our modes of being-in-the-world, is unjustifiable? Would it require us to stop that violence? If not, then on what grounds might such violence continue?

These brief comments, claims, and questions form the context and the ethical, political, and personal impulse or motivation for this book. This context has pushed me to articulate a critical theoretical response to that violence, one that can provide a starting point for challenging and hopefully reducing the amount of violence in human life. However, what concerns me most is the violence of the state, for it is the state that claims, more than any other entity or individual, and more exclusively, that its violence is legitimate, morally justified, distinct from the violence of (almost) all nonstate actors.

I argue in this book that there is no possible moral justification for a specific subset of violent acts: state violence. I offer an account of the condition that follows from accepting such an impossibility of justification: what I call moral horror. I, too, live my life on the bodies of those attacked by violence, specifically state violence. I can no longer accept that such actions are justified, even if I can barely imagine how I could lead my life as I do without them.

I return to the argument in a moment. But I would like to linger on the context of the argument to convey my sense of why I am arguing for what must surely seem to many a bizarre, at best counterintuitive claim, my own "strange doctrine" opposite to but just as unbelievable as Locke's. I have intellectual reasons for doing so, which will become clearer below and in the rest of this book. I have political reasons as well. How is one to challenge state violence if, as I claim in this book, every violent act of the state—and I do fully mean *every*—is morally unjustifiable? If not only the death penalty, not only war, not only the violence of jails or the brutality of the police but even the incarceration of the murderer found guilty in a court of law, or a drunken professor locked up for the night are morally wrong, then doesn't this commit me to Kropotkin's idealistic demand that "the first duty of the revolution will be to abolish prisons" because "anti-social acts need not be feared in a society of equals," for only "fraternal treatment and moral support" are required (Kropotkin 2002, 235)? Doesn't my argument commit us, or at least me, to not only an unrealistic view of human social life but to an idiosyncratic understanding of punishment even for those guilty for destroying the lives of others? Doesn't my argument commit me to a certain kind of anarchism as well as pacifism?

No.

Like most people I know and I assume like most people everywhere—even those of us who are highly critical of existing legal systems and the punitive "justice" they render—I am not eager to see individuals who have proven themselves to be extreme dangers to others walking among us. Although I do not think incarceration makes much sense for a far greater number of individuals than some may think—and that those incarcerated should not be as unjustly treated as they often are—I do not want a mass murderer to be living next door to me (or to you). My position does not commit me to Kropotkin's vision of a society of equals in which prisons would show themselves purely as spaces of injustice (although they are surely that now, and even if I am not opposed to a society of equals). My argument does not commit me to anarchism. On my view of what counts as an act of state violence, most pacifists would probably no longer count as (absolute) pacifists either. I think there are good reasons to put some people in jail, and there may even be good reasons to use military force.

All the good reasons in the world, however, will not change the moral unjustifiability of that violence. State violence, whatever good reasons we might have for employing it, is never morally justified. This puts us in a tight spot: state violence is unjustifiable, but at least for the moment it is difficult to imagine an alternative to some practices of state violence. This contradiction between a violence I know to be immoral but I cannot live without is the position or experience I call moral horror—the experience, briefly stated, of my acquiescence to or even support of an unjustifiable violence. Starting with moral horror, I think we can mount challenges to state violence in the hopes of severely limiting its use. For what I am arguing here is that the best political starting point for challenging state violence is attacking, without hesitation and continuously, any and all moral justifications of state violence. From an ethics of moral horror, one can begin to develop a politics resistant to state violence, for if one can only live uneasily, if at all, with the burden of moral horror, then it is necessary to lessen the horror by reducing state violence.

THE THEORETICAL CONTEXT

One can approach the phenomena of violence from any number of methodological perspectives, virtually all of which will employ empirical examples or methodologies with normative presuppositions or implications. My interest in this book, as I have already noted, is with those acts of violence that are justified as or simply called legitimate, specifically acts of legitimate state violence.

The focus on moral justifications of violence here differs in one important respect from the foci and aims of what we might call critiques of violence. Critiques of violence—which we find in diverse but related forms in Sorel, Benjamin, Arendt, Heidegger, Levinas, Adorno, Derrida, Galtung, Coady, Butler, and many others—are often a mixture of conceptual, phenomenological, and normative inquiry. I engage a number of these thinkers and their conceptualizations of violence, but as is apparent in chapter 4, I rely on what I hope is an uncontroversial definition of violence drawn in large part from the *Oxford English Dictionary*. Unlike critiques of violence, I do not differentiate the concept of violence into various species—legal, mythical, divine, psychological, social, epistemic, ontological, proletarian, revolutionary, and so on—and justify the extension or delimitation of the concept of violence to rule in or out one or another species. I do not spend much time showing what (if any) relations exist between the various species; nor do I provide a conceptual definition of violence which distinguishes it from neighboring concepts (e.g., force); nor do I spend any time on "hard cases" like violence in self-defense, nonstate violence such as terrorism, and so on. There is a large and still growing literature from psychology, sociology, political science and philosophy that I draw on in this book, but I do not, I think, add much to the conceptual and phenomenological inquiry into violence.

Rather, I deal with a subset of violent acts—state violence—that any concept of violence would surely include. Imprisonment, drone attacks, war, the death penalty, police actions, and similar acts of the state are surely violent—unless one distinguishes between legitimate and illegitimate violence in such a way as to transform state actions of the aforementioned kind into "legitimate uses of force." I am concerned with precisely this transformation in this book, and to the extent that what I am doing is a "critique of violence" it is only insofar as I share with other critics of violence a normative interest in violence that leads to the ethico-political idea of moral horror, the subject of chapter 5.

I see my project as a critique of moral justifications of violence, of those justifications of violence that transform prima facie violent acts committed by the state into "legitimate force." I acknowledge that my argument may undermine the moral justification of any act of violence, but I do not pursue that here. By focusing on what I assume are uncontroversial acts of violence by the state, I hope to clear some theoretical space for focusing on the moral justifications of state violence, justifications that along with the violence itself ought to horrify us.

I am interested, then, in those acts that fall under the concept of political legitimacy, including acts of war and internal security, from drone attacks to brief imprisonment for public drunkenness. This means that for the most part I will be dealing with normative matters, most of which center on, or more precisely are a subset of, the concept of political legitimacy.

Max Weber famously defines the state sociologically in terms of its specific means, that is, the use of physical force, and from these means he defines the state as "the human community that (successfully) claims the monopoly of the legitimate use of physical force within a given territory" (Weber 1946, 78). This sociological description of the state tends toward a de facto account of legitimacy, emphasized in the parenthetical *successfully*. Most political philosophers, however, understand political legitimacy in normative terms as well. Thus in its broadest sense, "political legitimacy" refers to some entity that has the moral or legal, de jure or de facto, power and/or authority to make and enforce law for and on some (usually territorially bound) group of subjects, citizens, and so on. This concept is central to thinking about politics. As the long debate over the concept of political legitimacy and whether it makes sense to say that any political entity is or can be legitimate reveals, the efforts of so many have failed to produce a generally accepted solution. The constant attempts, the centrality of the issue, and the failure to solve the problem once and for all, resemble the worry and compulsion to respond found in Immanuel Kant's admission that "it always remains a scandal of philosophy and universal human reason that the existence of things outside us ... should have to be assumed merely on faith, and that if it occurs to anyone to doubt it, we should be unable to answer him with a satisfactory proof" (Kant 1998, Bxxxix). To which Martin Heidegger, 140 years or so later, expressing exasperation rather than worry, responded by declaring that the " 'Scandal of philosophy' is not that this proof has yet to be given, but that such proofs are expected and attempted again and again" (Heidegger 1962, 249).

In the debate over political legitimacy, the analogue to skepticism—at least since Robert Paul Wolff's *In Defense of Anarchism* (1998)—is what has become known as philosophical anarchism, roughly speaking, the view that there cannot be or there are no existing legitimate states. The rejoinders to this position—in some cases literally Kantian—have invoked principles such as the "natural duty of justice," the principle of "fair play," of "gratitude," "(tacit) consent," and so on. The "Heideggerian" analogue to this debate has been the general disinterest in the project of articulating a justification for or refuting any argument for political legitimacy, a marked characteristic of much of what is poorly labeled "continental" political theory or some versions of "critical" theory. It is not, of course, that questions of state violence, punishment, law, legitimacy, and so on are not discussed in these strains of political theory—nothing could be further from the truth—but the idea that a goal of political theory or philosophy is to argue for (or refute an argument for) political legitimacy is not an idea one often finds in nonanalytic political theory (here Jürgen Habermas occupies a liminal position, partly because he is interested in legitimizing democratic political and legal institutions rather than the State as such and partly because he is clearly working between traditions of philosophy).

The Kantian and Heideggerian approaches to the question of political legitimacy—by which I simply mean the approach that tries to solve the problem of legitimacy and the approach that tries to diagnose and dissolve the form that problem has taken—stand in need of a little mutual contamination. The Kantian side of things fails to take seriously the criticisms of the foundational concepts and ontological premises common to traditional Western moral and ethical philosophies that have arisen in philosophy since at least Nietzsche. This lack of seriousness has meant that after philosophical anarchists show how no states are or can be legitimate, the consequences drawn from this demonstration end up seeming quite meager, nothing more than the removal of the "presumption" that we have an obligation to obey the law. After showing the absence of any obligation to obey the law, it turns out that the only thing that will really change is that we should not feel obligated or presumptively obligated to halt at that inexplicable stop sign in the middle of the desert or pay certain taxes. Our moral duties— whatever those are, and however philosophically grounded—will ensure the continuation of society and obedience to government, very much as we know it, and with all the morally justified violence that political legitimacy supposedly needed to legitimize. In short, moral duty will ensure what political obligation would seem to have safeguarded. That this view of morality and its conceptual and ontological underpinnings has been under attack for at least two centuries seems to have gone unnoticed, or simply deemed nihilistic, eccentric, and thereby safely dismissed and ignored.

On the other hand, the Heideggerian side of things has neglected why a justification of legitimacy is of such central importance in political thought, that is, that what the state (or whatever entity claims legitimacy and authority) does when it makes and enforces law—especially when it does the latter—is claim a right to engage in acts of violence that would be illegal, and depending on whom you ask, immoral if performed by anyone or anything else. In other words, the state requires an account and moral justification of its authority to enforce law because without it nothing distinguishes state violence from nonstate violence, more specifically, legal and morally justified violence from illegal and morally unjustified violence.[1] Although in the 1970s and 1980s discussions of a legitimation crisis were common, and in the 1990s through to today, attempts to show foundational paradoxes in politics (the paradox of founding, the paradox of politics, the paradox of democracy, etc.) that might expose the a-legitimacy of any state (rather than the illegitimacy of any state) were numerous, these accounts often failed to engage the Kantian side of things and, since then, the issue with important exceptions has ceased to capture the attention of many political theorists.[2] Often enough, the dubious morality of the state's use of violence

is argued for in relation to some (but not all) acts of state violence, and
when state legitimacy is otherwise put into question, the consequences
of losing the distinction between legitimate and illegitimate violence seem
not to be taken as seriously, as radically, as I think they are to be taken.[3]
It may be useful, then, not to synthesize these two traditions—for the ontological, anthropological, ethical, and political differences between the sides
will not allow for synthesis without interpretive violence—but to expose
them to each other. Thus, a second, theoretical impulse that motivates
my writing is that I am not satisfied with the arguments in analytic political
philosophy and continental political theory vis-à-vis the problem of state
violence, although I think that both "sides" need to be taken seriously
within theoretical considerations of legitimacy, violence, law, and so on.

However, I do not deal directly with arguments for the legitimacy of the
state. Rather, I deal with two debates in contemporary political theory—
philosophical anarchism and the paradox of politics/founding—which put
into question the legitimacy of the state. I have a few reasons for avoiding
arguments that attempt to justify the legitimacy of the state. First, to do
so would require writing a different book. The debate between philosophical
anarchists and their opponents is over four decades old, and I don't feel that
I have anything interesting to contribute to it. I do think that my argument
here might affect that debate but indirectly, for the state can be justified,
even (if not) legitimate—to use A. Johns Simmons's terminology—without
state violence thereby being legitimate. Thus, my concern here is not the
legitimacy of the state as such, but the legitimacy of state violence. Second,
although I tend to side with those positions that argue for the illegitimacy
or a-legitimacy of the state, I am interested in focusing on the consequences
of these positions for the legitimacy of state violence. In particular, I am
interested in how these positions tend to elide the problem of state violence
or fail to see how state violence is problematized by the illegitimacy of the
state. Although those who argue for the legitimacy of the state also thereby
legitimize state violence, this is an unsurprising entailment (or consequence)
of such arguments, whereas the opposite is the case for philosophical anarchism. Finally, and perhaps most important, I offer an argument for the
impossibility of justifying state violence that, if persuasive—and as I have
already suggested—could be useful to those who argue for and against
state legitimacy more broadly. All three reasons depend on the possibility
of conceptually and argumentatively distinguishing the legitimacy of state
violence from the legitimacy of the state. I think this can be done based

on the work of Walter Benjamin and it forms the methodology of the first chapter, so I postpone saying anything more about it for now.

My argument in this book, as I see it, draws on two main presuppositions. The first is the subject of the third chapter: I use an ontological "basis" for my claims, drawing on the work of Jean-Luc Nancy. I will not say much more about this here. But I would like to note that I do not think my argument requires Nancy's specific ontological claims to succeed, although there are certainly many ontological, metaphysical, anthropological, and political presuppositions and values on which my argument would make no sense at all, much less be persuasive. A certain version of the dignity of each human being could lead to an argument like mine—say, what we find in the work of George Kateb—although historically this has not been the case (Kant, recall, is one of many to start from such a concept and justify punishment, even a mandatory death penalty). What is required is some sense of the sheer uniqueness of all beings in the world, which amounts, as I see it, to a sensitivity to the movements of time and the plurality of spaces in the world. Although many might not be convinced by Nancy's ontology, and thus would discount my argument, beginning from some basic account of being—often in its broadest sense as opposed to any regional ontology—is unavoidable. I believe that the perception of the singularity of all beings is as intuitively plausible as the belief that, for example, all human beings have an inherent moral dignity, just as I believe that both perceptions or intuitions are often ignored or repressed in the service of (what we might mistakenly take to be) our needs.

The second, surely less contentious presupposition of my argument is that violent acts stand in need of moral justification, that is, violent acts are morally questionable (but not necessarily wrong or right). This might be stated as follows: violent acts are prima facie wrong. Although this might accord with some intuitions about violence as such, I would hazard to guess that in our everyday lives certain acts of violence are assumed to be prima facie right, for example, the acts of the police. The point, though, is that violence is morally questionable and thus in need of moral justification or explanation, something for which we have ample evidence from cultures all over the world. Insofar as violence stands in need of moral justification, the justifications provided become, just as much as the acts themselves, objects of critical contestation. As I have noted already, this is precisely the strategy I take in this book. The fourth chapter, in which I provide my argument for there being no possible moral justification of state violence, turns on the claim that, based on a certain understanding of violence and singularity, all justifications of violence are themselves violent, hence there is an infinite regress of justification that undermines the very possibility of justifying state violence. Thus, Nancyean ontology and the assumption that violence stands in need of justification are the bases of my argument (although, to repeat, I think there are other ontologies or accounts of dignity or singularity that could ground my argument).

MORAL HORROR

The ethico-political consequence I draw from my argument against the possibility of justifying state violence is the condition of moral horror. I devote chapter 5 to that argument, but I do not present the idea in the context of other affective orientations to politics. I was trained in a tradition of thinking about ethics and politics in which a strong sense of the tragic in human (and indeed in all) existence is combined with (or inspires) a fundamental affirmation of existence, one that neither denies nor passively accepts the tragic but affirms existence as tragic. Nietzsche, for example, writes in *Thus Spoke Zarathustra* that "Whoever climbs the highest mountains laughs at all tragic plays and tragic seriousness" (1966, 41) and in *The Gay Science* he imagines a dead-end of tragedy that might be resolved through a "comic solution," the solution of affirmative laughter (1974, §153). The affirmative laugh, for Nietzsche, declares that tragedy is not only present but necessary, fated, unavoidable, in human life; yet in the pleasure of laughter, we are to "rise above" the tragic precisely by denying the "metaphysical solace" of sinking into a doomed, passive resignation. As Gilles Deleuze—an important figure in the affirmative modes of political theory today—writes of Nietzschean affirmation, "To affirm is still to evaluate, but to evaluate from the perspective of a will which enjoys its own difference in life instead of suffering the pains of opposition to this life it has itself inspired. To affirm is not to take responsibility for, to take on the burden of what is, but to release, to set free what lives" (1983, 185). Jacques Derrida, also drawing on Nietzsche, argues that once "turned towards the lost or impossible presence of the absent origin," one possibility is "the Nietzschean affirmation, that is the joyous affirmation of a world of signs without fault, without truth, and without origin which is offered to an active interpretation. This affirmation then determines the noncenter otherwise than as loss of the center" (1978, 292). William Connolly, drawing on Nietzsche and Deleuze, has shown again and again the limitations and dangers of denying the tragic or of resignation in the face of it. For Connolly the tragic and a "philosophy of abundance" that generates and enables new modes of creative response to tragedy are both key components of an affirmative political ethos capable of responding to the increasing pressures and problems of "cowboy capitalism," environmental destruction, and the capitalist-evangelical resonance machines of the contemporary United States (Connolly 2008). For thinkers such as Nietzsche, Deleuze, Derrida, Connolly, and others in contemporary political theory and philosophy, relentless critique without affirmative vision is incapable of projecting a philosophically viable and politically effective response to the dangers and promises of our modernity.

The suggestion that we should acknowledge moral horror as a starting point for challenging state violence would seem to put me out of the affirmative politics camp, even with the necessary reminder that neither Nietzsche, Deleuze, Connolly, or others are in any way to be equated with Nietzsche's ass braying "yea-uh" to anything and everything. My position—for reasons that are made clearer in chapter 5—is more akin to Adorno's relentless negativity, required as the only possibility left for revealing, if only in a refracted glimpse, a reconciled, redeemed world. There is some truth to this.

I used the word *catastrophes* above, which comes from the ancient Greek word indicating a conclusion, overturning, or a sudden turn. It is a word that is liable to be misunderstood because it is not taken literally or etymologically enough, because it has become too domesticated and tamed. But if writers, artists, and philosophers after World War I were prone to thinking of their world as in ruins, destroyed, undone, broken; one has the feeling, in this moment, that it is not only the destruction of the old that we must confront but the destruction of a (recognizable) future. Whether it is environmental changes that will radically overturn both human and (some) nonhuman life; the realization of the ever more awesome dangers of global capitalism; continuous violence; ongoing genocide; the mainstreaming in Europe of racist and nationalist politics and the destruction of the social welfare state there as well as in the United States; or asteroids hitting the Earth; we don't need divine intervention to imagine the imminent destruction of (forms of) human life. These times are dark, to say the least.

However, articulating a clear-sighted recognition of the horrors within and the horror of human life is not the same thing as counseling despair and hopelessness, either a passive or active nihilism. The horror I am interested in is neither ontological nor a matter of Fate in need of an *amor fati* to affirm what cannot be changed anyway; nor is it a fall from grace. The horror is ours, our doing, and precisely for that reason it is in our power to lessen if not eliminate it. In "Personal Responsibility under Dictatorship," Hannah Arendt recalls Mary McCarthy's response to those who criticized Arendt's judgments of those Jewish individuals who were—cruelly, horrifyingly—required to select other Jews for (almost inevitably) death. Arendt writes:

> I had somehow taken for granted that we all still believe with Socrates that it is better to suffer than to do wrong. This belief turned out to be a mistake. There was a widespread conviction that it is impossible to withstand temptation of any kind, that none of us could be trusted or even be expected to be trustworthy when the chips are down, that to be tempted and to be forced are almost the same, whereas in the words of Mary McCarthy, who first spotted this fallacy: "If somebody points a gun at you and says 'kill your friend or I will kill you,' he is tempting you, that is all." And while a temptation where one's life is at stake may be a legal excuse for a crime, it certainly is not a moral justification. (2003, 18)

When we are threatened by others in the many ways and many modes others can threaten us, and when we are reminded of our vulnerability at the hands of others, we are tempted to respond with violence of various sorts. In the institution of the State we have placed the deadliest, most advanced, most effective, most wide-reaching, and seemingly most legitimate means of violence to keep threats at bay or punish those whose threats have been realized in deeds. Temptation, however, is no (moral) excuse. We opt for state violence for any number of reasons, but none of those reasons morally justify state violence. State violence is tempting, but only a temptation. It can be—it should be—resisted.

Thus, moral horror, however negative its affective register, should not lead to despair or resignation, even if it is all too predictable that precisely because moral horror is so horrifying we will close our eyes to it, avoiding it and the others it forces us to acknowledge. Moral horror cannot be eliminated as long as state violence exists, which may seem to reintroduce a fatedness that I am trying to reject. But first, that state violence exists is, again, something that we can change for it is a, it is our, temptation. Second, the point of recognizing moral horror is not to make ourselves feel worse about ourselves (and thereby perhaps ultimately makes us feel better) but to prevent as many acts (if not all acts) of state violence. Moral horror may be something I experience, but, as I argue later, it directs our responsiveness to the singular being that is the victim of state violence. Moral horror doesn't exist without a certain kind of responsive relation to others.

My argument here, then, calls for acknowledgment—in the Cavellian sense of the term—of moral horror, not affirmation. When one keeps in mind that thinkers of affirmation like Deleuze, Derrida, and Connolly are not asses who bray "yea-uh" to anything and everything (that is, but affirmers of a contingency and openness of Being that generates terrors and horrors and moments of creative and positive change), my position ends up looking less opposed to the politics of affirmation than it may appear.

THE STRUCTURE OF THE BOOK

Rather than being a collection of essays guided by an overlapping set of themes, this book present a continuous argument. Before outlining each chapter, I want to quickly justify two aspects of the structure that might be objectionable to some readers. The first aspect is the amount of exegesis. The second, related aspect is that the "state violence" part of this book takes up far more space than the "moral horror" part.

First, it is no secret that since the early twentieth century, philosophy has tended to diverge into two poorly named camps: "analytic" and "continental." I won't recite the various reasons these names are inadequate, nor how many philosophers have contested the distinction and distinctiveness of the camps, nor how the peculiarly Anglo-American story of the rise of behavioralism in political science in the 1950s shaped the institutional location of political philosophy and political theory. I take it as given that sufficient evidence exists—for example, in looking at citation patterns in leading journals of political theory and philosophy—for the assumption that a number of thinkers and arguments in one tradition will be almost entirely unknown, or known only in distortive caricature, to theorists working in the other tradition.

I do not want the argument of this book to be unintelligible to those not familiar with one or another thinker, be it A. John Simmons or Walter

Benjamin, Stanley Cavell or Jean-Luc Nancy, Jacques Derrida or Richard Brandt, Theodor Adorno or Noel Carroll. I aim to provide enough detailed knowledge of a particular argument for readers to understand where my argument differs from theirs and why that is so. I hope that my exegeses are faithful to yet distinctive enough to keep the attention of both the reader who already knows and the reader who doesn't. But I am not willing to accept the cost of a limited audience for this book for the benefit of a quicker path to my central arguments and conclusions. I hope that readers familiar with a theorist's arguments will suffer through a bit of repetition for the sake of what I hope is a controversial but important argument against the moral justifiability of state violence. I try to situate a particular exegesis in the context of my own argument at a number of points, and I hope that is enough to keep familiar readers reading. If not, then I would simply skip those parts of the book you find to be a rehashing of familiar ideas.

The second aspect of the book, the asymmetry between the discussion of the moral justification of state violence and the discussion of moral horror, is a consequence of the controversial conclusion I arrive at in the course of the former discussion. I briefly justify that asymmetry now, because I don't really feel it needs much defense. Simply put, if you are not persuaded by the first four chapters of the book, the fifth chapter will be largely beside the point. Persuading myself of the argument in the first four chapters has proven difficult, so I imagine that it is unlikely to be easily accepted by a reader. My aim has been to clear some room for the distinctiveness of my concern in chapters 1 and 2, to provide an ontological basis for my argument in chapter 3, and to show my argument against the possibility of morally justifying state violence in chapter 4. These chapters contain contestable readings of texts, contestable affirmations of an ontology, and contestable arguments on the basis of contestable definitions and that contestable ontology. In short, I have no doubt that the bar for accepting my conclusion is quite high, and I want to leap over that bar as best I can. If I can at least make my argument plausible, then the ethico-political project in chapter 5—which could surely be extended in a number of interesting and valuable directions—is, I hope, introductory and exploratory, a promissory note for future work.

To repeat, the first two chapters deal with positions within contemporary political theory that come closest to mine and for which I have a great deal of admiration and with which I am often in agreement. In chapter 1 I engage with philosophical anarchism, specifically the work of A. John Simmons, not only a prominent philosophical anarchist but, in my opinion, the most persuasive. Although largely in agreement with Simmons's argument on its own terms, I argue that philosophical anarchism elides the problem of the legitimacy of state violence insofar as the consequences drawn by Simmons for our understanding of the legitimacy of law, political obligation, and specifically state violence, are remarkably minimal and depend on extremely contestable moral commitments. Drawing on Walter Benjamin, I show that Simmons's justification of the moral legitimacy of law, and by extension, law's violence, relies on a set of moral claims that enable Simmons to justify the use of violence as a means but not violence itself. Even that justification, I claim, pushes the justification of state violence into the realm of moral philosophy, a space in which Simmons's own—often unargued for—commitments to forms of moral realism require defense against criticisms of morality and the moral subject from Nietzsche on. Thus, I show that Simmons's philosophical anarchist justification of the legitimacy of the law and its violence is importantly incomplete, and I suggest that the way he would complete it would not succeed.

Chapter 2 turns to arguments concerned with the paradox of founding/ politics, specifically as they appear in the work of Bonnie Honig, William Connolly, and Jacques Derrida. I begin by challenging the interpretation of Jean-Jacques Rousseau that orients Honig and Connolly in their accounts of the paradox of founding because in their own way they elide the problem of the legitimacy of state violence. In relocating the paradox of founding in Rousseau's *On the Social Contract*, I argue that Rousseau's paradoxical response to that paradox has important consequences for the legitimacy of state violence. Precisely because I endorse Honig's and Connolly's politics, I hope that my account of the paradox of founding furthers that politics. I turn to Derrida's account of the paradox of founding in "Force of Law" to argue that, perhaps surprisingly, he too elides the problem of the legitimacy of state violence through an unargued for commitment to law as the only means for actualizing an impossible to fully actualize justice. If the a-legitimate foundation of law undermines the legitimacy of law and its violence, why does Derrida remain so committed to law? I end the chapter by returning to Honig and Connolly to suggest that their contestatory politics is furthered by putting one political issue beyond contestation: the necessary illegitimacy of all state violence.

The next three chapters present my argument for the impossibility of morally justifying state violence and the consequence of that fact—the experience of moral horror. In chapter 3 I lay the ontological foundations of my argument through an explication of Nancy's *Being Singular Plural*. I begin by contextualizing Nancy's claims about being singular plural both within twentieth-century philosophy and, more specifically, in the reception of Heidegger's phenomenological analysis of being-with (*Mitsein*) in Being and Time. I then turn more directly to Nancy's text to bring both the "phenomenological experience" of singularity as well as its conditions. Nancy, along with others (including Adorno, Levinas, Derrida) emphasizes that insofar as all beings are singular, our cognitive, ethical, political, and legal attempts to "determine" the singular being are necessary for thought and experience to proceed but at the same time necessarily incapable of "capturing" the singular being *qua* its singularity. Thus for Nancy, there is a violence in conceptual (and other) determination that is necessary yet still deeply problematic. Nancyean ontology, I claim, gives us an account of the singular being and of the violence done to the singular through our appropriative acts from which we can begin to articulate an understanding of what is necessarily wrong about state violence.

Drawing on Nancy's ontology, chapter 4 presents my argument for the impossibility of morally justifying state violence. I begin by making plausible an addition to our definition of violence: those acts are violent that avoid, repress, or deny the singularity of beings to justify physical acts of violence. I argue for the plausibility of this addition by showing that two key components of our everyday definition of violence are accounted for by this definition: the notion of injury and the notion of physical acts of force. I move on to demonstrate how a certain set of acts—justifications—avoid, repress, or deny the singularity of beings to justify physical violence by looking at Kant's justification for punishment in *Groundwork of the Metaphysic of Morals* and Cavell's criticism of Rawls's *Theory of Justice*. If justifications of physical violence themselves can injure, and do so precisely by denying the singularity of the beings who are the object of violence, then we have a set of acts that fall under the (expanded) definition of violence, that is, a set of acts that are rightly defined as violent. But if acts that justify physical violence are themselves violent, then those violent justificatory acts need to be justified, too. However, those justifications will, for reasons Nancy (and others) help us see, also be violent. Thus, there is an abyssal justificatory process here, an infinite regression, and for this reason there can be no possible moral justification of state violence. I end the chapter by showing how my position differs from a similar problem in contemporary moral and political philosophy: the problem of dirty hands.

If there is no possible moral justification of state violence, I argue in chapter 5, we are left with what I am calling moral horror. I define moral horror as the experience of horror produced by the thought of the contradiction between the unjustifiable violence of the state and one's willingness to let that violence continue. I start the chapter by distinguishing moral horror from what I am calling "aesthetic horror" through a discussion of Susan Sontag's *Regarding the Pain of Others* and Adriana Cavarero's *Horrorism*. I offer an account of how moral horror comes about and why it is horror produced by the thought of the contradiction between unjustifiable state violence and the willingness to let it continue. My argument for how and why moral horror comes about turns on a seemingly unrelated problem: the distinction between the human and the animal. Drawing on Cavell's claim that horror is the experience of the precariousness of human identity (vis-à-vis the gods and the animal), I argue that the distinction between legitimate and illegitimate violence is part of what constitutes the distinction between the human and the animal. For this reason, when state violence is shown to be impossible to justify and we are thereby engaging in illegitimate violence, our sense of our human identity is threatened: we face the vision of our own inescapable animality, and this horrifies us. Moral horror comes about, then, through a cognitive dissonance that threatens our presumed humanity (over and against the animal). I end the chapter by tracing an ethics and politics in which, following Adorno, we learn not to repress our animality but to live as better animals, responding responsibly to the suffering bodies of those who are victims of state violence.

In the (In)conclusion I address two of my worries about the position I have argued for in this book. First, doesn't my position, by depriving state violence of any moral justification, leave state violence to the unrestrained domination of instrumental reason? Second, relatedly, have I deprived us of any moral ground from which to distinguish between "better" and "worse" violent states and practices of state violence? I respond to these objections without conclusively answering them, in the hope that further reflection will allow me to be able to deal with these problems in a more, shall we say, conclusive way.

1 THE STRENGTHS AND LIMITS OF PHILOSOPHICAL ANARCHISM

THE BASIC DEFINITION of state legitimacy as the exclusive right to make, apply, and enforce laws is common, clearly visible in Max Weber and contemporary political philosophy and found less explicitly in the classical contract thinkers.[1] A. John Simmons, drawing on Locke, writes that "A state's (or government's) legitimacy is the complex moral right it possesses to be the exclusive imposer of binding duties on its subjects, to have its subjects comply with these duties, and to use coercion to enforce the duties" (Simmons 2001, 130). Similar definitions—whether vis-à-vis legitimacy or authority—with slight alterations of terms and in conjunction with a series of other ideas and conditions (for example, "authoritativeness," background criteria, the difference between force and violence) can be found in Robert Paul Wolff (1998, 4), Joseph Raz (2009), Richard Flathman (1980), Leslie Green (1988), David Copp (1999), Hannah Pitkin (1965, 1966), and others. The point is that the justification of state legitimacy and the (corresponding) obligation to obey involve, more often than not, making, applying, and enforcing laws: political power.

Often left out of these discussions—with important exceptions—are the real practices of legitimate statehood, and perhaps for good reason. What philosophers who explore the question of legitimacy and authority are most often interested in—for a variety of reasons—is the relation of the individual to the state, that is, whether and to what extent a citizen (or sometimes a noncitizen) has an obligation to obey the state. As Raz notes, part of the explanation for this is that contemporary philosophical interest in questions of political obligation emerged in response to political events in the 1960s (Raz 1981, 105). However, focusing on the legitimacy/authority/obedience

1

relation obscures a particular practice always implicated in the problem of state legitimacy and a central (although not sole) reason we desire a justification for the right of the state to enforce its laws: the need to morally distinguish coercive force used by the state from immoral, unjust violence. Wolff's essay "On Violence" does acknowledge the problem, for if the state is not legitimate then "it is impossible to distinguish between legitimate and illegitimate uses of force," that is, between (morally justifiable) force and (immoral and illegal) violence (Wolff 1969, 607). The need for a moral distinction emerges from the impossibility of distinguishing state violence from nonstate violence at a purely descriptive level (excluding obvious differences in particular cases). The violence in the death penalty and in murder is the same: an agent kills someone. That a moral difference between the two acts must be found is clear if we are to avoid the conclusion that the state's use of force is always (unjust) violence.

For those who present arguments that secure the legitimacy of the state, whether classical or contemporary, the moral justification of state force/ coercion/violence and thus its distinction from nonstate violence is resolved by those arguments. As I show in a later chapter, such arguments engage in a justificatory violence that undermines those arguments, but one can understand why, the state having been legitimized, the only real concerns with practices of state force are the justice of particular laws and procedures of enforcing the law. State violence as such is elided or displaced as an issue meriting real philosophical analysis because it has already been morally justified.

The situation is quite different for those who self-describe or can be described as "philosophical anarchists." Those who deny the legitimacy or authority of the state (or a prima facie obligation to obey the law)—Simmons includes himself, Raz, Green, Wolff, Regan, and others among this group—face a real difficulty when it comes to the enforcement of the law. Quite consistently from his anarchist position, Wolff argues in "On Violence" that there simply is no morally relevant difference between violent acts committed by the state and violent acts committed by nonstate actors because there can be no legitimate states (Wolff 1969, 609; for a nonanarchist attempt to challenge the legitimate force/illegitimate violence distinction, see Coady 2008, 1–4, 21–42). Wolff's acceptance of the consequences of his position is an exception, however. Most philosophical anarchists—including Simmons, who I focus on here—do not seem willing or feel forced to move in this direction because the consequences of philosophical anarchism for most philosophical anarchists turn out to be not very radical at all (see Simmons 2001, 112–21; Smith 1973, 969). The reason is that the obligation to obey the law, once denied, removes only one moral reason for conforming to what the law demands of us. Other moral duties compel many, if not most, of the same actions, and thus we have other reasons for obeying the state and its laws that are just as morally compelling as a political obligation to obey a legitimate authority. Correlatively, state violence may be justified by other moral reasons even if the state lacks authority. In short, where political obedience fails to obligate us, moral obligations perform the same task, and where authority cannot justify state violence, other moral justifications do the same work. As we will see, if that morality includes a natural right and even a duty to punish those who break the natural law, then the problem of state violence is once again easily elided because it is too quickly legitimized.

Although I do not defend philosophical anarchism against its critics, I am sympathetic to its conclusions and believe them to be persuasive within the terms of the debate.[2] I find Simmons's work to be particularly compelling, rigorously and successfully argued, and thus the most important of the various defenses of philosophical anarchism. His basic argument for anarchism is simple: after surveying various grounds for political obligation (including gratitude, fair play, a natural duty of justice and consent), he shows that only express consent given under certain speech conditions could successfully ground a political obligation. Insofar as incredibly few individuals ever have consented or do or will consent to their state, then vis-à-vis the vast majority of individuals, there are no political obligations, and because state legitimacy requires authority, the state is illegitimate (Simmons 1979, 191–201). This position is so persuasive because it rests on the most intuitively powerful and theoretically coherent basis for the generation of an obligation: the actual, express giving of one's word. Not backing away from the fact that consent, for all of its theoretical and political promise, is virtually absent in political life, Simmons accepts the conclusion that existing states are illegitimate in relation to most of their citizens. Furthermore, he is rightly skeptical of "hypothetical consent" positions such as Rawls's in *A Theory of Justice* (1971) because they "have illicitly appropriated the justificatory force of voluntarism while being (like Kant) in no real way motivated by it" (Simmons 2001, 147). Simmons presents an almost purified (Lockean) picture of liberalism in which the power and right of an individual in conjunction with other equally powerful and rightful

4 ■ State Violence and Moral Horror

individuals to be the generator of political obligations (and, as it were, the political itself) faithfully reflects the "atomistic" side of liberalism while insisting that these prepolitical rights must be understood in conjunction with equally prepolitical duties. In short, we get two of the central founts of liberalism—natural law and natural rights—taken seriously in a coherent argument for the illegitimacy of existing states.

Insofar as one of my main arguments in this book is that there can be no moral justification of state violence, it is perhaps natural that I would be attracted to and convinced by arguments that deny the state the moral authority to enforce its laws. Yet I am dissatisfied by most versions of philosophical anarchism, and Simmons's exemplary version in particular, for two reasons. First, the very mild consequences of philosophical anarchism claimed by its defenders rest on a set of moral ideas resting on concepts and premises drawn from a metaphysical tradition that has been rigorously historicized and philosophically attacked since at least Hegel, Marx, Kierkegaard, and Nietzsche. This line of critique has continued into the twentieth century with Adorno, Foucault, Derrida, Arendt, and others. The failure to take seriously or even acknowledge this tradition of critique undermines the plausibility of the anarchist's claim that the loss of state legitimacy does not entail any radical consequences, for this claim uncritically substitutes moral for political obligations.

Second, as I have already suggested, the substitution of moral obligation for political obligation elides the problem of morally distinguishing state violence from nonstate violence, and thus threatens to turn state violence into a paradigm of injustice. As Thomas Senor has argued in response to Simmons, if a state lacks the right to punish its citizens, then when it punishes it is actually only "punishing" (for the authority to punish is part of the concept of punishment); furthermore, it is committing a genuine act of injustice: using violence without right (Senor 1987; see similar worries in Edmundson 1998, 33). As we will see, Simmons argues for the plausibility of the Lockean natural duty to punish to answer these worries; once again he moves the philosophical problem back to the terrain of a moral realism that needs defending not only against communitarians, constructivists, noncognitivists, and others within contemporary analytic moral philosophy but also against the criticism of Nietzsche, Marx, Foucault, and others. The elision of an analysis of state violence is linked to the moral theory underlying those who justify state legitimacy and, more important for me, the philosophical anarchists.

In this chapter, then, I present two arguments. First, I turn briefly to Walter Benjamin's "Critique of Violence" to emphasize Benjamin's reasons for removing the critique and analysis of violence from the means–ends relation that is found in natural law and positivism. Simmons is able to elide the problem of state violence because he defends (sometimes ambiguously) a Lockean moral realism about rights and duties, thereby subsuming violence back into a particular form of the means–ends relation within natural law. However, if Senor is right, and the loss of state legitimacy undermines the moral justification of state violence, we are forced to move the real argument over the consequences of philosophical anarchism to the (unpromising) field of moral philosophy, specifically metaethics.

Second, I argue that although Simmons briefly defends his (largely implicit) moral theory against (some) critics, he fails to account for the most powerful criticisms of the moral subject. I cannot go into the details of the criticisms of the modern (moral) subject that are so prominent in some nineteenth-century philosophers and, in the twentieth century, in post-Heideggerian philosophy and critical theory. But I hope to say enough to argue that Simmons's philosophical anarchism is limited by and subject to criticism for its commitment to a moral theory that is both more questionable than it acknowledges and enables a displacement of the problem of state violence that the justification of state legitimacy is partly designed to solve. To save the moral distinction between state violence and nonstate violence through recourse to the highly contestable field of moral theory is tough enough; failing to take seriously the most powerful criticisms of the modern moral subject only makes such a task harder and less persuasive.

BENJAMIN'S "CRITIQUE OF VIOLENCE"

Walter Benjamin's "Critique of Violence" argues for a number of claims about the relations of violence (mythical and divine) to law and justice. For my purposes, I want to focus only on Benjamin's argument for how we should approach and critique the problem of violence. I do so because it will set the terms within which I would like to question the (non)place of state violence in Simmons's work.

For Benjamin, the "task of a critique of violence can be summarized as that of expounding its relation to law and justice. For a cause, however effective, becomes violent, in the precise sense of the word, only when it bears on moral issues. The sphere of these issues is defined by the concepts of law and justice" (Benjamin 1978, 277). The first premise, then, is that violence is only properly ascribed to human acts (with the exception of divine violence, which is entirely opposed to all other human, mythical, legal violence), for only human acts—as opposed to natural disasters and the actions of animals—fall within the moral sphere. One might quibble with the claim that moral issues are defined (solely?) by the concepts of law and justice, for Benjamin leaves out other seemingly essential moral concepts (such as value or virtue, although the "value" of the law itself is explicitly at issue in the essay). But insofar as his primary concern is the relation of violence to law and justice, his neglect of other moral concepts does not affect his argument.

The second, more crucial premise in Benjamin's text is that "with regard to the first of these [law], it is clear that the most elementary relationship within any legal system is that of ends to means, and, further, that violence can first be sought only in the realm of means, not of ends" (Benjamin 1978, 277). That the most basic legal relationship is instrumental in character stands in need of justification.[3] The second feature of the premise—that violence is to be sought in the means, not the ends—is less controversial. No legal system—save perhaps totalitarian systems such as the Nazi state—has violence itself as one of its ends; on the contrary, a central aim of law is the reduction if not elimination of violence, and law employs putatively legitimate violence as a means to that end. To return to the first part of the premise, we must ask whether the means–ends relationship is so elemental within law.

Benjamin turns to the two most important philosophies of law to justify the claim. First, natural law gives us a criterion with which to judge violence: whether it is a means to a just or unjust end. For natural law "perceives in the use of violent means to just ends no greater problem than a man sees in his 'right' to move his body in the direction of a desired goal. According to this view ... violence is a product of nature, as it were a raw material, the use of which is in no way problematical, unless force is misused for unjust ends" (Benjamin 1978, 277–78). Benjamin cites Spinoza at this point, but he could just as well have quoted any number of modern contract thinkers. For Hobbes, natural right simply is "the liberty each man hath, to use his own power, as he will himselfe, for the preservation of his own Nature" including, of course, the violence that leads to the state of war (Hobbes

1997, chapter 14). Locke presents a more complicated case because our actions in the state of nature are restricted by natural law (as we will see when we turn to Simmons). For Locke we are either born with or acquire in the state of nature a right to punish others, that is, a natural right to use violence (Locke 1988, §7–8). In both cases, the right to use violence serves a just purpose and is thus justified by the ends of self-preservation or the preservation of humankind. In other words, violence is a means, justified by a just end. Of course, in Hobbes and Locke (and any number of other thinkers), the law itself, as well as particular laws, are means to ends (self-preservation, the protection of property, or any other end). In natural law, then, the means–ends relation of all law is clear, and the criterion by which to justify the means is the justness of the end.

Although one does not find the justification of violent means by just ends in legal positivism, the means–ends relationship remains. For "if natural law can judge all existing law only in criticizing its ends, so positive law can judge all evolving law only in criticizing its means. If justice is the criterion of ends, legality is that of means" (Benjamin 1978, 278). Benjamin, I take it, is referring to the important place of procedures (or of Hart's "second-ary rules") in positivism, procedures for enacting laws (which find their legitimacy in some basic law or foundational act) and more specifically what Rawls calls "pure procedural justice." Unlike perfect and imperfect procedural justice—both of which have an independent criterion by which to judge the procedure (although imperfect procedural justice cannot design fail-proof procedures to reach the desired end)—pure procedural justice "obtains when there is no independent criterion for the right result: instead there is a correct or fair procedure such that the outcome is likewise correct of fair, whatever it is, provided that the procedure has been properly followed" (Rawls 1971, 86). The use of violence as a means within positive law is justified by the propriety of the procedures through which it is used, the way they satisfy secondary "rules of recognition" (Hart 1961, 92). Here, too, the means–ends relationship is central to the structure of law, for the justness of a legal system under conditions where perfect and imperfect procedural justice are not possible or only rarely achieved requires that legal means—that is, legal procedures—are justified and executed properly to justify the ends attained by legal violence.

To be sure, more needs to be said to justify Benjamin's claim to the elemental place of the means–ends relationship in law. We have already seen enough to move on to Benjamin's disagreement with the way violence is understood by natural law and legal positivism and further to the proper way to approach the place of violence within law. The problem faced by natural law's solution to the problem of justifying violence is that natural law can only justify the use of violence as a means in particular cases; it cannot and does not justify violence itself. Benjamin writes:

> For what such a system [of natural just ends], assuming it to be secure against all doubt, would contain is not a criterion for violence itself as a principle, but, rather, the criterion for cases of its use. The question would remain open whether violence, as a principle, could be a moral means even to a just end. To resolve this question a more exact criterion is needed, which would discriminate within the sphere of means themselves, without regard for the ends they serve. (Benjamin 1978, 277)

In other words, whenever violence as a means is justified by a particular just end, what one is justifying is not the violence but the use of violence in that (and all other identical) case(s). Benjamin's claim is a condensation of a more complex argument. First, he argues that the normative justifiability of the means comes from the normative justifiability of the ends (just ends [normatively] justify the means). Second, he argues that the means as means, that is, as useful ways of obtaining an end, are justified by the ends (the ends instrumentally justify the means). Third, and crucially, he claims that within natural law the normative and instrumental justifications of the means collapse such that the usefulness of the means in obtaining a just end is the normative justification of the means. What is occluded in this collapse is a normative assessment of the means as such, without relation to ends.

For example, take the use of the death penalty. Undoubtedly, the death penalty can—in either a retributive, deterrence, or mixed theory of punishment—be justified as a means to achieve a just end (if the death of the criminal is a just end, then the use of violence is justified). However, this does not answer the question of whether the violence of killing is itself just, can ever be just, no matter what just ends it serves. Thus, it is left open whether "violence, as a principle, could be a moral means even to just ends." Benjamin draws a distinction between the justice of violence and the justification of the use of violence, and on the basis of this distinction he argues that natural law deals only with the latter and never the former.

Therefore, natural law cannot be the proper way to approach the relation of violence to law and justice.

On the other hand, legal positivism does offer, for Benjamin, a starting point for a critique of violence. It does so because insofar as violence is not the end of a legal system and no just end can justify violence itself, a critique of violence must look at violence solely within the realm of means, of actions. Insofar as legal positivism justifies ends by the justness of the means, it necessarily attends more closely to an analysis of the means. For this reason, legal positivism makes a fundamental distinction between kinds of violence pertinent to the use of violence as a means: the distinction between legitimate and illegitimate violence. This distinction rests on positivism's "positivism," as it were: that law is made, posited, in a particular historical time and space (Benjamin 1978, 279–80). What legitimizes certain uses of violence as a means is the historical foundation of that violence in a founding act (what Benjamin calls "lawmaking violence"). This founding act—if legitimate—would legitimize the violence of the state that is founded by the act (we return to problems with the founding act in chapter 2).

Thus, a critique of violence begins by attending to the distinction within positivism between legitimate and illegitimate violence, for that distinction, found on the "means" side of the means–ends relation, is an attempt to address violence itself, to make a moral distinction, however dubious, between "kinds" of violence such that one kind is morally justified regardless of the ends it serves. (One might add that the justification of violence in natural law is prospective in a sense, justified by what it achieves, whereas violence in positivism is retrospective, justified by the propriety of the act that legitimizes it.) For Benjamin the distinction between legitimate and illegitimate violence is central to the relation of violence to law, but that very violence, no matter how legitimate, irreparably divides law from justice (I return to this issue in chapter 2).

What is important for my purposes, however, is Benjamin's "methodology." If we want to criticize state violence, we must turn to the legitimacy/illegitimacy distinction, and to understand that we must turn to the founding act of the state (again, I return to this latter point in chapter 2). Philosophical anarchism, as exemplified by Simmons, denies the legitimacy of the state by denying that the only act capable of "founding" the authority of the state has taken place. In so doing, one would seemingly deny the right of the state to use violence to achieve its ends and thus collapse the moral distinction between legitimate and illegitimate violence, rendering state violence immoral and unjust. However, this is not at all the conclusion Simmons reaches.

THE NATURAL RIGHT TO PUNISH

In responses to his critics (including Senor)—some of whom claim that philosophical anarchism would quite naturally lead to actual (acts of) anarchism—Simmons often makes the same basic point:

> The anarchist conclusion is that most citizens have no political obligations and that governments lack the correlative political right to command and be obeyed. In particular, of course, this means that governments possess no right to use coercive sanctions to compel obedience to civil (as opposed to natural) law ... I have argued that the anarchist conclusion does not justify widespread disobedience, as it might at first seem to, and that in at least some kinds of states many citizens have morally compelling reasons to conform their conduct to law, even in the absence of political obligations. (Simmons 1987, 275; see also Simmons, 2001, 112–21)

In addition to a variety of natural duties we owe to others that compel us to conform to the law as well as a "balance-of-reasons" approach to moral reasoning that sometimes morally justifies "unrightful" actions (I return to this set of ideas later), Simmons argues that

> while it is certainly true that if there are no political obligations governments cannot have the right to enforce civil law, it is not obvious that they lack the right (or authority) to enforce natural law (or basic moral rules). If we possess a "natural executive right," governments (as sets of persons and also perhaps as punishers "authorized" by, say, naturalized express consenters) will have the same right to enforce moral requirements as individuals possess. I believe that one variation of Locke's "strange doctrine" of the natural right to punish is in fact true and in no way incoherent. (Simmons 1987, 276)

The full defense of Locke's "strange doctrine" comes a few years later in Simmons's *The Lockean Theory of Rights* (1992). Even in his brief response to Senor, one can see the important role Locke's natural right to punish plays in Simmons's anarchism. If we have no political obligations, and states have no political right to enforce law, for Simmons this does not mean that state violence is unjustified, for the state (or more precisely, the government or its officials) may have a natural right to punish those who break the natural/moral law. This position fits coherently with the justification/legitimacy distinction Simmons draws in *Justification and Legitimacy*, in which we can "justify the state by showing that some realizable type of state is on balance morally permissible (or ideal) and that it is rationally preferable to all feasible nonstate alternatives" even if the state is not legitimate (Simmons 2001, 125). If the key to criticizing legal or state violence is to begin with the legitimacy/illegitimacy distinction, Simmons, after undermining that distinction, restores it at a prepolitical level through an appeal to natural law. But if so, then on Benjamin's account, Simmons cannot have justified state violence (e.g., punishment) itself but only its use for certain ends presumed to be just. In the next section, the presumption of the justness of the ends in Simmons's work will be questioned. But here I would like to show how Simmons fails to get at the justification of violence itself precisely by transferring the justification of violence from the positivist moment of legitimate founding to the state of nature, ensuring that violence is justified in its use but not in itself. State violence is justified "naturally" and as "natural," and thus elided at the very moment its morally problematic status would be most obvious.

Locke's strange doctrine is announced early in the Second Treatise: "And that all men be restrained from invading others Rights, and from doing hurt to one another, and the Law of Nature be observed, which willeth the Peace and Preservation of all Mankind, the Execution of the Law of Nature is in that State, put into every Mans hands, whereby each one has a right to punish the transgressors of that law to such a Degree, as may hinder its violation" (Locke 1988, II, 7). Simmons's reconstruction and defense of this "natural executive right" to punish wrongdoers is interesting in a variety of respects, but I am concerned only with the implications of this right on the consequences for the legitimacy of state violence given the truth of philosophical anarchism. That there is a connection is noted by Simmons at the end of his discussion: "The Lockean account I have just defended is an account of what must take place if legal punishment is to be legitimate … It may be true that punishment in many or most civil soci-eties is not legitimate" (Simmons 1992, 165). The Lockean account is one in which the exclusive right to punish wrongdoers is given to the gov-ernment through a transaction, where each citizen gives up their natural executive right (as well as, on Simmons's account, some of their rights to self-government) to the state. Insofar as such transactions rarely if ever take place in any state (according to Simmons's anarchist position), most individuals have never given up their natural executive right to punish, and thus all states have such an exclusive right only in relation to the very few who have explicitly consented to the state. Thus, it would seem fair to say, as Simmons does, that most practices of legal punishment are illegitimate.

Of course, they are not really illegitimate even if the state does not possess and cannot morally justify an exclusive right to punish. The reason is that in defending a natural right to punish, the violence of punishment is naturalized (in the specific sense of the state of nature, often invoked by Simmons, as a logically but not temporally prepolitical state) within the framework of a natural law and realist moral theory. The illegitimacy of state practices of violence does not entail the moral unjustifiability of those practices because there is a prepolitical, natural moral justification for those same practices. The question becomes: what justifies the natural violence involved in the natural right to punish?

Locke's case appeals to many sources: to God, to the logical necessity that the natural law have real sanctions, to the grounds of a right to punish aliens, and so on. For Simmons, however, the explanation begins in part from the basic "principle" of Lockean moral theory, the fundamental law of nature, which is the right and duty to preserve humankind: "Specifically, the fundamental law of nature is, I think, meant to function in Locke's moral theory much as the principle of utility has been thought to function in some rule-utilitarian schemes. The superstructure of Locke's moral theory, then, is a kind of rule-consequentialism, with the preservation of mankind serving as the 'ultimate end' to be advanced" (Simmons 1992, 50). What we have, on Simmons's reading of Locke, is a basic means–ends structure neces-sary to any consequentialism, albeit a rule consequentialism that allows for a blending of utilitarian and deontological arguments (Simmons 1992, 58–59). Thus we can know the ultimate natural end for which any violence, however far down the instrumental chain, must be used: the preservation of humankind. Punishment and its violence—and presumably all other justified violence, say, of war or resistance—is justified by the ultimate just end of preserving humanity.

To return to the specific violence of punishment, it is perhaps surprising that Simmons does not rely entirely (or even largely) on a direct derivation of the right to punish from the fundamental law of nature. Largely to avoid Locke's divine foundation of the natural law, Simmons turns to the possibility that the natural right to punish is a matter of rights forfeiture on the part of the criminal, and for this claim he gives something closely analogous to (although not entirely identical with) a "fair play" argument (Simmons 1992, 148–61). Given the existence of moral rules (the law of nature), he argues, it is reasonable that only those who follow the rules deserve the protection of those rules. When a person commits a crime, they forfeit some (or all, presumably in the case of capital punishment) of their rights against being harmed by others. Thus the natural right to punish is the "special right" generated by the wrongdoing of the criminal that belongs to everyone in the state of nature so that they can punish wrongdoing to repair the damage done to the victim (although the right to that reparation belongs to the victim alone) and to preserve humankind through the usual deterrent effects of punishment.

However, there is a real problem with the rights forfeiture foundation of the natural right to punish. In basing the right to punish on rights forfeiture, there is a seeming advantage: the loss of rights against harm from others (and thus the corresponding right to punish when one forfeits those rights through wrongdoing) is given a voluntaristic basis that avoids the divine ground of moral obligation embraced by Locke (in favor of a secular ground of the same rights, something also present in Locke). If coherent, then the argument I have been making—that Simmons's position is thoroughly naturalistic and thus cannot justify violence itself—would fail, for even if what is at issue in the right to punish is no longer the legitimacy of the state based on consent, the natural right to punish would have a "historical" basis in a voluntary system of rights and duties based on fair play. In short, the violence involved in the right to punish would be legitimized not by its naturalness but by a historical, voluntaristic ground.

Indeed, Simmons describes life under moral rules in the state of nature as a conception of social interaction akin to the "fair play" image of political society, that is, one in which our reception of benefits within a system of cooperation is the ground of our obligation to obey the rules. He writes: "Perhaps the most 'natural' way to view forfeiture involves maintaining that any reasonable or fair system of protective rules (laws, conventions) must specify (explicitly or implicitly) that one's status under the rules depends on respecting them; any rights the rules may define are guaranteed only to those who refrain from violating them" (Simmons 1992, 153). In criticizing the principle of fair play as a ground of political obligation, Simmons rests his case largely on the fact that only a clear acceptance of benefits that almost amounts to or collapses into consent could ground political obligation on the fair play view, but very few citizens have accepted benefits in the "right" way. Moreover, others who receive or accept benefits most likely do not accept the vision of society within the fair play view as one of a "cooperative scheme" (Simmons 1979, 136–42). In short, fair play fails as a ground of political obligation both because very few people accept benefits in the right way and because few view their society in the right terms.

Surely the same arguments apply to the fair play rights forfeiture view Simmons paints. Is it really all that natural to think of individuals in the state of nature viewing themselves as members of a "moral cooperative scheme" in which they know, explicitly or implicitly, that one's status within the system depends on respecting its rules? Is there, as it were, a meta-natural law, or secondary natural law, that reason can discover in which we know our rights are contingent on following the rules? Surely we are bound to obey the natural law even in the absence of any acceptance of benefits or even consent and, further, even if we do not participate in anything like or believe we are participating in anything like a cooperative scheme. If such a rule is "implicit," this would undermine any kind of voluntaristic basis for our participating in the natural law "cooperative scheme," just as the mere reception of benefits cannot generate an obligation to obey the law. The voluntaristic picture of life under moral rules in the state of nature—one that mirrors the picture of life within a political order where obligation is grounded in fair play—seems incoherent on the face of it; even if coherent, this view appears to radically change the conception and point of natural law. The real argument for the right to punish must then be the purely natural one, in which our right to punish, the right to use violence, is justified by the just ends of punishing individuals to achieve the highest end: the preservation of humankind.

But what about the violence itself? Has it been justified, or only its use? Can violence ever be a moral means to even just ends, as Benjamin asks? Put differently: is there a natural right to violence, as Benjamin claimed to be the position of natural law, a violence that is "as it were a raw material"? (Benjamin 1978, 278).

If the answer, certainly for Hobbes and complexly for Locke and Simmons, is yes, and no matter what restrictions one puts on violence it is undoubtedly natural (in the sense of prepolitical), then a serious problem emerges in Simmons' anarchism. If consent alone could legitimize the state and its violence (Simmons 1979, 191); if, as Simmons repeatedly notes, the principle of consent, expressing the artificial nature of political obligation, is central to Locke's (and Simmons's own) sense of political legitimacy (see also Simmons 1993, 37); and few people have consented to their governments, thus all states are illegitimate; then practices of state violence should be illegitimate but are not because even illegitimate artificial governments have a legitimate natural right to punish. There are three problems here. The first is that one is led to wonder why we need to authorize the state at all—much as Buchanan argues—given that the legitimacy of state violence (and presumably state lawmaking), even on Simmons's own anarchist account, is morally justified even without being authorized. The second problem is that the artificial, created character of political power equally seems to lose its importance insofar as the only real "wrong" a government can commit when it lacks the exclusive right to punish is to interfere in the equal right of another person or entity to punish the wrongdoer (and is that really an important moral wrong, or even a real practical difficulty if governments, as we know, are capable of maintaining standing armies, police forces, legal systems, and so on). A natural account of the legitimate use of state violence obviates the moral necessity to legitimize that violence through any artificial act of consent.

The third problem is the one I have been emphasizing: violence is too quickly assumed to be morally unproblematic, and the use of violence to achieve just ends (and restrictions on that use) becomes the only pressing matter. In Simmons we see how a natural law thinker, even one who offers persuasive arguments for the illegitimacy of existing states based on the importance of consent (and thus on positivist claims for the importance of founding in thinking about state legitimacy) elides the problem of violence because of a natural law framework that reduces the moral problem of violence back to its usefulness in achieving just ends. That there is something morally problematic about state violence given the illegitimacy of existing states is acknowledged, but too quickly forgotten or solved through recourse to a moral theory grounded in natural rights and laws. I now turn to the questionability of that theory.

SIMMONS'S DEFENSE OF NATURAL LAW/RIGHT

The closest Simmons comes to defending his moral theory is in his response to "natural rights skeptics" in *The Lockean Theory of Rights*. Before turning to that defense and how it fails to answer to the most powerful criticisms of the philosophical bases of natural right/law theory, I want to note my agreement with Simmons on a basic point. In a footnote Simmons argues:

> It is, I think, often tempting to allow historical and social explo-
> rations, which sometimes show us how moral concepts come into
> use and become firmly entrenched, to deflect our attention from
> the project of determining whether moral judgments using those
> concepts are justified or valid. That the two are distinct projects
> seems to me undeniable. To maintain the contrary would be like
> arguing that because the church is responsible for our view of God,
> there is no independent question of the meaningfulness, truth,
> or justifiability of religious propositions. This is not, of course,
> to argue that explanations of how our moral language comes into use
> or its role in our lives is not relevant to the latter kind of question,
> but only that he first project cannot be a simple substitute for the
> second. (Simmons 1992, 115–16)

I return to the context in which Simmons makes this point in a moment, but I think he is right. Pointing out the history—especially if that history is particularly violent, unsettling, racist, sexist, and so on—of a concept need not entail anything vis-à-vis its meaningfulness or justifiability or truth. When Simmons admits that the history of a concept is relevant to the deter-mination of its truth, I imagine he is referring (at least in part) to the fact that before we can determine the truth of an idea, we must at least under-stand that idea, and such an understanding is aided by understanding the historical context within which the idea emerged. Similarly, of course, we also need to understand the philosophical context of the idea.

However, I would phrase the point slightly differently because there is a form of historico-philosophical criticism—for example, what we find in Nietzsche, Heidegger, Foucault, and others—in which the historiciza-tion of ideas is purposefully interwoven with philosophical argumentation (and for philosophical reasons). Far from being a confusion, such crit-icism relies in part on a philosophical interrogation of history, that is, history itself is taken as an object of philosophical analysis and as a matter of philosophical importance. For Nietzsche and Foucault, genealogy is precisely a historical method that is philosophical and relies on a con-ception of history that has been subjected to philosophical analysis. That the most important and powerful criticisms of the modern moral subject often proceed by blurring the distinction between historicization and phil-osophical argumentation is not surprising, for temporality itself becomes a matter of ontological, anthropological, and historical concern given the criticisms of the modern (moral) subject one finds in many nineteenth- and twentieth-century thinkers. Thus, I want to be clear that my own response to Simmons does not collapse the history/philosophy distinction in the way he warns against (and which I agree with), but it does not accept the distinction as it stands.

Although Simmons does not offer a full defense of his moral theory, he does acknowledge that "the 'common core' of natural law doctrine seems to amount to little more than this: that there are universally binding ('objec-tively valid') moral rules, knowable by use of our natural faculties ... Natural law theory, in this sense, implies some form of value objectivism—a position that is controversial enough, of course, but one that is still well within the mainstream of active theoretical debate" (Simmons 1992, 103). He further acknowledges that this position does commit him to some version of moral realism (Simmons 1992, 104).[4] We also find a tentative acknowledgment of the coherence of "ethical pluralism," that is, that we can work with a plurality of irreducible ethical principles in grounding moral rights and duties (Simmons 1992, 59). Finally, in deciding what to do in cases of conflicts between rights, duties, principles, and prudential concerns, Simmons argues for a "balance-of-reasons" view in which, depending on the case, rights can be overridden by prudential concerns, one right can override another, or rights can serve as "trumps" (Simmons 2001, 108).[5]

Many of these positions inform Simmons's response to "natural rights skeptics," for example, Marxists, Hegelians, and communitarians such as Charles Taylor, Alisdair MacIntyre, and Michael Sandel as well as to utilitarians such as Jeremy Bentham. I ignore his response to Bentham (for whom rights are famously "nonsense on stilts") and focus primarily on his response to the various communitarians, for in that response Simmons comes closest to addressing some of the criticisms of the moral subject we find in Nietzsche et al., but he deflects the problems in ways that do not address the real nature of the criticisms.

Simmons first responds to Taylor's claim in the essay "Atomism" that the idea of natural rights rests on a concept of an "extensionless subject, epistemologically a tabula rasa" (as quoted in Simmons 1992, 104). To this he responds:

> It is hard to assess the complaint at this level of generality ... The only salient meaning "natural" seems to have for Locke in connection with rights ... is "nonconventional" or "logically nonpolitical." If this is what a natural right is, the defender of natural rights is not obviously committed to any more than the existence of objective (not essentially conventional) moral rules defining rights ... The standard (but not only) epistemological and metaphysical positions accompanying these views are admittedly realist in character [Simmons is referring here to moral realism, not, I think, to realism more broadly] ... But since moral realism and objectivism are clearly still live issues in moral philosophy, neither of these commitments for the natural rights theorist is obviously damning. (Simmons 1992, 104–5)

Without defending Taylor specifically, I would like to show how Simmons misses the point of the criticism. For the issue of the *subject* of rights, that is, how we philosophically understand the bearer of rights—metaphysically, ontologically, epistemologically, and anthropologically—rests on a set of Cartesian and post-Cartesian ideas that have been a common object of criticism from a number of philosophers (including Friedrich Nietzsche and Martin Heidegger, Michel Foucault and Jacques Derrida, but also Ludwig Wittgenstein and the American pragmatists). Taylor's criticism cannot be met, as Simmons goes about it, by claiming that "natural" means "prepolitical" in Locke. What is at issue in the criticism is how we philosophically conceive the subject, and this is a matter of philosophical importance for Heidegger, to take just one example. In Heidegger's criticism of Cartesian ontology in *Being and Time*, he argues that the picture of the human being's relation to its world that we find in modern philosophy is one of a subject standing against a world of objects to which it relates through forming mental representations of that world. Heidegger shows that a phenomenology of everyday human existence reveals that the representational stance of a subject vis-à-vis objects is a derivate mode of human being, arising out of a more basic relation in which human beings are always already engaged with "objects" without the mediation of representational mental states. It is the Cartesian picture of the human subject that is being questioned by Taylor, not its "naturalness." To be sure, addressing Taylor's "complaint" would then require reading any number of prominent philosophers who dispute the truth of the Cartesian subject.[6] But the point is that not only in the continental tradition but equally in the analytic tradition, the conception of the subject we find in Descartes has been challenged (of course, it is has also been defended).

This general issue becomes more specific and pertinent when Simmons defends his position against those who would argue that natural rights "must be derived from or somehow turn on facts about human nature" (Simmons 1992, 105). These critics, he notes, often argue that one cannot read off moral facts from natural facts, that there is no human nature to "read," and that natural rights theories based on human nature are far too general to apply to the variety of real-world contexts they are supposed to help us navigate. To the first criticism—that one cannot read off moral facts from natural facts—Simmons responds that Locke, at any rate, does not do any such thing; rather, "his argument concerns not what is 'natural' for humankind in this simple sense, but rather what is rational. To the extent that his derivation of natural rights relies upon facts about human nature, it relies only upon relatively uncontroversial and extremely general claims (about, e.g., rationality, desire for self-preservation, moderate sociableness, etc.)" (Simmons 1992, 105).

The problem with this response is that our understanding of human rationality is one of the central issues in or consequences of criticisms of Cartesian anthropology and ontology. Nietzsche argues—along with Freud and a number of researchers in contemporary neuroscience, philosophers of science and mind, and the like—that consciousness is only a part (he thinks the smallest part) of our thinking:

Man, like every living being, thinks continually without knowing it; the thinking that rises to consciousness is only the smallest part of all this—the most superficial and worst part—for only this conscious thinking takes the form of words, which is to say signs of communication, and this fact uncovers the origin of consciousness [which, for Nietzsche, is the need to communicate in order to receive help and protection from others] … You will guess that it is not the opposition of subject and object that concerns me here: this distinction I leave to the epistemologists who have become entangled in the snares of grammar (the metaphysics of the people). (Nietzsche 1974, §354)

The issue is not just one for the philosophy of mind, for the centrality of consciousness and rationality to intentional action and thus to morality is part of Nietzsche's general criticism of morality, just as it plays a central role in Simmons's brief response to natural rights skeptics. The point is not that anyone should be satisfied with Nietzschean or any claims about human rationality simply because the claims are reasonable and defensible. Rather, the point is that both contemporary philosophy and contemporary neuroscience have made it difficult to make uncontroversial claims about rationality. Insofar as a moral theory is based on claims about rationality—and in natural rights theory, rationality plays a crucial, if not the most elemental role (save, in certain theories, God)—then one needs to address the controversy. That the capacity for rationality—perhaps along with some other capacities—plays that role in Simmons's argument is clear, for he explicitly acknowledges that where there is no rationality (or the other capacities necessary for the possession of natural rights), those individuals have no natural rights (Simmons 1992, 113).

The other communitarian criticism Simmons responds to is the Hegelian and post-Hegelian idea that individuals are necessarily situated within communities constituted by roles, norms, rules, and a history that "encumbers" any self such that it makes no sense to speak of a presocial natural individual bearing rights. I agree with one aspect of his response: at least for Locke, who understands the state of nature as a social place, there is no obvious contradiction between the claim that selves are (partly) products of social relations and roles and that they have the right, perhaps even the duty, to criticize (so as to genuinely accept) those roles (Simmons 1992, 111). The real meat of the criticism, as Simmons sees it, is that only within certain societies can the capacities necessary for having and employing rights come into being, and thus there can be no "self-sufficient moral agent" (Simmons 1992, 113). To this, he reiterates the claim that the state of nature can be social, and thus changes the import of the criticism: it is not that capacities for rights cannot develop in the state of nature, but that they might not, depending on the social context. Simmons allows for such a possibility and thus grants that natural rights theories need not claim that natural rights are universally held by all human beings:

> Those who are not persons (moral agents) are not under the moral law. The natural rights theorist (and certainly Locke) is not com-mitted to asserting that all human in all places at all times have rights, but only to the claim that all persons naturally acquire certain rights along with their personhood. But being a person or moral agent does not, in the way Taylor suggests, presuppose any particular conventions, rules, laws, or practices. Many different kinds of arrangements, both political and nonpolitical, can clearly suffice for the development of those minimal capacities necessary for Lockean agency or personhood. (Simmons 1992, 114)

Related to this criticism of Taylor is Simmons's response to Alisdair MacIntyre's account of the loss of moral bearing in the modern world, epit-omized in the invention of the modern moral subject, the bearer of natural rights. The tale MacIntyre tells in *After Virtue* is well known, but to the claim that the modern bearer of rights was invented, Simmons responds:

> But it is possible to tell other kinds of stories in which the "modern individual," the person who bears natural rights, is not so much invented as discovered. We have seen ... how on certain theo-logical views, rights-talk, and the perception of natural equality on which it rests, is naturally suppressed. It is even more plain that rigid social classes and hierarchies of certain sorts, as well as the economic forms of life that shaped and accompanied them, greatly reduced the visibility of equality, and consequently also prevented the perception of shared natural rights ... It would, then, be far from surprising, and certainly not unintelligible, if persons in other cultures and times possessed the natural rights of which Lockeans write, without any general social recognition that this was the case. (Simmons 1992, 115)

The claim that no particular conventions, rules, laws, or practices must be presupposed to be a person or moral agent and the second claim that a story can be told about the historical emergence of natural rights in which the modern bearer of rights is "discovered" rather than invented (by a particular set of conventions, rules, laws, etc.) raises the question: what about the work of Foucault? For throughout Foucault's work we are told a "story"—grounded in historical evidence and philosophical analysis (contestable to be sure)—of the "invention" of the modern subject, in particular the modern moral subject, as a bearer of rights. This process takes place through very specific "rules, laws, or practices" that produce a subject/object of power through regimes of power/knowledge in which techniques of power informed by scientific inquiry into the human being feed back into those scientific inquiries.

It is unsurprising that we find in Foucault an explicit rejection of the discovery narrative, especially in its visual metaphors of a movement from blindness to vision, darkness to light (in a footnote Simmons refers to blinders that required removal to see the rights-bearing subject; Simmons 1992, 115): "Before the end of the eighteenth century, man did not exist ... He is a quite recent creature, which the demiurge of knowledge fabricated with his own hands less than two hundred years ago: but he has grown old so quickly that it has been only too easy to imagine that he had been waiting for thousands of years in the darkness for that moment of illumination in which he would finally be known" (Foucault 1994, 308). Simmons would no doubt disagree with the implication here—later stated explicitly—that humanity is disappearing and because of this event we are tempted to think that people could not possibly be dying at such a young age. But the point is that Foucault—in much greater historical detail than MacIntyre—offers a historical narrative and philosophical analysis of the invention of Man. In "Man and his Doubles" in *The Order of Things*, Foucault identifies the creation, within philosophy and the social sciences, of man as a subject/object of knowledge, an "empirico-transcendental doublet" through which investigation into the empirical contents of finite humanity are differentially repeated and grounded through inquiry into the transcendental subject of knowledge (most obviously in *The Critique of Pure Reason*). Although natural rights theories and the politics they inform are not always explicitly at issue in *The Order of Things*, it is clear that the empirico-transcendental doublet, that "enslaved sovereign, observed spectator" is central to at least Rousseauian and Kantian moral and political theories (Foucault 1994, 312). To the extent that Locke, as Simmons suggests, shares affinities with Kant, one might further that suggestion by looking at how the Lockean subject shares with the Kantian subject its empirico-transcendentality (Simmons 1994, 39–46). If it could be shown—as I think it can—that the Lockean rights-bearing subject, in spite of Locke's empiricism, draws on features of the transcendental subject we find in Kant, then the Lockean subject might also be more susceptible to the charge of being invented rather than discovered. However, an invention narrative might be countered by a discovery narrative; for this reason a persuasive response to MacIntyre requires not just the assertion that a discovery narrative is plausible but an actual historical account.

Foucault does not just offer a historico-philosophical account of the birth of the modern philosophical subject. Especially in *Discipline and Punish*, *Madness and Civilization*, and *The History of Sexuality*, we are given further historico-philosophical analyses of the specific rules, laws, and conventions— specific techniques of power/knowledge—that produce the modern subject/ object. In *Discipline and Punish*, for example, it is shown that the modern "soul"—the transcendental side of the empirico-transcendental doublet— is produced through disciplinary techniques within a number of modern institutions. That the soul is the object of intervention within disciplinary institutions does not, however, mean that the body—as it were the "empirical" side of the doublet—is no longer the target of power. Rather, the production of the soul is a new technique of producing and continually intervening in the soul/body such that the soul/body learns to discipline itself. Though produced through discipline, "it would be wrong to say that the soul is an illusion, or an ideological effect. On the contrary, it exists, it has a reality, it is produced permanently around, on, within the body by the functioning of a power that is exercised on those punished–and in a more general way, on those one supervises, trains and corrects" (Foucault 1994, 29). This modern soul is not a substance but an element in which techniques of power and scientific inquiry flow, producing, among other things, the object of the "moral claims of humanism," that human being who is to be liberated through the recognition and protection of its rights (Foucault 1994, 30). In linking the production of the modern soul to the liberatory moral project of humanism, Foucault emphasizes that the modern moral subject is produced through an effect of a "subjection" more "profound than himself" (Foucault 1994, 29). The modern soul is a "prison of the body," and along with the techniques of power that bring this soul into being, the soul itself is a "factor in the mastery that power exercises over the body" (Foucault 1994, 29).

If it is true that the rights-bearing subject is a product of specific rules, laws, and conventions—and that this can be shown through historico-philosophical analysis—then Simmons's defense of natural rights theory becomes even more untenable as it stands and requires a response to critics like Foucault. The issue raised by Foucault's work is not (only) that the rights-bearing subject is only found in and intelligible within specific societies that produce the capacities necessary for rights-claiming. Foucault is at pains to show that the modern moral subject, a bearer of rights, is produced through a subjection more profound than itself such that the claiming of a right is, normatively considered, a paradoxical act. The freedom sought in the claiming of a right rests on a subjection (even to oneself) that makes the rights-claiming subject possible. Foucault's analytic and normative arguments are often hard to distinguish, and one can be as impressed by the analysis as one is frustrated by the difficulties of identifying, much less affirming, Foucault's normative project (see the first three chapters of Fraser 1989). But one cannot simply assert, as Simmons does, that a discovery historical account of the rights-bearing subject is possible, even plausible—no doubt it is logically possible—without providing a detailed historical narrative (or even a citation to one). One cannot also assert that no particular rules, laws, or conventions are required to produce the capacities necessary to bear rights when detailed historical and philosophical arguments to the contrary stand by to refute the claim.

In short, Simmons's undefended appeal to moral realism must at least be supported in response to what J. M. Bernstein, in a discussion of the ethical views of Adorno and Horkheimer and Bernard Williams, distinguishes as the "intelligibility" in modernity of moral realism (Bernstein 2001, 98–106). Rather than the question of whether moral realism is true—recall that I have not claimed that Nietzsche, or Foucault, or Heidegger, or anyone else has shown moral realism to be false—Bernstein argues that given the progressive demythologization and disenchantment of (at least) the Western world, moral realism cannot be held in the same way that premodern, thick ethical concepts were subscribed to. As Simmons admits, moral realism is but one (plausible) contender in moral theory today. But so many of the consequences of Simmons's philosophical anarchism depend on a commitment to that moral realism that its defense is necessary, especially in response to those critics—like Adorno, Nietzsche, Williams, Habermas, and others—who have radically called into question the plausibility and/or truth of the moral realist position.

THE LIMITS OF PHILOSOPHICAL ANARCHISM

Nothing I claimed in the last section amounts to an argument; they are just suggestions, or questions, to Simmons. To Simmons's attempt to make natural rights theories plausible in the face of various forms of skepticism toward those theories, I have only argued that the most powerful criticisms of those theories may come from writers—for example, Nietzsche, Heidegger, and Foucault—who make no appearance in Simmons's defense. The reason for doing so is that however much I am persuaded by Simmons's anarchist arguments, the consequences drawn from that argument rest on moral ideas, concepts, and presuppositions that have been rightly questioned. Within analytic moral philosophy, as Simmons acknowledges, debates over moral realism, noncognitivism, relativism, constructivism, and others are ongoing, but those debates rarely acknowledge the kinds of criticisms I have outlined here. In addition to the debate over the possibility of legitimizing the state and the debates within analytic moral philosophy, I suggest that an inclusion of further forms of criticism like the ones I have noted would productively add to ongoing discussions in analytic political philosophy.

Foucault's work also moves us away from questions of legitimacy—which rest on a somewhat but not entirely outdated seventeenth-century connection of sovereignty and law—to a "capillary" micro-physics of power. To that extent, the whole debate over the legitimacy of the state tends to lose its importance, and thus my interest in philosophical anarchism and its conclusions might appear to be superfluous. However, this is both to mistake Foucault's position—which does not deny that sovereign, disciplinary, and biopolitical power can and do coexist—and to forget the moral issue central to the problem of the state's legitimacy: whether and how we can morally distinguish state violence from nonstate violence. To be sure, I have argued that Simmons's work displaces state violence. But he does not displace or ignore the moral justifications needed for state actions. On one hand, then, I do not think that even for Foucault raising the moral question of the legitimacy of the state is anachronistic; on the other hand, I do think that Foucault and his many inheritors in contemporary political theory have criticized, and then forgotten that question, specifically vis-à-vis practices of state violence. In the next chapter, I show how arguments within contemporary political theory for an unavoidable paradox of founding within political communities—one that renders state legitimacy always questionable—displaces the moral problem of state violence in a particular way, even as the paradox of founding is invoked (in part) to question specific practices of state violence.

2 THE STRENGTHS AND LIMITS OF THE PARADOX OF POLITICS

IN THE PREVIOUS CHAPTER I began by appropriating Walter Benjamin's approach to a critique of violence to show that A. John Simmons's anarchism displaces the moral problem of state violence within legal positivism insofar as he regrounds state violence on a natural right to punish. For this reason, my general agreement with the anarchist position has compelled me to seek alternative ways of approaching the problem of the moral legitimacy of state violence.

In this chapter I explore the strengths and limits of a problematic within contemporary political theory that I am not only persuaded by and sympathetic to but far more intellectually indebted to: what is called the "paradox of founding" or the "paradox of politics." For William Connolly and Bonnie Honig, the paradox of founding can be explicitly traced to Paul Ricoeur's essay "The Political Paradox," although the recognition of a paradox of founding or politics by other philosophers—especially Rousseau—is clear (Ricoeur 1992). I return to Ricoeur later, but the paradox of founding is akin to yet different from the anarchist's denial of the state's legitimacy. The theorist who identifies and affirms the paradox of politics/founding, to borrow a phrase from Benjamin, "demands of all violence a proof of its historical origin" (Benjamin 1978, 280). Once the historical origin of the state is examined, however, the contingent genesis of the state calls into question the legitimacy it claims for itself. One can always ask: "What legitimizes a founding act?" Far from being merely a theoretical problem, one need only look at the many "constituent moments" Jason Frank identifies during the revolutionary period in the United States to see the very real and complicating political difficulties and promise of speaking without,

27

or by speaking transforming, authority (Frank 2010). Once asked, inquiry into the conditions of legitimacy for a founding act tends toward an infinite regress, one that can only be stopped by a (nonetheless a-legitimate) coup de force (Derrida 2002, 241; Frank 2010, 6).

Rather than denying (the possibility of) state and/or legal legitimacy on the basis of the infinite regress, some theorists who accept this paradox claim that the state/law is neither legitimate nor illegitimate. For example, Derrida argues that "Since the origin of authority, the founding or grounding [*la fondation ou le fondement*], the positing of the law [*loi*] cannot by definition rest on anything but themselves, they are themselves a violence without ground [*sans fondement*]. This is not to say that they are in themselves unjust, in the sense of 'illegal' or 'illegitimate.' They are neither legal nor illegal in their founding moment" (Derrida 2002, 242). The paradox of founding haunts any political community that claims legitimacy precisely because it is founded in time and space.[1] One can, as Derrida notes, perform a historical regress to find the conditions that enable the founding of law, but those conditions will also require legitimacy and the abyss of justification will not be crossed. The "mystical" foundation of law—the fact that the ground of Law rests in the mystical, violent power of the performative to inaugurate—signals the deconstructability of law and is thus not only a political danger (for law is force, violence) but a political chance (for law is perfectible, in "relation" to and with an undeconstructible justice that law must but cannot render).

Carl Schmitt is aware of the paradox, too. In *Political Theology* he writes: "The exception reveals most clearly the essence of the state's authority. The decision parts here from the legal norm, and (to formulate it paradoxically) authority proves that to produce law it need not be based on law" (Schmitt 2005, 13). For Schmitt, the paradox is not really a paradox at all, for the fact that authority proves that to produce law it need not be based on law only proves the irreducibility and ultimate autonomy of the decision in determining any legal situation. For him, one might argue, the "solution" to the paradox is to deny the paradox: there is only a paradox if one thinks that all legal decisions must be determined by norms to be properly legal (see also Schmitt 2008a, 124).

For still other theorists of the paradox of politics/founding such as Connolly and Honig, the paradox of politics/founding emerges from a reading of Rousseau.[2] For both thinkers, Rousseau shows that the relation between a legitimate legal order and a democratic people is always vexed, for it is a legitimate law that cultivates the type of democratic citizen that will approve the correct, hence legitimate, laws. But to get such a law in the first place, the democratic people would already have to be formed and educated properly by correct, legitimate laws. As I would put it (somewhat following Honig), democratic sovereignty and legitimacy ought to—but never can—coincide. The paradox is affirmed by Honig and Connolly because the fact of the paradox opens the possibility—to be urgently actualized—of an agonistic, contestatory democratic politics that denies any claims by a political community to be "truly" sovereign, truly democratic, fully legitimate. Such a politics is not only responsive to the fact of pluralism in modern societies but sensitive to what Connolly calls "pluralization," that is, the further fact that surprising and unexpected new constituencies, rights claims, political subjectivities, and problems emerge into politics, often unsettling established legal and political relationships and in turn provoking reactionary political movements. The contestatory politics argued for by Connolly and Honig encourages recognition and an (always cautious) affirmation of the unsettling, evental nature of politics and encourages others to affirm it as well (rather than deny or repress what provokes change).

I am persuaded by Derrida, Schmitt, Honig, and Connolly that there is a paradox of politics/founding, and the political possibilities and consequences drawn from that paradox in Derrida, Honig, and Connolly (but not Schmitt) have shaped my own thinking in this book. Yet I am resistant to the formulations of the paradox in Honig, Connolly, and Derrida because I locate the paradox of founding in a different part of Rousseau and thus draw a different set of conclusions for the problem of legitimate state violence. For this reason, I try to open their politics (which I heartily endorse) to a reconsideration of the legitimacy of state violence.

In this chapter I first turn to Honig and Connolly to contest their reading of Rousseau, specifically the claim that the paradox of politics/founding in *On the Social Contract* can be found in book II, chapter 7. I do so because in locating the paradox where they do, the "lesson" of the paradox of politics/founding they draw can lead toward the dismissal of the kinds of questions about the morality of state violence asked by analytic political philosophers, questions that are still valid and valuable. In offering my own reading of the place of the paradox of founding/politics in Rousseau, I hope to show that my way of approaching the problem of state violence could further the kind of contestatory politics Honig and Connolly affirm.

In short, although I differ in my understanding of Rousseau, I largely agree with the political lessons Honig and Connolly draw from him.

On the other hand, although I agree that Derrida's formulation of the paradox of founding/politics gets at the root of the relation between the paradox and state violence, I find his politics unjustifiably legalistic and thus insufficient for negotiating the politics of state violence. It is unclear to me why, as Derrida argues, justice can only and must be enforced through a law that can never render justice. Rather, I understand the neo-Kantian (as it were) (non)relation between the unconditional and the conditioned that creates the aporia, and I also understand that Derrida's position is partly a response to the political dangers of Benjamin's absolute distinction between a mythical law and a divine justice. Moreover, I am generally a big fan of the rule of law. What I do not think Derrida has shown, however, is that we must accept the quasi-Kantian ethical structure his politics rests on, and my concern is that, strangely enough for a text called "Force of Law," the moral problem of state violence may in fact be, in its own way, displaced or repressed in Derrida's politics because of this structure.

In this chapter I hope to show both what I affirm and what I am hesitant about in discussions of the paradox of founding, and thereby set the stage for my own arguments about the morality of state violence in the next three chapters.

CONNOLLY, HONIG, AND THE ROUSSEAUIAN PARADOX OF FOUNDING

The paradox of politics/founding, for Honig and Connolly, is to be found in book II, chapter 7 of Rousseau's *On the Social Contract*. In that chapter—"On the Legislator"—Rousseau writes:

> In order for an emerging people to appreciate the healthy maxims of politics, and follow the fundamental rules of statecraft, the effect would have to become the cause; the social spirit, which should be the result of the institution, would have to preside over the founding of the institution itself and men would be to be prior to laws what they ought to become by means of laws. Since the legislator is therefore unable to use either force or reasoning, he must necessarily have recourse to another order of authority, which can win

over without violence and persuade without convincing. (Rousseau 1978, book II, chap. 7)

Although this passage does express a tension present just after the founding moment and continuing throughout politics, I would like to argue that it is not a paradox of founding at all, nor is it a paradox of politics. There is a paradox of founding in *On the Social Contract*, noticed by Rousseau, just as there is a paradox in Hobbes, Locke, and any other theorist (although not always acknowledged) that is forced to confront the facticity of the historical genesis of a putatively legitimate political community. This facticity generates a paradox of politics/founding, and it does indeed haunt any political community (although it is also true that theorists try to solve the paradox). To show this, I turn to another section of *On the Social Contract*.

First, let's return to the famous passage just cited. For Connolly, this is a paradox of founding, the paradox of the founding of the "general will": "For a general will to be brought into being, effect (social spirit) would have to become cause, and cause (good laws) would have to become effect. The problem is how to establish either condition without the previous attainment of the other upon which it depends. This is the paradox of political founding" (Connolly 1995, 138; see also Connolly 2005, 135). Rousseau and many political communities attempt to resolve this paradox, often by locating and confining its existence and solution to the founding moment such that the present is not haunted by the paradox. In this way, the "paradox of sovereignty dissolves into the politics of forgetting," and a continuing foundational violence is concealed (Connolly 1995, 138).

For Honig, partly following Connolly, the passage in Rousseau reveals a paradox of politics (as such?) that is, in the passage cited, located at the founding moment but not confinable to it: "But the seeming quandary of chicken-and-egg … takes off and attaches to democratic politics more generally … The problem that Rousseau casts as a problem of founding recurs daily" (Honig 2007, 3). The paradox of politics manifests and is responded to in numerous ways, but it is unavoidable, partly because in a democracy "the people are never so fully what they need to be that a democracy can deny credibly that it resorts to violence, imposition, or coercion to maintain itself" (Honig 2007, 5). The paradox also emerges in the necessity within democracy for democratic judgment and decision, thus undermining any "authoritative" attempt to impose norms that will then be properly decided on through democratic procedures. That even norms and authoritative utterances, within democracies, must be decided on by the democratic people—and such decisions are irreducibly decisions rather than determinative judgments following from norms and reasons—means that ineluctably, a decision will cut through the paradox of politics without solving or dissolving it.

Although I largely agree with Honig and Connolly, I am nonetheless resistant to their claims that they are analyzing a paradox of founding/ politics because I am not sure the passage in Rousseau reveals a (genuine) paradox of politics, and moreover the attention paid to that passage ignores what I and others (including at times Honig and Connolly; see Connolly 2005, 134) take to be a real paradox of founding that is a genuine paradox within and of politics as such.[3] To show this, I return to Rousseau.

The first thing to notice in book II, chapter 7 is that founding (Masters's contestable translation of *instituer*), although mentioned (hence support for the claim that a paradox of founding is on display), is not really the subject of the chapter "On the Legislator" at all. In chapter 6 ("On Law") Rousseau begins as follows: "Through the social compact we have given the body politic existence and life; the issue now is to give it movement and will through legislation. For the original act which forms and unites this body does not thereby determine anything about what it should do to preserve itself" (Rousseau 1978, book II, chap. 6). Rousseau is quite clear that before law can be and is given to the body politic, that body politic itself must be formed, must have existence and life.[4] Moreover, the purpose of law is not to found the people but to give it movement and will. I return to this social compact and the coming into being of the body politic in a moment (for there we find a paradox of founding); for now, what is important is to see that the social compact and the moment of founding are distinct from the moment of legislating.

However, in the passage cited, and in other places in book II, chapter 7, Rousseau does employ the term *translated* as "founding" (*instituer*). In its first appearance, Rousseau writes that "one who dares to undertake the founding of a people (*d'instituer un peuple*) should feel that he is capable of changing (*changer*) human nature"; just prior, he had analogized the legislator to a "mechanic who invents (*invente*) the machine" and, citing the authority of Montesquieu, notes that "the leaders of republics create (*font*) the institutions" (Rousseau 1978, II, 7). Finally, of course, there is the passage cited above in which a legislator presides over "the founding of the institution itself" (*que l'esprit social, qui doit être l'ouvrage de l'institution, présidat à l'institution meme*). If this is not simple inconsistency in terminology, why does Rousseau speak of "founding" a people after having already noted, just one chapter before, that the act which forms and thus presumably founds the body politic is distinct from the act of giving a people laws?

Of course, one answer is surely that Masters mistranslates *instituer* as "founding" (given that Rousseau throughout his book employs *fonder, fond, fondement,* and so on). That aside, the answer lies in the metonymic chain linking many of the verbs and nouns used in book II, chapter 7: founding (*instituer*); institution (*institution*); invent (*invente*), create (*font*); changing (*changer*); constitute (*constitue*) and constitution (*constitution*). What is most often at issue in book II, chapter 7 is not the founding of "the people" but the founding of the "institution" (whatever that is). Recall that the founding of the institution is what is being referred to in the famous passage from book II, chapter 7 (the people are referred to as "emerging" but not "founded"). The institution is also that which is made more "solid and perfect" by the legislator's ability to alter man's constitution (*la constitution de l'homme*) (Rousseau 1978, book II, chap. 7). Finally, in a crucial passage, Rousseau writes: "The legislator is an extraordinary man in the State in all respects. If he should be so by his genius, he is no less so by his function. It is not magistracy, it is not sovereignty. This function, which constitutes the republic, does not enter into its constitution (*Cet emploi qui constitue la République n'entre point dans la constitution*)" (Rousseau 1978, book II, chap. 7).

What is the institution to which Rousseau is referring? It cannot be the government, of course, for the legislator does not institute the government; the people do, although not through a contract (Rousseau 1978, book III, chap. 1). Is it the State itself? How can it be since he refers to constituting a republic, and a republic is a form of state ruled by laws (which implies that there can be a state not ruled by laws). Of course, Rousseau also adds immediately that "every legitimate government is republican," but it is clear that what is at issue here is a legitimate government, not a legitimate State, for in a footnote Rousseau adds that "in order to be legitimate the government must not be confounded with the sovereign, but must be its minister. Then monarchy itself is a republic" (Rousseau 1978, book II, chap. 6). Is the institution in question the people? But in what sense could the people be an "institution" even if they are instituted (and etymologically, *instituĕre* in Latin can refer to founding but also establishing, ordaining, beginning, teaching, arranging, etc.)? Finally, there is the fact that the legislator does not enter into the constitution of the republic even as he constitutes it (i.e., the legislator is a foreigner), for the legislator is neither a magistrate nor sovereign. The legislator has no power save his ability to persuade without reasoning. The legislator does not institute the law (for he has no authority to do so); he does not institute the people (for they must already be a people to be given the law); presumably, then, he constitutes the Republic, institutes it, constitutes the institution of Law that defines the Republic, but not by founding it.

Rather than founding the people, the state, the Law, or the government, the legislator constitutes the institution of Law by transforming, changing, inventing, and (re)creating the nature of a people such that they will learn to adopt good laws. The institution of law also requires a legislator to invent the machinery of law, like a good mechanic. Without harping too much on the machine metaphor in the text, it does appear that Rousseau—along with the stated aim of legislation, to give will and movement to the body politic—virtually reverses the Hobbesian image of an artificial, mechanical State in which "the Soveraignty is an Artificiall Soul, as giving life and motion to the whole body" (Hobbes 1997, introduction; for a discussion of this image see Schmitt 2008b, 32–50). In Rousseau, the sovereign, the legislative power, is "the heart of the State," whereas the government is "its brain, giving movement to all its parts." Thus, the death of the state occurs not when the brain dies, for "the brain can become paralyzed yet the individual is still alive. A man can remain an imbecile and live"; the death of the state occurs "as soon as the heart has ceased to function" (Rousseau 1978, book III, chap. 12). For Hobbes, the sovereign gives life and motion to an artificial, inert machine. In Rousseau the sovereign people is the necessary and sufficient condition of life, but that living being requires a supplementary machine, the institution of law that binds a legitimate republican government, to make it move. The legislator transforms the nature of a people so that they will authorize the machinery of Law. This task is undoubtedly crucial to the success of a newly founded people, and the tensions it reveals between democratic sovereignty and the possibility of political legitimacy are real and pressing. But the legislator does not solve a paradox of founding.

Is this moment in Rousseau's text, although not a paradox of founding, a paradox of politics (as such)? I'm not sure why it is, for a simple reason: the paradox only exists if we are committed to democracy, that is, the sovereignty of the people. Honig is absolutely right that within democracies marked, as everything is, by the tenses and multiple durations of time, the formative and reflexive relation between the law and the people is such that a people will never be "well constituted" enough to guarantee that the right laws will always be chosen. Moreover, I agree with Honig and Connolly that this "failure" is to be affirmed, for it opens a space for contestation and political engagement that is too quickly shut down by proceduralists and deliberativists of various stripes. Nonetheless, a paradox of politics ought to be found in all political communities no matter their structure of rule or ethos, and I do not see how the paradox of politics identified by Honig within democracies is or could be ubiquitous within politics as such. For this reason I return to Rousseau to argue for the existence of a paradox of founding that is a paradox of and within politics.

The founding moment in Rousseau is described in book I, chapter 5, titled "That It Is Always Necessary to Go Back to a First Convention." Rousseau tells us that the reason it is always necessary to go back to a first convention is that a people cannot be formed without such a convention, for no matter how many people are subjugated by the same individual(s), individuals cannot become a people until they have unanimously decided to become a people. This first convention, this first unanimous agreement of all, "is the true basis (*le vrai fondement*) of society" and prior to those acts by which a people gives itself to a government (Rousseau 1978, book I, chap. 5). The social compact itself, then, is a unanimous decision by a group of people living in the state of nature to unite and direct the existing force of each such that it stops those "obstacles to self-preservation" that can prevail in the state of nature (Rousseau 1978, book I, chap. 6). Rousseau does not say much about this moment, but "Instantly, in place of the private person of each contracting party, this act of association produces a moral and collective body, composed of as many members are there are voices in the assembly, which receives from this same act its unity, its common self, its life and its will" (Rousseau 1978, book I, chap. 6).[5]

Articulated through the concept of law, the paradox of founding is as follows: the sovereign that is by definition absolutely above any and all law must also be absolutely subjected to the law. The dual-aspect character of Rousseau's thinking—for example, that an individual is both citizen and subject, the same body politic sovereign when active, State when passive —tries to unify this paradox, but unsuccessfully. This is nowhere more present than in book I, chapter 7: "On the Sovereign." Rousseau argues that although a particular individual is both subject to the sovereign (as a private person) and sovereign (as a citizen) does not mean that the obligation is pointless or without force (for generally one cannot be obligated to oneself) because "there is a great difference between being obligated to oneself, or to a whole of which one is a part" (Rousseau 1978, book 1, chapter 7). On the other hand, the sovereign—being one vis-à-vis itself (rather than vis-à-vis itself *qua* individual subjects)—cannot obligate itself to itself and thus "it is contrary to the nature of the body politic for the sovereign to impose on itself a law it cannot break … It is apparent from this that there is not, nor can there be, any kind of fundamental law that is obligatory for the body of the people, not even the social contract" (Rousseau 1978, book I, chap. 7). This is the sovereign right to be above the law, even the most fundamental law, because it is the origin of law.

However, in the next paragraph Rousseau writes: "But the body politic, or the sovereign, deriving its being solely from the sanctity of the contract, can never obligate itself, even toward another, to do anything that violates that original act, such as to alienate some part of itself or to subject itself to another sovereign. To violate the act by which it exists would be to destroy itself, and whatever is nothing, produces nothing" (Rousseau 1978, book I, chap. 7). We have gone in one paragraph from a sovereign that cannot (logically) obligate itself to itself and thus cannot be bound by any law— even the social contract itself—to a sovereign that can never obligate itself, whether to itself or to another (say, a nation-state or sovereign power) to violate the social contract. The social contract both can and cannot be violated, the sovereign both is and is not above the law.

The paradox might be avoided if Rousseau is only claiming that the sovereign cannot obligate itself to break the social contract. For on one hand the sovereign can never obligate itself to itself; in the case of obligating itself to others (which it can do), the reason could be nothing other than an (unstated) duty to self-preservation. Yet the reason given by Rousseau for the impossibility of the sovereign violating the social contract is a matter of logic: insofar as the social contract is the origin of the sovereign, to destroy that origin would be to destroy itself, and if the sovereign does not exist, then it cannot act at all, hence it cannot violate the social contract. This response is telling for two reasons. First, it resorts to paradox to solve a paradox. Rousseau appears to recognize that insofar as the sovereign is and must be self-grounded—grounded only in the act that produces it—it cannot rely on any natural duties or divine grounds that would limit or bind the sovereign. The sovereign truly is absolutely sovereign, and thus cannot be bound even by its own founding act. Yet if so, this renders the body politic inherently unstable, liable to self-annihilation at any moment. Rather than find an external limitation on sovereign power, Rousseau employs a paradox of action to show that the founding paradox is, however real, incapable of endangering the body politic. The structure of the paradox of founding is not confined; it spills over into Rousseau's discussion of the legitimacy of state violence.[6]

Rousseau's most extensive discussion of state violence is found in book II, chapter 5, "On the Right of Life and Death." The chapter is revealing because of the many twists and turns the brief argument takes, a path that may have much to do with the paradox of founding and the distinction between civil society and the general will. Rousseau's basic argument is simple: one enters the social contract to better secure one's life, but such a choice is not without risks. The main risk is that one's survival is aided by but therefore conditional on (the will of) the prince such that "the citizen is no longer the judge of the risk to which the law wills that he be exposed, and when the prince has said to him 'It is expedient for the State that you should die' he ought to die" (Rousseau 1978, book II, chap. 5). One's life, in the State, is a "conditional gift of the state" (Rousseau 1978, book II, chap. 5).

The problem—revealed here by Rousseau's reference to the will of the prince rather than the sovereign—is that the sovereign cannot act in specific, particular cases, as Rousseau acknowledges. Thus, "this condemnation is not to be made by the sovereign. It is a right that the sovereign can confer without itself being able to exercise." Given this rather bizarre idea, Rousseau's next sentence turns apologetic: "All of my ideas fit together, but I can hardly present them simultaneously" (Rousseau 1978, book II, chap. 5). But what is a right that can only be conferred, not exercised? Why can't the sovereign exercise it in spite of Rousseau's restriction of the lawmaking power to general acts? Is this a problem of simultaneity in presentation or of real paradox?

Attention to the rest of the chapter only makes matters more complicated. If the sovereign can confer a right to kill but not exercise it, the object of that violence both is and is no longer a citizen. Recall that Rousseau's justification for the right of the sovereign to kill is that the citizen now lives a conditional life; when it comes time to killing the citizen, the "guilty man is put to death ... less as a citizen than as an enemy ... such an enemy is not a moral person, but a man, and in this case the right of war is to kill the vanquished" (Rousseau 1978, book II, chap. 5). The point seems obvious, but it is necessarily obscure. Rousseau's argument requires the citizen to lose his citizenship status, for to be a citizen is to be (in part) sovereign, and the sovereign is "beyond" law. How can a citizen be (part of a) sovereign and yet still be bound by law such that the sovereign can confer a right to another to kill that citizen for violating a law it is not (as sovereign) bound to? On the other hand, if the citizen were merely a man (or a moral person), then the justification of state killing would be stuck at the start because the argument is made solely on the grounds that citizenship is both advantageous and risky, one risk being death at the hands of the State. Rousseau's argument requires the object of state killing to be both citizen and person, sovereign and subject, active and passive. Yet all of these complications are overlooked when Rousseau gives the sovereign and the sovereign alone the right to pardon. At the very least this violates the "no particular acts" restriction on sovereignty.

These confusions make it difficult to see where and how state killing receives its justification. Nowhere is this clearer than in the sovereign's right to kill that it cannot exercise. Again, we have an acknowledgment that the sovereign must be absolutely sovereign, unbounded; but an unbounded sovereign leads to serious theoretical and political difficulties. At the very moment that paradox is acknowledged it is quickly and paradoxically overcome. Lost in plain sight is the body of the killed, that citizen/enemy/person whose death is supposedly legitimized by Rousseau's arguments for transforming our illegitimate chains into legitimate bonds. Rousseau is not alone in his dual acknowledgment and avoidance of the paradox of founding and its implications for the legitimacy of state violence.[7] He seems peculiarly incapable of not showing his hand, of heeding his demurral at the end of his discussion of state killing to feel his heart and hold back his pen.

The paradox of founding in Rousseau is a paradox of politics because every political community is founded, contingently, in a specific time and place, and thus its claims to legitimacy are always unfoundable, deconstructible, even as they aspire to the validity and legitimacy Rousseau associates with the perpetually present and indestructible general will. Moreover, this paradox of founding is a paradox of politics that persists within political communities. Every time the state acts violently—when the state acknowledges its violence, that is—the moral justness of its acts depends in the first instance on the legitimacy the state claims for itself, and in that very claim it raises anew the justification of that claim, hence the paradox of founding. State violence, whether in its most mundane and apparently most justifiable form (say, putting an abusive spouse in jail) or in its most horrifying acts of killing, can always provoke the question of state legitimacy, the paradox of founding and, as I argue in the following chapters, the absolute immorality and horror of state violence.

THE POLITICAL CONSEQUENCES OF THE PARADOX OF FOUNDING

For Honig and Connolly, the paradoxes of politics are identified because they are there; but they are affirmed because they open spaces for and of political contestation that can be and are often closed through various forms of violence. Honig claims that the failure of the legislator to authoritatively determine the decisions of the political community is the "ineliminable moment of popular sovereignty in a nation ... For democratic theory this is a good thing, for Rousseau's lawgiver, therefore, cannot help but inaugurate or represent a contestatory politics" (Honig 2007, 6). Thus, in affirming the paradox of politics "we get neither deliberation nor decision as such; we get a politics, in which plural and contending parties make claims in the name of public goods, seek support from various constituencies, and the legitimacy of outcomes is always contestable" (Honig 2007, 14).

Connolly's political project, aided in part by affirmation of the paradox of politics, is the development of an ethos of pluralization infused by critical responsiveness to emergent claims and subjectivities, a politics in which

at least a significant minority of those implicated in it [i.e., the territorial and institutional conditions of democratic political life] understand that the porous understandings they share rest upon contestable foundations, that there are numerous differences among them grounded in a matrix of uncertainty, and that a laudatory way to respond to these uncertain commonalities and shared uncertainties is to cultivate respect for a politics of democratic governance and contestation that limits ways in which contested changes are to be initiated and disturbed traditions to be retained. (Connolly 1995, 154)

To this, as I have already said, I am in full agreement.

However, Honig notes in passing what I find left out of the paradox of founding literature. She mentions that the paradox of politics means that the people "are never so fully what they need to be (virtuous, democratic, complete) that democracy can deny credibly that it resorts to violence, imposition or coercion to maintain itself" (Honig 2007, 5). Obviously, what interests me here is the reference to a violence that enables a democracy to maintain itself. To what kind of violence is Honig referring? My sense is that the violence is not only or even primarily practices of state violence. But why do I get that sense? It is not because Honig (or Connolly) are not aware of or responsive to practices of state violence; rather, where and how the paradox of founding/politics is identified and affirmed contributes to deemphasizing not practices of state violence, but questions about the moral justification of state violence as such. For in identifying the paradox of politics in a tension between the authority of a transformative pedagogical law and a democratic sovereign people the founding moment is understood in terms of the (often violent) practices of political subject formation, practices that Honig and Connolly show to be necessarily incomplete because paradoxical. It is political subjectivity (whether of the individual or the community) and its relation to authoritative norms—whether they be those of the law or of cultural, religious, ethnic, racial, gender, and sexual identity—that is at stake in the paradox of founding.

I repeat: I am in full agreement with Honig and Connolly on the importance of the paradox they analyze as well as the politics they affirm. But in locating the paradox of founding/politics in the act that creates a political community, we get a different problem, a problem within any political community: the problem of morally justifying state violence. If the paradox of politics is affirmed to help inaugurate a more contestatory politics, such a politics best responds to the legitimacy of state violence by approaching the problem in a different way. I return to this difference later, after first engaging with the political consequences Derrida draws from the paradox of founding.

DERRIDA AND THE FORCE OF LAW

Derrida's most extensive engagement with law is found in "Force of Law." It is in the first half of that essay—in which he identifies various aporias that haunt legal judgment and (de)constitute the necessary but impossible relation between justice and law—that the paradox of founding is described. But it is the much more contentious, sometimes disturbing, reading of Benjamin's "Critique of Violence" in the second half of the essay that I focus on. In the first half of the essay, an ethical and political project is driven by the aporia of law and justice. That aporia—in its many forms—is the impasse that arises from the fact that although law claims to make justice forceful by rendering it, and justice itself demands that law enforce it, put into effect, law never can render justice because justice is unconditional and all law is conditioned. This aporia generates an ethical and political demand, one that compels an obligation to be constantly vigilant vis-à-vis justice, to never think that or act as if a legal decision has satisfactorily, without remainder, rendered justice (Derrida 2002, 250–58). In resisting the complacency of a procedural politics in which our only responsibility is to ensure the propriety and fairness of the institutions and institutional rules and processes that render justice, Derrida urges us toward a politics of active, vigilant responsiveness to others to whom we owe a duty of rendering infinite justice that can never be discharged by procedures of justice that nonetheless are necessary for justice to be effective.

However, the unconditional, infinite justice that drives Derrida's ethics and politics in "Force of Law," as well as his insistence that law cannot (even though it must) render justice bears marked resemblances to Benjamin's distinction between the mythical violence of a generalizable law and the divine violence of an always singular justice that will bring to an end the epoch of the Law (Benjamin 1978). Thus, the purpose of Derrida's turning to "Critique of Violence"—besides those he explicitly gives—would seem to be that Benjamin's text deals precisely with the essential violence and force of law as well as the possibility of thinking a justice beyond law, albeit for Benjamin, a justice beyond law that acts violently and destroys law. This latter danger is what, to my mind, compels Derrida to make, in the postscript to "Force of Law," the rather startling and suspect claim that Benjamin's divine violence, which kills without spilling blood, could lead one to think of the Final Solution (Derrida 2002, 298).[8] Yet Derrida appears to mean what he says insofar as he links Benjamin to discourses of the fall, originary authenticity, the criticism of Enlightenment, and so on, themes he explicitly associates with the names, and hence politics (however complicated), of Heidegger and Schmitt (Derrida 2002, 298). Derrida's criticisms of these other themes are quite familiar, going back to his earliest texts. There is nothing to indicate that he does not intend the analogy between divine violence and the gas chambers (although there is reason to think that provocation may play a large role in such a claim).

If Derrida means to associate Benjamin's text with the possibility of mass extermination, of violence without spilling blood, then what exactly is the danger of thinking a justice destructive of law? It strikes me that Derrida's worries here are less (or not only) philosophical and more ethical and political. These two sides of the issue converge in a passage dealing with Benjamin's endorsement of a sphere of nonviolence found where "a civilized outlook allows the use of unalloyed means of agreement," the sphere "of human agreement that is nonviolent to the extent that it is wholly inaccessible to violence: the proper sphere of 'understanding,' language" (Benjamin 1978, 289). This nonviolent sphere is defined by its rejection of, its imperviousness to, violence, which for Benjamin means everything having to do with the sphere of law. Derrida cautions that "we shall see in a moment how this nonviolence is not without affinity to pure violence" (Derrida 2002, 285). Pure or divine violence shares with nonviolence its opposition to law, and in this complicity there is, on one hand, a philosophical "error" and, on the other, an ethico-political danger.[9] The ethico-political concern with pure, divine violence is that a pure, infinite, singular justice that destroys the law—and Derrida equates divine violence with pure, infinite justice, the justice he is articulating—cannot and does not give reasons for what it does (at least none that we finite humans can know) and is thus not bound in any way by rules, therefore running the danger of becoming indistinguishable from the worst violence to befall human beings.

The problem is that, as Benjamin claims, it is "less possible" and "less urgent for humankind, however, to decide when unalloyed violence [that is, pure or divine violence] has been realized in particular cases" (Benjamin 1978, 300). The reason we cannot know when divine violence has been realized is that "only mythical violence, not divine, will be recognizable as such with certainty, unless it be in incomparable effects, because the expiatory power of violence is not visible to men" (Benjamin 1978, 300). In other words, Benjamin argues that distinguishing pure, divine violence from mythical (or other) violence—the violence that destroys law from the violence of law—is impossible with any certainty (save, I take it, for clear and obvious miracles), for what distinguishes the two—the expiatory power of divine violence—is not visible to people. For that reason, Benjamin predicts that "the premise of such an extension of pure or divine power is sure to provoke, particularly today, the most violent reactions, and to be countered by the argument that taken to its logical conclusions it confers on men even lethal power against one another" (Benjamin 1978, 298). For Derrida, divine violence "is the most just, the most historic, the most revolutionary, the most decidable or the most deciding. Yet, as such, it does not lend itself to any human determination, to any knowledge or decidable 'certainty' on our part. It is never known in itself, 'as such,' but only in its 'effects' and its effects are 'incomparable'" (Derrida 2002, 291).

The problem with a justice destructive of law, pure violence, is that it lacks any boundaries, any contamination with and by its opposite—law—which, for better or worse, introduces a degree of knowledge, reason giving, certainty, order, structure, responsibility, and so on into human affairs. Divine violence, which cannot be known with any certainty, must, within the finite world of human affairs, appear virtually indistinguishable from other forms of violence, presumably or even especially the worst forms of violence: for example, mass genocide. What divine justice lacks is any capacity or reason to justify itself in human terms, for only God can decide just ends (Benjamin 1978, 294). If the only justification of justice can come from God—and God acts justly through divine violence, expiating violence without blood, the existence of which cannot be known by men except in its incomparable effects—then just violence becomes indistinguishable from arbitrary violence, lawless violence. Justice indistinguishable from injustice is unacceptable. Or as Derrida writes toward the end of the first part of "Force of Law," "Abandoned to itself, the incalculable and giving [*donatrice*] idea of justice is always very close to the bad, even to the worst for it can always be reappropriated by the most perverse calculation" (Derrida 2002, 275). Derrida's hesitancy and finally his break with Benjamin is a response to his worry, both philosophical and ethico-political, about the idea of an infinite justice that destroys law. However irreducible justice may be to law, Derrida insists that justice must be enacted and enforced through law; the reasons, as we have seen, are not only philosophical but also ethical and political.

However, this forces on us a question: why law? If it is granted that pure justice requires a "phenomenal" institution to be enforced (which is what Derrida gives a philosophical argument for), then why is it the particular phenomenal institution that is law—beyond, of course, the long history of the connection of justice to law—that is required for that enforcement?[10] Derrida's commitment to law throughout his later work can be seen by turning to his other texts dealing more explicitly with ethical and political themes (Derrida 1994, 83–83, 2001, 22, 2005a, 150; this commitment can also be seen in Beardsworth 2005). What is it about law that requires justice to be enforced through law? Are there no other domains, institutions, micro- or macropolitics, or social practices through which our responsibility toward the singular other can be "enforced?" Is it simply the case that the regimes of law that have developed in the West since the Jews and Greeks are so firmly—however contingently—a part of our political concepts and practices that no other possibility can be imagined for organizing and judging claims to justice? Or is there an essential relationship between law and justice, a relationship that excludes other possible modes of actualizing, to the degree possible, justice?

One might think that the advantage of law is that is it susceptible to legitimation through foundational acts, giving a voluntary basis to the force of law and hence morally distinguishing such force from nonlegal violence. If so, then the force needed to effectively render justice would itself be morally justified, thus, as it were, "purifying" the procedures through which justice is "tainted" by the force of law. However, as we have seen, Derrida argues for an ineluctable paradox of founding. Within "Force of Law," the lack of a fully founded legal system is not to be bemoaned; on the contrary, this makes the law deconstructible and thus opens the possibility of justice. However, that deconstruction as/and justice is opened by the an-archy of the origin does not at all address the issue I am raising, namely, why law alone must be the institution through which justice is enforced. If law is legitimate force, force in the name of justice, and Derrida has shown that the legitimacy of law rests on an a-legitimate violence, then how can law claim any special right or privilege as the institution through which justice must be enforced?

The issue, of course, is the moral justification of the state violence that law employs to enforce, however impossibly, unconditional infinite justice. If state violence, often enacted through law, were capable of legitimation, then one can see how law might be the privileged institution and site of those practices and procedures that enforce justice. Lacking such legitimacy, the force of law is morally problematic, and if we are to affirm law as the privileged institution for the rendering of justice despite the illegitimacy of its violence, then we will have to find other arguments and justifications (a truly worthwhile and important project). However much I admire and affirm Derrida's call to resist the temptation of thinking justice has ever been done, such a call requires taking more seriously the possibility that because law's force is always, already, and only unjust, immoral violence, it cannot be the privileged vehicle of rendering justice.

THE LIMITS OF THE PARADOX OF FOUNDING

I left off my discussion of Honig and Connolly with the claim that neither directly addresses the moral problem of state violence in light of and because of their understanding of the paradox of politics/founding. I have just argued that Derrida, on the other hand, has an important theoretical account for the paradox of founding but—analogous to Simmons—does not draw the right consequences from his theoretical position and ends up affirming the necessary and sole relation of law to justice without offering sufficient argument for that relation. In both versions, there is an elision of the problem of state violence (although what is elided is different).[11]

What cannot be claimed about any of these thinkers, though, is that they are not cognizant of, interested in, or responsive to practices of state violence. For example, Connolly's fascinating analysis in "The Desire to Punish" of the subterranean currents of desire and ressentiment that inform legal judgment and punishment shows how such desire undermines the concepts of individual agency and responsibility that feed into punishment as well as the surety and moral purity of the judgments about action that set into motion practices of punishment. Connolly also comes close to the position I articulate later when he writes, in response to the punishment of Dontay Carter—an African American resident of Baltimore convicted of killing one white man and kidnapping two other white men—and after having put into question many of the traditional grounds for punishment, that "I continue to prize my security and mobility. But now a larger part of me thinks and (sometimes more precariously) feels that Carter should be imprisoned only to protect others from the fate suffered by his victims, and only as long as the probability is high that he will repeat such acts in the future" (Connolly 1995, 72). This position, which appears quite similar to utilitarian deterrence (especially Bentham), is not utilitarian, for it acknowledges not only that punishment is an evil that is counterbalanced by the good it will bring (à la Bentham); rather, it acknowledges, in emphasizing "feeling," that both the desire to punish and the desire not to punish, carefully cultivated and worked on, exceeds the rational determination of action relied on by utilitarians (of course, affect, feeling, and desire play a strong role in early utilitarianism).

Yet Connolly's example, revealing as it is, is perhaps overdetermined. The long and continuing history of violent racism in Baltimore and the United States generally is undeniable. Choosing a murder case in which an African American killed a white man—in a highly segregated city with one of the highest murder rates in the nation, most of it not "black-on-white" crime—is not accidental, for the reporting of black-on-white crime is guaranteed to be more extensive. Moreover, the example allows Connolly to delve more deeply into the dynamics of punishment, the interplay between the desire for security, for revenge, and for an ethos of critical responsiveness and the cultivation of an affirmative politics. But in choosing such a rich and compelling example, Connolly may overlook the more mundane— extremely mundane—examples of punishment that take place even more often within political communities. The example also may deflect attention from other cases in which horrific crimes committed by clearly guilty individuals who need to be "put away"—and whose incarceration or death are least likely to provoke pangs of conscience—tests the possibility, somewhat hesitantly affirmed by Connolly, that one can discern a trace of revenge in a "general economy of desire" (Connolly 1995, 63).

Ten years later, in *Pluralism*, Connolly argues—this time in conversation with Giorgio Agamben's conception of sovereignty—that the paradox of founding one sees in Rousseau cannot be overcome, but it can be better negotiated by loosening the strict logic of paradox that informs Agamben's arguments in *Homo Sacer*. Rather than trying to transcend sovereignty and delimit it conceptually, we should understand that "the sovereign is not simply (as Agamben and Schmitt tend to say) he (or she) who first decides that there is an exception and then decides how to resolve it. Sovereign is that which decides an exception exists and how to decide it, with the that composed of a plurality of forces circulating through and under the positional sovereignty of the official arbitrating body" (Connolly 2005, 145). In situating sovereignty within a broader set of (bio)political and (bio)cultural forces, Connolly can offer a more nuanced set of possibilities of responding to acts of sovereign power. Thus, when a positional sovereign such as a court decides, "We owe positional respect to the institution called upon to make authoritative decisions when the pressure of time compels them. That responsibility is met by a presumption of obedience to Court decisions and by public admission that democratic constitutionalism needs such a body in a non-parliamentary system. But to express partiality for democracy is to accept other responsibilities as well" (Connolly 2005, 146). These other responsibilities include active struggles to identify and publicize moments when sovereign authorities employ un- or antidemocratic ethoi such that sovereignty undermines the possibility of a pluralist democratic ethos and politics. Thus, "We meet our first responsibility to sovereignty by a presumption to obedience that might be overridden on some occasions; we meet the second by contesting publicly the partisanship against democracy exercised by the Gang of Five [i.e., the Supreme Court justices who decided *Bush v. Gore*]" (Connolly 2005, 146).

What about cases in which judicial decisions employ state violence against convicted individuals? Do we have a presumption to obedience in such cases? Similar questions are at issue in discussions of philosophical anarchism, and given the role of foundational moments to morally distinguish state violence from nonstate violence, the paradox of founding deeply problematizes this presumption of obedience in all cases where the state uses violence. As I have been repeating, if that violence is morally unjustifiable, and if, as Robert Cover argues, all legal decisions take place in a field of pain and death, then the acts of some sovereigns at some times— no matter how positional—do not merely stifle democratic possibilities and pluralism: sovereigns inflict unjustifiable acts of violence against literally millions of individuals each year (Cover 1986). I appreciate and concur with Connolly's criticism of Agamben on theoretical and political grounds, but I am still not convinced that the moral problem of state violence has been adequately addressed in his discussions of the paradox of founding.

For my argument in this book, there is no best or worst case of state violence, against which I test my own claim that all state violence is unjustifiable. Nor will I argue that sovereignty is always violent and, for that reason, to be overcome (although I have argued for such a position in the past and still feel inclined at times to do so; see Arnold 2009). Every case of state violence poses the same question, whether one is thrown into a drunk tank or sentenced to death: what morally justifies that violence, distinguishes it from nonstate or nonlegal violence? But not every act of sovereignty poses this question, for not all acts of sovereignty are violent. While the moral problem of state violence I am posing is, as it were, transcendental—that is, it asks about the conditions of possibility for morally justifying state violence and whether such conditions can, a priori, obtain—this does not mean that the state itself or sovereignty as such is unjustifiable. It also means that we cannot only attend to what Derrida might call the "empirical" injustices of practices of state violence, especially in legal practices. The legal system in the United States—legal systems everywhere—are unjust for a variety of reasons, including racist, sexist, homophobic, and xenophobic laws; unjust and discriminatory enforcement of the laws; and extralegal conditions such as poverty that are not only partly shaped by law but inadequately responded to through law. As Honig, Connolly, Derrida, and I agree, these practices need to be vigorously contested.

But must we vigorously question as well even the most boring, mundane, and currently acceptable practices of punishment and state violence more broadly? If so, why and how? The former questions I answer affirmatively in the following chapters. But to foreshadow my answer to the question of how we should contest all practices of state violence, I suggest that the politics advocated by Honig, Connolly, Derrida, and others who affirm the paradox of founding might be usefully informed—and problematized—by a particular approach to the problem of state violence, albeit an approach I am hesitant to affirm myself.

The paradox of politics that shows the state to always be a-legitimate decides, as it were, the question of the moral justifiability of state violence in advance. If the state is a-legitimate, then the violence of the state cannot be justified by justifications of the state's legitimacy, and thus cannot be morally distinguished from other violence *qua* violence (it can of course be distinguished in any number of ways, some of which are called "moral"). Unless one finds other moral grounds to morally justify state violence, then state violence is unjustified, immoral, unjust because it is violence. Although mostly a Pyrrhonian skeptic, and thus very worried about the certainty of my claim here, I want to say that it just is the case that the paradox of politics/founding, if true—and I think it is—shows that state violence is always morally wrong. There is, I wish to say, nothing more to be said about the matter.

Contestatory politics—and the ethos that informs it in Honig, Connolly, Mouffe, Derrida, and others—is crucial for the kind of political community we do and ought to live in. Given the fact of pluralism and pluralization, such a politics is also necessary if we are to avoid the worst in politics (and it is useful for striving toward the best). We do best to approach the problem of state violence by contesting it in light of its moral unjustifiability, that is, not by contesting the morality of state violence itself in particular instances or by leaving open to further analysis the possibility of legitimizing state violence, but by contesting what is to be done given the inescapable injustice of that violence. Contestation and more active resistance is necessary to challenge the manifestly racist, sexist, homophobic, classist, and other injustices of law. But those are, as it were, the easy cases (easy insofar as I see no drawbacks—save to those who benefit from the law's injustices— to ridding the law of its "empirical" injustices). The difficult cases arise when we ask the political question in light of the transcendental question: whether any punishment by the state is morally justifiable at all, and if not, what we are to do or say about the imprisonment of the serial killer or Thoreau. For if such actions are unjustifiable, necessarily violent—but they are, say, in the case of the serial killer, actions we will take nonetheless—then how can contestation proceed? It is as if we would be fighting not our shadows but our flesh and blood minds and cognizant bodies, contesting ourselves, or some part of ourselves: after all, we are allowing, sometimes endorsing, such practices even though we know we cannot morally justify them. If my arguments in the next two chapters are persuasive, then the ethics and politics I suggest in chapter 5 seem to me to be an important and necessary addition to the politics I admire and affirm in Honig, Connolly, and Derrida.

3 THE "CONCEPT" OF SINGULARITY

IN THE PREVIOUS TWO CHAPTERS I examined two views in contemporary political thought that—as the next few chapters will show—share many of the impulses and political values of my own arguments against the possibility of morally justifying state violence. In each chapter I argued that, however differently, philosophical anarchism and the paradox of politics elide the moral justification of state violence even when normative judgments about particular practices of state violence come under critical scrutiny. My goal in the previous two chapters has been to set the stage for my claim that there is no possible moral justification of state violence. The aim of this chapter is to examine the ontological and philosophical basis for that argument, specifically the concept of singularity.

Singularity and the concepts akin to it are a prominent motif and object of exposition in a great deal of philosophical texts, especially within the continental tradition but also at moments in the analytic tradition. Undoubtedly the concept means different things and is employed in response to different problems, within different thinkers. But it is striking that, for example, the medieval concept of haecceity, of "thisness" and individuation, can be found throughout the work of Deleuze and in analytic metaphysics (see especially Deleuze and Guattari 1987, 233–309; Rosenkrantz 1993). No doubt this connection is partially a result of a common set of sources, including Leibniz, Duns Scotus, Bertrand Russell, and others. Russell's "individuals," the objects named by proper names, are subjects of propositions that, like Aristotelian substances, can take predicates but cannot be predicated of anything else (Russell 1993, 141–43). The theme of proper names in relation to singularity has also been taken up many times by Derrida, just as Saul Kripke, John Searle, Peter Strawson, and others have also taken an interest in proper names.[1]

In a different vein, Heideggerian authenticity can be understood as the task of achieving singularity. Insofar as the resolute anticipation of one's ownmost possibility—being-towards-death—is a possibility that is nonrelational and rips me out of the anonymity of *das Man*, that is, is an existentiell modification of my self and projects, authenticity is the way in which Dasein becomes, as it were, a Dasein (Heidegger 1962, 307–11).[2] Criticizing Heidegger, but nonetheless formally repeating him in many ways, Emmanuel Levinas argues that the uniqueness of the self emerges in an absolute, undischargeable responsibility for the other, specifically the other's death. (Levinas 2000, 20, but see also 43, 162, 182). Hannah Arendt also notes that while all beings have the property of alterity or otherness, human beings achieve distinction, manifest their "whoness" through witnessed free action in the space of appearances (Arendt 1998, 176). Levinas's and Arendt's works, which unlike Heidegger's are more explicitly ethical and political, draw a link between singularity (or its related concepts and figures) and the relation to other(s), a link we can see in Derrida and contemporary theorists inspired by Levinas and Derrida (e.g., Derrida 1995, especially chapter 4; Critchley 1999a, 1999b). Only somewhat surprisingly, the concept of singularity or something quite like it also plays a crucial role in the work of two liberal political theorists, George Kateb and Richard Flathman. Flathman refers specifically to a singularity that is a "radical form of self-enacting individuality" (Flathman 1998, 45), whereas Kateb identifies as an aspiration of democratic individuality an "impersonal individuality," a kind of manifestation of one's "soul" (Kateb 1992, 90). The list goes on (it includes Kierkegaard, Nietzsche, Bergson, Adorno, and others).

One cannot reduce to a unity the varied and sometimes conflicting uses of the concept of singularity in the thinkers I have just identified. Nor can one neglect that outside of philosophy, singularity is a concept within mathematics and physics (a concept that some philosophers, such as Deleuze, employ within their work, and about which I can say nothing). What seems to be at issue for all philosophers interested in singularity, individuation, nonidentity, deictic speech, authenticity, uniqueness, and so on is a basic perception marked (depending on the thinker in question) by either the definite or the indefinite article (and deictic expressions more generally): here or there, and now, is "a boy," "a rock," "a redness" (not "the boy" or "the rock"). As Russell claimed, "the only thing that distinguishes 'the so-and-so' from 'a so-and-so'" is the implication of uniqueness" (Russell 1993, 176). For philosophical reasons that are important but beyond the scope of the argument here, thinkers such as Deleuze and Nancy see singularity in the indefinite article, whereas Russell finds it in the definite article (this may mark a difference between the singular and the individual that again is important but beyond the scope of this chapter). The point remains the same. The uniqueness of a spatially and temporally singular "thisness" is something so strikingly pervasive in our experience, and yet so difficult to describe or define or conceptually determine, that it is no surprise that philosophers who refuse to subsume that uniqueness under a general concept (which would somehow destroy that uniqueness) have found the singular being to be so intriguing.

There are other reasons for philosophical interest in singularity, especially within twentieth-century continental philosophy. One central reason, as I see it, is as much ethical and political as it is philosophical. It can be found, for example, in the preface of Levinas's *Totality and Infinity*: "We do not need obscure fragments of Heraclitus to prove that being reveals itself as war to philosophical thought, that war does not only affect it as the most patent fact, but as the very patency, or the truth, of the real … The visage of being that shows itself in war is fixed in the concept of totality, which dominates Western philosophy" (Levinas 1969, 21). Levinas's linkage of "actual" war to Western philosophy's war—the war waged against singularity and exteriority, against the Other—is not unique. For Adorno and Horkheimer, "totalitarian" Enlightenment thought "aimed at liberating human beings from fear and installing them as masters," and yet in and through the process of Enlightenment "the wholly enlightened earth is radiant with triumphant calamity" (Horkheimer and Adorno 2002, 1). The calamities of the twentieth century are intimately linked in *Dialectic of Enlightenment*, just as in *Totality and Infinity*, to a mode of conceptualization in which the "nonidentical" is ruthlessly subjected to conceptual determination and physical violence. One can question, of course, any claim to an internal connection between the Western philosophical tradition and the horrors of the twentieth century, but it is clear that such a link—tying together the philosophical desire for and claim to totality and the political realization of totalitarianism, often manifested in a complicated relation to Hegel—is an impetus for much of the philosophical interest in singularity.

However one accounts historically or philosophically for the attention paid to singularity, I am struck by the problematic obviousness of the singular: in this or that space, at this moment, there is a being. In particular, I have been most impressed by the work of Jean-Luc Nancy, especially his essay "Of Being Singular Plural." My initial interest in Nancy stemmed from what I took to be his (implicit) elaboration and critique of a line from Arendt's *The Human Condition* that has always fascinated me: "In man, otherness, which he shares with everything alive, becomes uniqueness, and human plurality is the paradoxical plurality of unique beings" (Arendt 1998, 176). That uniqueness is intimately tied to—in fact, partially constituted by—plurality and that plurality "consists" in unique beings (and is thus partially constituted by those unique beings) is a paradox that Nancy develops into an ontology, one that begins to rework Heidegger's existential analytic by giving prime of place to *Mitsein*, "being-with." The co-primordiality of singularity and plurality is a distinctive feature of Nancy's thought, distinguishing it from Heidegger as well as from Levinas and (in a more complicated way) Derrida, giving to his thought a more explicitly political bent. Perhaps the only other philosopher who shares this focus on the singular plural is Deleuze, albeit from within a different philosophical and nonphilosophical inheritance.[3]

The concept of singularity that we find in Nancy helps me in my attempt to undermine the possibility of moral justifications of state violence. Undoubtedly states commit acts that can be rightly described as physically violent, which is why moral justifications for that violence—often taking the form of moral justifications of the legitimacy and authority of the state—need to be given. However, as I hope to show in the next chapter, any attempt to morally justify that violence must deny the singularity of the being on which violence is being committed. If one can describe as violent the attempt to justify physical violence by denying the singularity of the object of that physical violence, and if all beings are singular, then in morally justifying any state violence, we are committing violence. But this, as it were, justificatory violence itself must be justified, or any attempt to morally justify state violence will be unjustifiable violence and hence doomed to fail as a moral justification. This abysmal failure of justification is the reason there can be no moral justification of state violence. The details of this argument will be spelled out in the next chapter.

Clearly I have a great deal to show. Here I elaborate Nancy's exposition of singularity in "Being Singular Plural." I do so first by comparing his appropriation of Heideggerian *Mitsein* to two other important criticisms of *Mitsein* to see more clearly the origins and goals of Nancy's ontology. I then examine the plural of being singular plural and then the singular of being singular plural. Finally, I examine Nancy's claim that we always "appropriate" the singular being such that we always "do wrong" by that being.[4]

NANCYEAN SINGULARITY

Nancy's most exhaustive analysis of singularity is found in an essay radicalizing the Heideggerian existentiale of *Mitsein*: "Of Being Singular Plural."[5] Given Nancy's explicitness about his rethinking of fundamental ontology on the basis of a radicalization of *Mitsein*, it is no surprise that commentators on his work often emphasize this point. However, Nancy's project is often seen in isolation from other philosophical attempts to rethink *Mitsein*. As a way of showing what is distinctive about his response—and to discuss in more detail than is often given the "immanent" reasons for Nancy's beginning with *Mitsein*—I turn briefly to two other opposed philosophical attempts to rework Heidegger on precisely this point. Hubert Dreyfus and Frederick Olafson—two prominent interpreters of Heidegger—find Heidegger's account of *Mitsein* in *Being and Time* to be flawed and incomplete, and they respond to this failure in ways that diverge from Nancy's response in many respects.[6]

The existentiale of *Mitsein*, of being-with, emerges as part of Heidegger's analysis of everyday being-in-the-world. Dasein not only encounters tools it employs for its projects or objects it perceives and thinks about; it also encounters other people, other Daseins. Insofar as these others are not other things or objects—they are other Daseins who share the same structure of being-in-the-world—Heidegger shows that "This being-there-too with them does not have the ontological character of a Being-present-at-hand-along-'with' them within a world. This 'with' is something of the character of Dasein; the 'too' means a sameness of Being as circumspectively concernful Being-in-the-world" (Heidegger 1962, 154). The "with-ness" of Dasein's existence means that human plurality is fundamental to and in human existence; "too-ness" means that the way human beings are with other human beings is similar: humans share the same structure of being-in-the-world or, as Nancy would put it, sharing is part of the structure of being-in-the-world. Here as elsewhere in *Being and Time*, Dasein is not understood as an ontologically distinct subject, whether in its everyday encounters with things or in its relations to Others. Others are not "added" to a distinct "I," creating an "inter-subjective" relation between Daseins. Rather, " 'With' and 'too' are to be understood existentially, not categorially. By reason of this with-like Being-in-the-world, the world is always the one that I share with Others. The world of Dasein is a with-world" (Heidegger 1962, 154). Even when no one else is around, Dasein is always being-with; thus a relationship to the plurality of other Daseins is part of the existential structure of everyday being-in-the-world: to be a human being, to Dasein, is to be-with-others.

Heidegger's methodological approach to the analysis of *Mitsein* leads him into a set of problems and claims that become objects of criticism for Nancy, Olafson, and Dreyfus. Heidegger examines the phenomenon of *Mitsein* by asking "who" Dasein is in its everydayness (Heidegger 1962, 149), that is, by asking what concrete way of Being-a-self is taken up by average, everyday Dasein (Heidegger 1962, 152). This has the benefit of revealing that Dasein is always being-with (rather than an "I" that is a stable subject constant across time and ontologically distinct from others) because Dasein is, for the most part, a "One-self," the kind of average, common self that does what "one" does, says what "one" says, and so on. But for this reason Dasein "itself is not; its Being has been taken away by the Others" (Heidegger 1962, 164). Rather than answering the question "who is Dasein?" with, as it were, "I," Dasein is for the most part a One-self, understanding itself in terms of *das Man*, the One: the anonymous, undifferentiated self of the average, everyday common world. Dasein understands itself and its world, for the most part and most of the time, according to prevailing norms within a given society: a father understands himself according to the norms of fatherhood (say, being the breadwinner and complaining about his wife's spending habits); a student understands himself in terms of norms of studenthood (complain about grades, demand that more money be spent on extracurricular activities); a professor understands herself according to the norms of the professoriate (my work is brilliant but unappreciated; the dean is the enemy). As Heidegger paradoxically puts the point, "Everyone is the other, and no one is himself. The 'they,' which supplies the answer to the question of the 'who' of everyday Dasein, is the 'nobody' to whom every Dasein has already surrendered itself in Being-among-one-another" (Heidegger 1962, 165). He often attempts to foreclose any tendency to read normativity or critical judgment into his phenomenological descriptions, but given the terms he uses to describe Dasein's life as *das Man*—subjection, tranquilization, anonymity—and given further the need for Dasein to resolutely anticipate its own death so as to break out of *das Man* to "choose" authentic existence, it is very difficult not to see a cultural critique of mass society in Heidegger's supposedly normatively neutral investigation into the phenomenon of Being-with.

For Olafson and Dreyfus, this latter issue and other serious problems dog Heidegger's account of *Mitsein*. Olafson notes,

> Unfortunately, this theory of Mitsein was not developed in the works that followed Being and Time; and the fact that it was not is a serious indicator of the course that Heidegger's later thought was to take ... Whatever the reason, the theory of Mitsein is not developed, either in Being and Time or later, in a way that contributes to the definition of the relationship which one Dasein stands to another in grounding the same world. (Olafson 1987, 72)

In *Heidegger and the Ground of Ethics*, Olafson returns to the theme of *Mitsein*. He argues for a position in some ways akin to Nancy's argument: "Although Heidegger developed the concept of *Mitsein*, neither that concept nor its ethical implications can be said to have been at the center of his thought about being as such ... That was unfortunate since it tended to minimize the role of being as the founding condition of the possibility of a world in which many ek-sistent beings can acknowledge one another with the framework of a relationship based on a common truth" (Olafson, 1998, 97–98). For Olafson, an "amplification" of the place of *Mitsein* reveals the conditions for relationships in which Truth is capable of being discovered and the conditions of ethical community (as well as the foundation of ethical duties).

Drefyus also finds *Mitsein* to be a central but confused aspect of *Being and Time*. For "as it stands Heidegger's Chapter IV [on *Mitsein*] seems just a short chapter on the problem of other minds and the evils of conformism, whereas, it is in fact, the last nail in the coffin of the Cartesian tradition. Indeed, the discussion of the way public norms are established makes this in many ways the pivotal chapter of the book" (Dreyfus 1991, 144). The problem is that in combining a phenomenological analysis of Being-with and a cultural critique of conformist society, Heidegger confuses the reader and is confused about the phenomenon he is describing, thus preventing *Mitsein* from being what it is: the intersubjective side of Heidegger's more general destruction of the modern philosophical tradition's Cartesianism. Dreyfus understands *Mitsein* and *das Man* as the "ultimate 'ground' of intelligibility" in the same sense that Wittgenstein describes a public language (wherein people agree not only in judgments but in forms of life) as the background set of practices that make possible shared understandings (Dreyfus 1991, 157). That Dasein's world is a shared world means that *das Man*, however powerful in its "subjection" of Dasein to its norms, is nonetheless to be understood in an ontologically positive manner as the condition of possibility of intelligibly encountering things and people at all (Heidegger himself is explicit about this positive function; see Heidegger 1962, 167).

Dreyfus's Wittgensteinian interpretation of Heidegger sparked a debate between him and Olafson over how best to read *Being and Time*, especially *Mitsein* and *das Man*. For my purposes, the actual debate is less important than the way each philosopher understands the importance of *Mitsein*.[7] For Olafson, *Mitsein* is a necessary condition for making truth-claims, but I focus on his important claim that *Mitsein* can serve as a ground for ethics. Heidegger provides, Olafson claims, a kind of post-Hegelian dialectic of recognition in which we recognize another Dasein as Alter Ego, as another Ego with whom we share the same structure of being-in-the-world. This identity in difference can be the ground of an ethical relationship because recognizing the Alter Ego as Dasein, as different from us but identical insofar as it too is Dasein, is something we cannot avoid (although we can pretend to question this recognition, as Olafson sees occurring in other minds' skepticism) given that *Mitsein* is an *existentiale* of Dasein. Thus, refusing to acknowledge the Alter as Alter Ego is one (unethical) way of actualizing *Mitsein* rather than denying it. Acknowledging and being responsible to our own Dasein requires us to acknowledge and be responsible to *Mitsein*. Insofar as our actions affect the interests of others who are Daseins, too, we must offer reasons for our actions when they adversely affect the interests of others, for such others share a way of Being with us, that is, being-in-the-world (Olafson 1998, 53). In short, Olafson sees *Mitsein* as the ground of ethics because it is, as it were, an "immanent" constraint on an individual Dasein: insofar as being Dasein is being-with others who are also Dasein, then my actions require taking their interests seriously and accounting for them when I act. Olafson's account focuses on the individual and the other, the Ego and the Alter Ego, to show that the Ego and the Alter Ego are ontologically bound to each other both in questions of truth and in ethical community, that is, in epistemology and morality.

Dreyfus's focus, on the other hand, is to argue for *Mitsein* as the public ground of all intelligibility. The individual—as either Ego or Alter Ego—that is the focus of Olafson's reconstruction of *Mitsein* recedes, and what comes to the fore is the way *Mitsein* makes possible any encounter with, disclosure of, beings. This applies not only for Dasein, whose own self is made possible by the various "possible selves" available within a given culture, but for beings other than Dasein (e.g., computers, quarks, sporks). Without the preexisting set of practices, words, judgments, beliefs, skills, and so on that are taught both explicitly and more often implicitly to newcomers into a culture, there simply would not be any intelligible encounters with beings at all. If for Heidegger what is at issue is often how beings can be encountered, which is to say how they are intelligible as what they are, then the answer is: *Mitsein* and *das Man*, the shared practices constitutive of any culture. *Mitsein* becomes one more way the Cartesian subject is shown to be only one (privative) mode of actualizing Dasein's existence (a mode that appears when the *zuhanden* breaks down and the *vorhanden* is disclosed). Insofar as Dreyfus emphasizes the ontological status of *Mitsein* and downplays the cultural critique of *das Man*, ethical questions are not really at stake in his interpretation of *Mitsein*. It is construed not as the ontological relationality between individuals who all share the same ontological structure of being-in-the-world (as in Olafson) but as the condition of intelligibility that no individual can possess or take ownership of (although they can modify norms of intelligibility in distinctive ways, i.e., become authentic). For this reason Olafson can claim to find a "cultural determinism" in Dreyfus's interpretation, one in which individuals are products of their cultures, even when they authentically modify an existentiell possibility of existence.

In Olafson what we share is the same structure of being-in-the-world: we are each individually identical in our difference. In Dreyfus what we share are a set of practices that precede and postdate us, and serve as the ground of intelligibility such that beings can be disclosed. Both philosophers, following Heidegger, assume that *Mitsein* is centrally a matter of humanity, of the human being.

Nancy's radicalization of *Mitsein* proceeds very differently. Perhaps most important of all, he does not restrict *Mitsein* to humanity:

> This thinking is in no way anthropocentric; it does not put humanity at the center of "creation"; on the contrary, it transgresses humanity

in the excess of the appearing that appears on the scale of the totality of being ... In humanity, or rather right at humanity, existence
is exposed and exposing. The simplest way to put this into language would be to say that humanity speaks existence, but what
speaks through its speech says the whole of being ... If existence
is exposed as such by humans, what is exposed there also holds
for the rest of beings. There is not, on the one side, an originary
singularity and then, on the other, a simple being-there of things,
more or less given for our use. On the contrary, in exposing itself
as singularity, existence exposes the singularity of Being as such
in all being. The difference between humanity and the rest of being
(which is not a concern to be denied but the nature of which is,
nevertheless, not a given), while itself being inseperable from other
differences within being (since man is "also" animal, "also" living,
"also" physio-chemical), does not distinguish true existence from
a sort of subexistence. Instead, this difference forms the concrete
condition of singularity. We would not be "humans" if there were
not "dogs" and "stones." A stone is the exteriority of singularity
in what would have to be called its mineral or mechanical actuality. But I would no longer be a "human" if I did not have this
exteriority "in me," in the form of the quasi-minerality of bone:
I would no longer be a human if I were not a body, a spacing of all
other bodies and a spacing of "me" in "me." A singularity is always
a body, and all bodies are singularities ... Existence, therefore, is not
a property of Dasein; it is the original singularity of Being, which
Dasein exposes for all Being. (Nancy 2000, 17–18)

In this long, dense passage, what becomes clear is first Nancy's rejection
of Heidegger's anthropocentric claim in *The Fundamental Concepts
of Metaphysics* that man has a world and is "world-forming"; the animal
is "poor in world"; and the stone is "worldless" (Heidegger 1995, 177).
What humans can do that other beings cannot do is ex-pose Being because
Dasein can speak. But as Nancy insists, what is spoken of or about in human
speech is what being is for all beings, human and nonhuman. *Mitsein* is not
an existentiale of Dasein alone but holds for all beings; in fact, Being-with
is Being. Thus, as we will see, all beings are singularly plural and plurally
singular because being-with is Being, is the condition of possibility of beings
coming to presence. This means that Being-with, for us humans, means

not only being-with-other-humans but being-with-other-beings. Humans share a world with all beings. Moreover, human beings are themselves only possible—in a very materialist sense—because they are "composed" of a plurality of singular beings (calcium, amino acids, proteins, water etc.). Nancy's explicit materialism distinguishes him from Olafson and (differently and more complicatedly perhaps) Dreyfus.

Second, Nancy's response to *Mitsein* begins from a very different but clearly central feature of *Being and Time*. Heidegger begins *Being and Time* by raising the question of the meaning of being: "Do we in our time have an answer to the question of what we really mean by the word 'being'? Not at all. So it is fitting that we should raise anew the question of the meaning [*Sinn*] of Being" (Heidegger 1962, 20). Heidegger defines meaning much later in *Being and Time* as "that wherein the intelligibility of something maintains itself," by which he claims that the meaning of anything is its intelligibility to Dasein within a significant referential context (Heidegger 1962, 192). For example, the "meaning" of the hammer is its intelligibility as that which I use to drive a nail to make this desk because I am or because I hope to become or so that I can (continue) to be a carpenter. Thus, the meaning of being "in general" is its intelligibility within the significant referential context of Dasein "in general." But if Dasein is also Being-with, and if any particular understanding of Being, any particular meaning at all, as Dreyfus and Olafson would agree, is partly made possible by Being-with, then meaning itself refers to others necessarily. There is no meaning, and therefore no meaning of being, without (a reference to) others. Olafson employs this idea to show how *Mitsein* makes possible truth-claims; Dreyfus uses this idea to show *Mitsein* and *das Man* as the ground of intelligibility.

Nancy follows the logic of this idea to show that insofar as meaning is only possible in a world shared by many beings, meaning itself must be understood as essentially shared. If the meaning of being is what we are after, then we have to understand not how meaning can be shared but how meaning is sharing: "There is no meaning if meaning is not shared, and not because there would be an ultimate or first signification that all beings have in common, but because meaning is itself the sharing of Being. Meaning begins where presence is not pure presence but where presence comes apart in order to be itself as such. This 'as' presupposes the distancing, spacing, and division of presence" (Nancy 2000, 2). Nancy's emphasis on *as* alludes to Heidegger's exposition of the "as-structure" of interpretation (see Heidegger 1962, 188–95). Only insofar as a being is not purely what it is can it be interpreted as what it is (only insofar as the hammer is not primarily vorhanden, not seen as an isolated present "object" with present "qualities" can the hammer be understood as a hammer within a significant referential context). The as-structure requires that the hammer, if it is to be understood as a hammer, must be relational through and through. The hammer is what it is only when related to, in communication with, sharing with other beings (the hammerer, to be sure, but also the nail, the wood, etc.). If being is presence, then the meaning of presence—what makes presence intelligible, significant, understood as what it is within a referential context—is the sharing that such presence requires. No sharing, no being, no meaning of being.

For this reason, Nancy radicalizes *Mitsein* not only because he thinks Heidegger failed to fully develop the concept and, when he did develop it, made crucial mistakes with disastrous political consequences (see Nancy 2008). For Nancy, the investigation into the meaning of being demands that Being-with be not only correctly described but taken as the "minimal ontological premise." Being-with is Being, is what allows beings to come to presence at all. Unlike Olafson and Dreyfus, Nancy's concern is not to "fix" Heidegger's mistakes and improve the existential analytic but to draw out the neglected ontological status of *Mitsein* to develop a new fundamental ontology: Being-with is Being.

I return to some of these issues in more detail later as well as note when Nancy agrees and disagrees with Olafson and Dreyfus (and others). My hope is that Nancy's distinct approach to *Mitsein* and his reasons for that approach are now clearer.

BEING SINGULAR PLURAL

The strange syntax of *Being Singular Plural* is meant to indicate that the three terms are co-primordial, and Nancy's writing, in all of its density and complexity and difficulty, is an attempt to be faithful to the co-primordiality of being singular plural. For this reason, as Henk Oosterling rightly admits, "writing about Nancy's forceful philosophy is difficult because of his écriture" (Oosterling 2005, 82). Oosterling's solution is to "mime" Nancy's writing, but I find such a task beyond me and often unhelpful. At the cost of infidelity, I try to be more schematic in my exposition of Nancy's ontology. Thus, I begin with the plural of being singular plural before moving on to the singular.

As we have already seen, Nancy radicalizes *Mitsein*: "it is necessary to refigure fundamental ontology (as well as the existential analytic, the history of Being, and the thinking of Ereignis that goes along with it) with a thorough resolve that starts from the plural singular of origins, from being-with" (Nancy 2000, 26). Some of the reasons for this claim were discussed already, but Nancy also shares Olafson's worry about *Mitsein* in Heidegger's and Dreyfus's interpretation: *Mitsein* is often understood in its negative, mass conformist actualization in contemporary culture, but this description actually hides the phenomenon. For Olafson, there are any number of innocuous ways in which *Mitsein* "shapes" us without "subjecting" or "dominating" us. For his part, Nancy also finds Heidegger's phenomenological descriptions of the *with* to be prejudiced and thus distorted by his account of being-with as, for the most part, the domination of *das Man*. For Nancy the problem with Heidegger's analysis of being-with as primarily the everyday experience of subjection to an anonymous "they" is that "Heidegger confuses the everyday with the undifferentiated, the anonymous, the statistical" (Nancy 2000, 9; see also Nancy 1993a, 88–98). It is not that Heidegger is totally mistaken, but for Nancy the possibility of *das Man* and its attendant features of impersonality, anonymity, and subjection lies in a more primordial mode of being-with: the singular-plural. The very constitution of the everyday—which Heidegger takes as his theme in *Being and Time*—must be thought as each day of the everyday, each day a new day, a new series of events, new moments of becoming, new relations, and new turns (Nancy 2000, 9). This more primordial mode can only be understood if being-with is thought through completely as being itself. The consequence of this move is that "Being is put into play as the 'with' that is absolutely indisputable. From now on, this is the minimal ontological premise. Being is put into play among us; it does not have any other meaning except the dis-position of this 'between'" (Nancy 2000, 27). We must begin from the with. The with is the condition of possibility of there being any beings at all, of any beings coming to presence. No being can come to presence, can be, without being with other beings. Thus, "Being Singular Plural means the essence of Being is only as co-essence" (Nancy 2000, 30).

But co-essentiality "signifies the essential sharing of essentiality, sharing in the guise of assembling, as it were. This could also be put in the following way: if Being is being-with, then it is, in its being-with, the 'with' that constitutes Beings; the with is not simply an addition" (Nancy 2000, 30). The with constitutes beings. Insofar as Being shares and is shared, it is "between" all beings: the with, plurality, is essential to the singularity of each being. Singular beings, then, are always already with other singular beings, not as an accident or as something in addition to their singularity but on the condition of there being a plurality of other singular beings. However, and importantly, singularity is not "achieved" by overcoming or canceling out plurality, as if plurality were the condition of singularity in the sense that it is only by standing out against other beings that a being can be singular.[8] The link between singularity and plurality is also not merely linguistic or conceptual (in the sense that the two concepts only mean anything due to their oppositional structure); nor is the link to be thought in terms of a mode of being released from the with because Dasein escapes from *das Man* through an irreducibly nonrelational "experience" (such as the resolute anticipation of one's death, as in Heidegger). This marks a fundamental difference between Nancy's position and that of Heidegger and Levinas.[9] For both Heidegger and Levinas singularity is found either in the mode of nonrelation or in the relationship with a singular Other. In both cases singularity is thought without plurality, for even in Levinas, plurality comes in the form of the third party, in the ontological space of calculation, decision, and compromise: the space of politics (Levinas 1998, 158–162). More importantly, for both thinkers it is the "experience" of singularity, a singularity without plurality that must (re)ground the political, for it is only through the "experience" of singularity that a renewed relationship to the plural is possible. Against these positions, Nancy thinks the singular-plural.

Position, Ex-position, and Singularity

Singular beings, then, do not stand out against the plurality of other beings, for singularity is in the mode of plurality, just as plurality is in the mode of singularity. The condition of possibility for the singular-plural is the with. Why? Largely because the concept of "with" implies a between, a space, and a time. Central to Nancy's thinking of the with is a critical appropriation of the identification of being with positing or position, an identification drawn from Kant's refutation of the ontological proof for God's existence. Kant claims that "Being is obviously not a real predicate, i.e., a concept of something that adds to the concept of a thing. It is merely the positing [Position] of a thing or of certain determinations in themselves" (Kant 1998, A596/B624). When I say that something is, Kant argues, all I am saying is that the possible object of a concept is in fact, here and now (or in the case of God, always and everywhere), actual. Kant's famous example is that there is not "more," that is, the predicate "being," in the concept of a hundred actual dollars (or thalers, or guilders) than in the concept of a hundred possible dollars. That I have a hundred actual dollars does not mean that the actual existence of the hundred dollars adds something to the concept "hundred dollars." The only difference is that I can pay for something with a hundred actual dollars. That being is position means that a possible being is actually here and now. Nancy cites this moment from *Critique of Pure Reason* and adds "the very simplicity of 'position' implies no more, although no less, than its being discrete, in the mathematical sense, or its distinction from, in the sense of with, other (at least possible) positions, or its distinction among, in the sense of between, other positions" (Nancy 2000, 12). Thus, if Being is simply the position, the setting into place, of a being—its presentation in and to experience here and now—then the implication of the spatial term *position* is its relation to other positions. Each being, the position of each being, implies other possible positions/positings/beings. Thus, Nancy concludes, "every position is also dis-position, and considering the appearing that takes the place of and takes place in the position, all appearance is co-appearance" (Nancy 2000, 12). Every position, every place, implies the dis-placement of place that is the between, the with. For a being to be, to be posited, to be placed, to appear, it must also be dis-placed, placed between or with other places. For this reason, every being, in its singularity, is—to use another important concept in Nancy—exposed to other singular beings. If being is position made possible by dis-position, by the between or the with, then each being is ex-posed, its position is always already outside of itself, appearing to other beings. Without the dis-positional capacity of the with, nothing could appear because there would be no space for a being to make an appearance.

But each space is not without time and the spacing of time, time thought of as contemporaneity and simultaneity. If beings are always together with other beings, then they are together simultaneously: " 'Together' means simultaneity (in, simul), 'at the same time.' Being together is being at the same time (and in the same place, which is itself the determination of 'time' as 'contemporary time'). 'Same time/same place' assumes that 'subjects,' to call them that, share this space-time, but not in the extrinsic sense of 'sharing'; they must share it between themselves" (Nancy 2000, 60; see also Nancy 1993b, 66–73). There is simply far too much philosophical background to these claims about time to deal sufficiently with them here, and Nancy admits that long analyses are needed at this point in his text (which he does not provide).[10] But the basic outline of the idea of temporality here is relatively clear. If beings are always with other beings, positioned and thus dis-positioned, and hence ex-posed to each other, then they can only be with each other if they are at the same time. This means that they cannot share time in an "extrinsic" sense, as Nancy puts it, for example, in the way that a time share beach condo is shared by a few friends. When friends share a time share, what they share is not time or themselves but the condo. When beings share time, Nancy argues, what they share is that time, not because they each own a piece of it but because they each are (of) it. This might lead one to think that insofar as time is thought of as simultaneity, as sharing a time that beings are, then the difference or separation between beings would disappear (this is why Levinas, for example, turns to time as radical diachrony). But, Nancy adds, "simultaneity is not a matter of indistinction; on the contrary, it is the distinctness of places taken together. The passage from one place to another needs time" (Nancy 2000, 61). Claiming that beings are with other beings because they share a simultaneous time does not collapse the distinction between singular beings because beings are always positioned in a specific place (and two beings cannot occupy the same place). Beings are always in this space at this time together with beings in those spaces at this (same) time. Time, of course, moves on, and thus there are always, every day, each day, each moment, singular time-spaces, singular space-times.

Nancy's emphasis on a simultaneous and dis-positioned space-time, however abstract, draws on a rather straightforward perception or intuition. Here is—to greatly simplify the scene—"a boy," "a girl," "a swing set," "a dog," "a sandpit." Each of these beings are here, now, in a space-time which is also "a here," "a now," singular as the beings "occupying" this singular space-time. Undoubtedly the swing set is mass-manufactured, and when I go to a different playground the next day I see the "same" swing set. There, too, are "a boy," "a girl," and so on; but of course, that swing set is not the swing set from the day before and neither are the children the same. When I return to the playground of the previous day the swing set is not the same swing set. Two days ago it was drab and noisy (cloudy day, rusty chains); today it is quiet and bright (I need to wear a hat; the city finally responded to the complaints); a boy is playing on it, but he isn't swinging so high and he looks nervous (he has a bruise on his knee from the other day.) For Nancy, these differences are not accidental. These different beings, scenes, times, and spaces are what they are because of being singular plural. Beings are singular plural because of singular plural space-times. That we do not often notice these things—more precisely, that we cannot often notice these things—is a matter I return to later. In moments of attention or more often passivity, I "perceive" (Nancy would say "receive") the singular plural of a situation, specifically the singular plural space-time of a situation, an experience predictably common, if unpredictably occurrent, within human experience. If philosophically ex-posing these moments requires a great deal of abstraction, the moments themselves couldn't be more concrete. This brief summary of the with has led us to a point where, I hope, we can turn to singularity, keeping in mind that singularity cannot really be thought without the plural.

A singular being, bluntly stated, is an origin, one of a plurality of origins in and of the world. Nancy means (in large part) by origin—more specifically, by origin-of-the-world—that each singular being is irreducible, incomparable, inassimilable to anything else (be it a concept, a totality, a particular value), and at the same time, that each singular being is, in some sense, "world-creative," "creating" the world from out of itself in each turn of its existence (Nancy 2000, 6).

This is, again, abstract. What does it mean to say that a singular being is an origin, both irreducible to anything else as well as world-creative? Nancy begins from a rather common statement: "People are strange." What do we mean when we say this? For Nancy, "this phrase is one of our most constant and rudimentary ontological attestations" (Nancy 2000, 6). What it attests to is that central to the experience of being a human being among other human beings—in fact, all beings—is precisely a multiplicity where we sense that others are somewhat like me but still very different. As Nancy notes, "people"

clearly states that we are all precisely people, that is, indistinctly persons, humans, all of a common "kind," but of a kind that has its existence only as numerous, dispersed, and indeterminate in its generality. This existence can only be grasped in the paradoxical

> simultaneity of togetherness (anonymous, confused, and indeed
> massive) and disseminated singularity (these or those "people(s),"
> or "a guy," "a girl," "a kid"). (Nancy 2000, 7)

The human cannot be thought without both of these modes of human experience, the one in which humanity seems to be a particular "kind" (however one defines it) and, at the same time, comprised of distinct and discreet individuals (a kid).

The strangeness of people emerges from both modes of experiencing humanity (often experienced simultaneously). The reason for this strangeness is that " 'People' are silhouettes that are both imprecise and singularized, faint outlines of voices, patterns of comportment, sketches of affects" (Nancy 2000, 7). Whether it is a matter of peoples as a mass (nations or races) or as individuals, the experience of strangeness emerges from the unshakeable sense that what we "know" and "experience" of another person—even those we know well—is inevitably imprecise, gleaned from minute habits, from particular turns of speech or tones of voice, and inevitably dis-concerting, bringing us close to others only in a mode of distancing, of separation. What is disconcerting about others is not a matter of installing one's own way of life as the norm and seeing the lives of others as deviant (Nancy 2000, 8). Rather, "from faces to voices, gestures, attitudes, dress, and conduct, whatever the 'typical' traits are, everyone distinguishes himself by a sort of sudden and headlong precipitation where the strangeness of a singularity is concentrated" (Nancy 2000, 8). What we find strange in others is that concentration of singularity, the fact that out of the imprecise sketches and drafts we perceive in the ways of others we can discern something unique, unlike anything or anyone else, including myself. People wouldn't be strange to us if they were not both accessible to us in some way—if, that is, there was only sketch without concentration—and different, close to us and far away, closeness in the mode of being far away. This experience of singularity is not itself a "perception," as if it was something we actively constituted through either Kant's or Husserl's transcendental subject. Rather,

> this very humble layer of our everyday experience contains another
> rudimentary ontological attestation: what we receive (rather than
> what we perceive) with singularities is the discreet passage of other
> origins of the world. What occurs there, what bends, leans, twists,
> addresses, denies—from the newborn to the corpse—is neither

primarily "someone close," nor an "other," nor a "stranger," nor "someone similar." It is an origin; it is an affirmation of the world, and we know that the world has no other origin than this singular multiplicity of origins. The world always appears [*surgit*] each time according to a decidedly local turn [of events]. Its unity, its uniqueness, and its totality consist in a combination of this reticulated multiplicity, which produces no result. (Nancy 2000, 8)

Recall that Nancy takes up Kant's understanding of Being as position; where he differs from Kant is that it is not the subject—meaning the transcendental, spontaneous "I"—that posits a being, for this would mean that the with is also a positing of the subject (and then we are back in the subject/object distinction of modern philosophy with all of its subsequent problems). The other being appears not because of the constitutive activity of consciousness but as a singular origin of the world, as a being that surges into being and to which I am and must be, in the first place, receptive, responsive. People, all beings, are strange because they surge into being, are irreducible to the constitutive activities of consciousness, and thus are necessarily and always separate even when close by. Each being appears to us as if the world began anew from it, as if it was incomparable to everything else even as it appears, and must appear, with everything else.

Thus, our response to the singular being is, in the first place, not a process of forming it through the forms of time and space, and then schematizing it under a concept such that we are able to fully understand it or identify it. Rather, all we can do—but this is already quite enough—is ex-pose ourselves to that being.[11] To be ex-posed by and to another being is, as the term suggests, to be undone by that being, to be, as it were, put out of place, outside of oneself, to become strange in the presence of the other's strangeness. To be ex-posed to the singularity of another being is to be open to that being; insofar as that openness consists of being ex-posed, being put of place, out of one's own place "we reach it [the other being] to the extent that we are in touch with ourselves and in touch with the rest of beings" (Nancy 2000, 13).[12] The key phrase here is "in touch"; we can touch ourselves, be in contact with ourselves only insofar as we are not ourselves, insofar as we do not completely coincide with ourselves. On this dual condition of touching—that we are ex-posed out of ourselves and exposed to other beings—the singular being can be "experienced" in its singularity. To gain what Nancy calls access to the origin is not and cannot be to appropriate the other being, to make it our own: "Access is 'coming to presence,' but presence itself is dis-position, the spacing of singularities. Presence is nowhere other than in 'coming to presence.' We do not have access to a thing or a state, but only to a coming. We have access to an access" (Nancy 2000, 14). The singular being is not a thing or a state but a movement of coming-to-be, an appearing; for us to access that other being as it comes-to-be, we must ourselves come-to-be. This coming-to-be implies the singular being's world-creative "power." In short, to be exposed to the singular being I must expose myself: I must cede my constitutive, identifying, and determining powers, "not be myself" so that this ecstatic "me" may receive the singular being.

The last issue I would like to address before concluding this exposition of Nancy is that in ex-posing ourselves to singular beings we are, or rather should be (in Nancy's term) curious about the other being (Nancy 2000, 19).[13] Our curiosity stems from the strangeness of the singular being, its uniqueness in the world "other beings are curious (or bizarre) to me because they give me access to the origin; they allow me to touch it; they leave me before it, leave me before its turning, which is concealed each time. Whether an other is another person, animal, plant, or star, it is above all the glaring presence of a place and moment of absolute origin, irrefutable, offered as such and vanishing in its passing" (Nancy 2000, 20). To be curious about another being is not, as in Heidegger, a sign of our inauthenticity; nor is it another way of expressing the later Heidegger's *Gelassenheit*. Curiosity is engagement with the being; it is to have "an affair with it" (Nancy 2000, 20). The opposite of this curiosity, of this engagement with the singular being, is the attempt to appropriate the origin. This is the great danger:

> If we do not have access to the other in the mode just described, but seek to appropriate the origin—which is something we always do—then this same curiosity transforms itself into appropriative or destructive rage ... This desire is the desire to fix the origin, or to give the origin to itself, once and for all ... This is why such desire is a desire for murder, and not only for murder but also for an increase of cruelty and horror, which is like the tendency toward the intensification of murder; it is mutilation, carving up, relentlessness, meticulous execution, the joy of agony. (Nancy 2000, 20)

I want to stay with this point for a moment because it is crucial for my later argument about moral horror and for the way I will understand (in chapter 4) how moral justifications of physical violence can themselves be understood as violent. Appropriating the origin (i.e., avoiding, denying, repressing, refuting), the singularity of a singular being is something we always do. There are no doubt many reasons why we tend to overlook or deny the singularity of all beings, but surely one main reason can be found in Henri Bergson. If it is the case that we are capable—as art shows—of perceiving more of the world, more in the world, then we tend to perceive, that is because there is "in normal psychological life, a constant effort of the mind to turn away from what it has a material interest in not seeing. Before philosophizing one must live; and life demands that we put on blinders, that we look neither to the right, nor to the left, nor behind us, but straight ahead in the direction we have to go" (Bergson 1992, 137). Our perception is shaped in action-oriented contexts—that is, most of the contexts within our lives—by the necessity to negotiate those contexts successfully, and doing so requires us not to attend to what might be attended to in other contexts. If I am driving, it behooves me to not notice the singular tire, the singular exhaust pipe, of the car in front of me. I ought to notice the brake lights, and insofar as I am noticing the brake lights it is, as Heidegger would put it, a sign that is intelligible as an indication that this car is slowing down and I might want to as well (all of which only makes sense within the significant referential context of an everyday activity). Unbalanced attention to the intensity of the redness of the brake light is likely to cause me trouble. There are, then, perfectly sensible and irrefutable pragmatic reasons for "appropriating the origin."

Moreover, it might not only be the case that to communicate we require a language that inevitably and invariably fails to name just this singular being. It might also be the case that to even begin to do more than receive singularity—that is, to understand it in any way, or perhaps even to move beyond receptivity and respond to it in any way—we must rely on our discursive understanding (there is no intellectual intuition). If there is any kind of ethical or political imperative to respond to the singular being as singular, such a response, if it is to be more than passivity and receptivity, must approach that being in one way or another. But in so doing, the singular being will always be missed, always be appropriated. In short, if it is the case, ontologically, that the singular being cannot be appropriated, it is no doubt the case that appropriating the singular being, denying its singularity, is something we (must) always do. Acknowledging this ever-actual impossibility in any aspect of human life has, I would argue, salutary effects for what we know (it demands a certain kind of Greek skepticism) and for how we relate to others. In regard to the specific case of state violence, acknowledging the ways we cannot, but must, appropriate the singular being produces, I argue, an experience of moral horror that demands an ethical and political response to the horrific actuality of state violence.

I hope this schematic analysis of Nancy's *Being Singular Plural* has put me in a position to turn from the ontological foundations of my argument in this book to that argument itself. I must now show how a Nancyean conception of singularity can help us articulate an addition to the ordinary definition of violence that, if plausible, will form the crux of my argument for the impossibility of morally justifying state violence.

4 SINGULARITY AND THE IMPOSSIBILITY OF JUSTIFYING STATE VIOLENCE

IN THE PREVIOUS CHAPTER, I ended with Nancy's claim—common to Derrida, Adorno, Bergson, and others—that we always appropriate, or miss, or repress, the singular being. In this sense, I suggested, we always "do wrong" to the singular being, always "mistreat" it. Derrida, Levinas, Adorno, and others often use the term *violence* to describe thought's comprehension of the singular object, a term loaded with significance and obviously central to my own project. But I have my own hesitations about the use of the term *violence* in these thinkers, especially as the problem of defining violence is central to any account of the legitimacy of state violence. As we will see, "defining" violence is even more crucial to my argument, for in some respects my entire move from the singularity of all beings to the impossibility of morally justifying state violence depends on the plausibility of my addition to the ordinary definition of violence.

In this chapter, I first attend to the problem of defining violence. I show, through a series of examples, what I mean by my addition to the ordinary conception of violence: we can call "violent" those acts that avoid, repress, or deny the singularity of beings within the process of morally justifying physical violence. The burden of this chapter is first to make plausible this definition and second to show how this definition undermines the possibility of morally justifying state violence. I try to demonstrate the plausibility of my addition to the definition of violence by showing that it contains two ideas central to our ordinary understanding of violence: the concept of injury and the concept of physicality. I show that this plausible definition undermines any possible justification for moral violence by arguing that if justificatory acts in the service of legitimizing physical violence are themselves violent, then an infinite regress becomes unavoidable, and thus state violence can never be justified. I end the chapter by examining the problem of dirty hands to exemplify how my approach to the problem of state violence is distinct as well as my own way of framing the "situation" in which we find ourselves given the unjustifiability but continuing use of state violence. In so doing, I set the stage for the next chapter on moral horror.

DEFINING VIOLENCE

As C. A. J. Coady and Allan Bäck have noticed, defining violence is a contentious practice in which it is difficult to avoid "some degree of sharpening and legislation" or "stipulation" (Coady 2008, 21; Bäck 2004, 219). The risks and rewards of expanding or delimiting the definition of violence are obvious. Vittorio Buffachi, in a concise summary of philosophical work on violence, notes that what one gains in precision by delimiting violence to, say, physical acts of force against persons (or property), one loses by failing to account for modes of violence that seem just as pervasive and destructive as physical violence, such as psychological violence (Buffachi 2005, 195–96).[1] On the other hand, widening the definition of violence— to include, for example, "structural violence"—runs the risk of making violence so pervasive a feature of human life that the concept loses all precision, even as it accounts for a variety of phenomena rightly described as violent.[2] Granting that any definition of violence will be to some extent stipulative and assumes risks by departing from ordinary conceptions of violence (whatever they are), I nonetheless try to develop, starting with the concept of singularity, an addition to the usual definitions of violence that is close enough to ordinary language and experience as well as more broadly accepted definitions to be plausible, while still expanding the concept of violence to include a specific range of acts: claims, judgments, and justifications.

The *OED* defines violence first as "The exercise of physical force so as to inflict injury on, or cause damage to, persons or property; action or conduct characterized by this; treatment or usage tending to cause bodily injury or forcibly interfering with personal freedom." The definition strives for normative neutrality and somewhat succeeds, but it surely leaves out a whole range of phenomena that can be understood, however contestably, as violent. In its sole focus on the physical, one is left to wonder whether years of emotional abuse of a child by a parent might be rightly understood as violence. It also leaves out the possibility that language in its performative power may wound and injure (Butler 1997). These issues aside, the *OED* definition certainly captures what many would accept as basic features of violence: physical injury caused by intentional acts of force to people or their property, where injury is understood either as damage to person or property or as restrictions on one's liberty (in a physical, almost Hobbesian sense of the term).

I would like to add to the concept of violence, as noted above, acts that avoid, deny, or repress the singularity of a being in the course of morally justifying physical violence. This "definition" includes as acts of violence a number of judgments, claims, and conceptual determinations, be they political, legal, or philosophical. At this point one might ask: why not simply follow Nancy, Adorno, Derrida, Levinas, and others and argue that insofar as violence is always done to the singular being in acts of cognition and identification, both physical and "cognitive" violence is done to the singular being in all acts of state violence, and if such violence is always wrong, then state violence must always be wrong?

A significant reason for my wanting to include in the definition of violence I am defending a reference to physical violence is that the paradigmatic cases of violence against singularity itself are far less clear than cases of physical violence, and they certainly do not form part of the ordinary conception of violence. For example, violence against singularity is captured in Adorno's claim that "The subject must make up for what it has done to non-identity," that is, has done to identify, conceptually determine, define, and thus repress the nonidentical in the subject's quest for a dominating knowledge through totalizing, identifying thought (Adorno 1973, 145). One can see it too in Levinas's argument that the Face of the Other opens the possibility of murder but also announces the ethical command that calls the subject to assume a responsibility not to kill. Against the war that rages throughout the totality of Being and in conceptual determination, the presentation of the face of the other is "preeminently nonviolence ... it is peace" (Levinas 1969, 203). Derrida, criticizing this text of Levinas, denies the possibility of a pure nonviolence. Instead, and somewhat akin to Adorno, insofar as "no philosophy responsible for its language can renounce ipseity in general—hence no philosophy can escape the violence of egoity—violence is irreducible such that there is always an economy of violence that can strive for a relative peace" (Derrida 1978, 131). In short, the claim is that violence is done whenever the other singular being—be it the Other or any being—is determined in some way, approached or appropriated, judged. For Derrida and Adorno—and as we have seen, for Nancy as well—such violence is ultimately unavoidable, for the price of coherency, of knowledge and cognition, is precisely the violence done to the object of knowledge, to that which is thematized or revealed. Appropriating the singular being is something we always do.

Several problems emerge here. First is a problem akin to one Buffachi identifies: the concept of violence seems to have become so extended as to be continuous with being a subject, hence experience itself, and thus one wonders what work the concept of violence is doing or how the ordinary conception of violence relates to this much wider concept. These problems are matters, one might say, of conceptual accuracy. One can see in Levinas's *Difficult Freedom* this almost global extension of violence:

> But violence is not to be found only in the collision of one billiard ball with another, or the storm that destroys a harvest, or the master who mistreats his slave, or a totalitarian State that vilifies its citizens, or the conquest and subjection of men in war. Violence is to be found in any action in which one acts as if one were alone to act; as if the rest of the universe were there only to receive the action; violence is consequently also any action which we endure without at every point collaborating in it. (quoted in de Vries 1997, 16)

Even the examples of violence listed by Levinas are questionable, for I am not sure why playing a game of billiards gives rise to a series of violent acts, much less why simply acting as if I am alone or being acted on in ways I do not entirely go along with makes me responsible for or a victim of violence.[3]

A second problem is normative: violence is usually thought of as wrong, injurious, and thus in need of justification when employed. The idea that violence is ubiquitous in experience means that all of our existence, thoughts, and actions must be, in some sense, wrong, and further that the violence of capital punishment and the violence of conceptual determination—say, in identifying a particular individual as a rational animal—are, again in some sense, the same. To be sure, Adorno affirms the former claim, at least as predicated of the unredeemed world we live in; the latter claim surely stands in need of further elaboration, for although identitarian thought may be linked to or justify physical acts of violence, it is unclear whether we can or should use the (unqualified) term *violence* for both.

Third, there is, as I would like to put it, a political problem with this use of the word *violence*. If one is interested in challenging practices of state violence—as I am in this book—those practices are most often cases of physical injury or physical impingements of liberty (in the Hobbesian sense). They are surely linked to conceptual determinations, judgments, and performative speech acts of many kinds—the judicial verdict, the demonization of the enemy, the disciplinary knowledge that helps produce the prisoner as subject—but as a political matter, I am more interested in how these judgments and determinations activate a set of physical acts that are more obviously and identifiably "violent," more obviously and identifiably morally dubious.[4] Beyond the "obviousness" of physical acts of violence, I also like to attend to the political nature of state violence. Judith Butler rightly cautions us against a "generalization of the thesis that all normativity is founded in violence" because she is "not at all sure about affirming or denying a transcendental thesis that would dismiss power from the equation" (Butler 2010, 169). In this passage Butler is referring to the claim I discussed above, that is, that violence is a transcendental within human existence, and thus she is referring primarily to the violent formation of the subject. But a similar set of reasons justifies my own caution in accepting the same transcendental arguments for the ubiquity of violence vis-à-vis state violence. In short, I assume that for many people there is—however questionable the distinction may sometimes be—violence and "violence," that is, there is physical injury or destruction and there is the "violence" one finds in so much twentieth-century French and German philosophy. Although there may be links between "violence" and violence in particular cases, there is no immediate reason to think that there is an internal, essential relation between the two, that is, that where there is violence there will always be (or have been) "violence."

On the other hand, it is not an implausible extension of the concept of violence to include under it some speech acts, determinations, and judgments, for example, hate speech and emotional abuse. The reason is that however seemingly nonphysical, hate speech and emotional abuse are certainly injurious. *Injury*, etymologically, includes the idea of wrongness, of a privation or absence of rightness, and the injuriousness of hate speech makes it an act of violence.[5] However much hate speech may include conceptual, transcendental, or epistemological violence—or as I am putting it, avoiding, denying, or repressing singularity—hate speech is more clearly injurious, whereas it is unclear how just any conceptual determination of an object alone (say, the determination that this being before me is a rose) could be injurious.[6] In short: what is wrong, injurious, as such, with appropriating the origin, determining the object, identifying the nonidentical? Where is the injury? For if the physicality of violence in acts that deny singularity is not so obvious, then including such acts in the definition of violence requires (at the very least) some specific account of the injuriousness of avoiding, denying, or repressing singularity.[7]

For this reason I feel pressed to give my addition to the definition of violence some plausibility by including within it injuriousness and a reference to physical violence. Given that physical violence is included in my addition to the definition of violence (albeit as a first-order phenomenon that is being justified), the real burden of my argument here becomes showing the injuriousness of avoiding, denying, or repressing singularity to morally justify physical violence.

The injury done to singular beings by avoiding, denying or repressing their singularity in order to morally justify physical violence is …

And here there is a problem. Although I have an intuitive sense of what is wrong here, it is very difficult to articulate it in propositional form. Making plausible the addition to the definition of violence I have given might best be achieved by pointing to examples in which the singularity of a singular being is avoided, repressed, or denied in a justification for how that being is treated such that the justification itself constitutes an injury and hence is violent. I would like to begin with two examples that will allow me to flesh out my intuition into something more concrete. The first example shows how a moral justification of violence avoids the singular being only so as to violently strike the singular being. The second example shows how justifications can be said to injure (hence showing the idea of injuriousness necessary to my argument within justificatory acts).

FIRST EXAMPLE

In his discussion of punishment in *The Metaphysics of Morals*, Kant provides an argument against Beccaria's claim that capital punishment is wrong. Beccaria argues that because no individual can be said to have consented to losing his life in case he becomes a murderer, such a provision cannot be in any original social contract, hence the state does not have the right to kill. Kant's response is to emphasize that we are punished not because we (once) will(ed) to be punished, which is Beccaria's framing of the problem, but because we "willed a punishable action." The crux of Kant's argument rests on a famous distinction:

> Saying that I will to be punished if I murder someone is saying nothing more than that I subject myself together with everyone else to the laws, which will naturally also be penal laws if there are any criminals among the people. As a colegislator in dictating the penal law, *I cannot possibly be the same person who, as a subject, is punished in accordance with the law*; for as one who is punished, namely as a criminal, it is pure reason in me (homo noumenon), legislating with regard to rights, which subjects me, as someone capable of crime and so as another person (homo phaenomenon), to the penal law, together with all others in a civil union. (Kant 1996, 6:335, emphasis added)

Although homo phaenomenon is the only possible object of violent punishment, Kant insists that he is not the same person as the one who legitimizes the punishment through legislation, homo noumenon. Yet this cannot be entirely true, for if homo phaenomenon were really a completely different person, then homo noumenon could not be that which is respected when we punish homo phaenomenon: homo phaenomenon both is and is not the same homo as homo noumenon. Kant needs phenomenal and noumenal man to be both identical and distinct for his justification of punishment to work.

In punishing other human beings, respect for homo noumenon determines the propriety of punishment, but it is homo phaenomenon who, as the spatiotemporal appearance of a particular individual, receives the violence of punishment. One can even honor and do justice to the honor or dignity of homo noumenon by killing homo phaenomenon (and thereby homo noumenon too? But how can one kill what does not make a spatiotemporal, i.e., finite, appearance in the world?). In all of this what seems left out, not taken into consideration, not an object of respect but merely a means for getting to the homo that really matters, is homo phaenomenon. It is homo phaenomenon that within the Kantian system is singular because only homo phaenomenon ex-ists, as we saw in the discussion of Nancy.[8] Existence for Kant, Nancy claims, is simply the presentation to experience of a being; homo noumenon cannot, by definition, be present in and to experience. Even if each individual has absolute value, absolute dignity, that is because "rational nature exists as an end in itself" (Kant 1964, 96), where such a principle "is not borrowed from experience" (Kant 1964, 98). What is dignified about each human being, what is to be respected in each human being, is their rational nature. Yet this rational nature cannot appear as such in phenomenal life, as Kant always makes clear, and thus without any spatiotemporal appearance, homo noumenon can exceed all empirical determinations only by being entirely incapable of being posited, of actually being presented within experience. The innocent victim in all of this is precisely the singular appearing being, the one who receives a violence that, *qua* appearance, he cannot possibly deserve (as even Kant admits, for homo phaenomenon is determined by causal forces and thus not responsible for what it does; see Kant 1996, 5:97–98. For Kant, only homo noumenon is responsible).

Kant's justification for punishment in these sections is based on a distinction in which what is of moral importance and justifies punishment is radically distinguished from what suffers the violence of punishment, such that a variety of justifications for violence are made possible and used even for acts that on the surface seem almost comically sadistic. It as if violence cuts through the undeserving singular appearing body to reach a deserving noumenal phantom it can never strike, a phantom that nonetheless is the basis on which violence against that body (that "other person") is justified. This justificatory process, in which what is of moral value justifies a violence against that which, as such, cannot be of moral value, is one way of avoiding, denying, or repressing the singularity of a being to justify physical violence. Violence rendered against a body that does not deserve—cannot deserve—such violence is justified such that the violence is not only not wrong (morally indifferent) but morally right, just, required. The injury lies in the unjustifiable transformation of a wrong into a right, that is, the injury committed is the repression, through a process of justification, of the fact that a wrong has been committed at all. What is admitted to be undeserved is justified as deserved not because the object of violence deserves it—the object of violence cannot, in principle and always, deserve its punishment—but because of an impossible to delineate (non)connection between what deserves punishment (homo noumenon) and the object of punishment (homo phaenomenon).

If Kant can justify punishment based on the responsible freedom of will of a rational being, he cannot justify the use of violence against a never responsible appearing body, and therefore he cannot justify a fundamental wrong done against that body. Yet such a justification is precisely what he provides. Kant's justification of punishment denies the singular being such that what is wrong, what is admitted to be irredeemably, unjustifiably, violent, is made right.

SECOND EXAMPLE

The previous example aimed to show how a moral justification of violence succeeds only by denying the singular being within the justification. In this example I want to show how a justification itself can injure.

In a long discussion of Wittgenstein's arguments about the possibility of knowing whether another person is in pain, Stanley Cavell reads such questions as symptomatic of a set of "myths" about the body in its relation to the "soul," specifically the idea that the body "veils" the interior life of the other, keeping us out and, sometimes, the other in (Cavell 1999, 368). The other knows their pain, but I do not, because the pain is "inside" their body and I am "outside." When I raise the question of whether the other is in pain, how I might know such a thing, Cavell argues that "the block to my vision of the other is not the other's body but my incapacity or unwillingness to interpret or judge it accurately, to draw the right connections [the right connection here being seeing the expression of pain as pain]. The suggestion is: I suffer a kind of blindness, but I avoid the issue by projecting this darkness upon the other" (Cavell 1999, 368) The blindness in question is what Cavell eventually calls "soul-blindness," lacking "the capacity to see human beings as human beings," an idea that is internally linked to two key Cavellian concepts: acknowledgment and avoidance (Cavell 1999, 378). He diagnoses the skeptical problem of whether we can know with certainty the pain of others as one in which the fundamental fact of human finitude obscures our need not so much to know (the other's pain) but to acknowledge that pain (where acknowledgment is a way of enacting knowledge): "Acknowledgment goes beyond knowledge (goes beyond not, so to speak, in the order of knowledge, but in its requirement that I do something or reveal something on the basis of that knowledge)" (Cavell 1976, 257). To acknowledge someone's pain is to act in the face of the fact of it, to respond to that pain, to show one's knowledge of that pain not by proving one's certainty of it but by responding to it. To avoid that pain is to acknowledge it in a certain way for "the concept of acknowledgement is evidenced equally by its failure as by its success. It is not a description of a given response but a category in terms of which a given response is evaluated ... A 'failure to acknowledge' is presence of something, a confusion, an indifference, a callousness, an exhaustion, a coldness" (Cavell 1976, 264).

Blindness, avoidance, and acknowledgment are ways of relating to others, that is, actions, judgments, denials, justifications, and excuses (as well as the refusal of these actions, judgments, etc.). These issues return in Cavell's later criticism of Rawls in *Cities of Words* and *Conditions Handsome and Unhandsome*, where, crucially for my interests here, the blindness in question is caused or expressed in a justifier by a justification of or a way of justifying the justness of a response to suffering, to a claim of injustice. Cavell knowingly takes out of context Rawls's assertion in *A Theory of Justice* that if someone has constructed a rational life plan but for reasons beyond his control fails to achieve his goals, then the person is not to be blamed or to blame himself: he is "above reproach" (Rawls 1971, 422). Cavell tries to connect this sense of one's conduct as above reproach—through the idea of what "can be said"—to the terms of social cooperation in which individuals "can say to one another that they are cooperating on terms to which they would agree" (Rawls, quoted in Cavell 2004, 177). Whatever the textual merits of this connection, Cavell argues that Rawls allows fortunate individuals in a reasonably just society to say to those less fortunate individuals who cannot point to an unjust institution responsible for their less fortunate position that more fortunate individuals and the society as a whole are above reproach (Cavell 2004, 177–78). In other words, given that individuals in the original position would choose a distributive scheme that includes inequality, then unless a specific inequality is a function of an unjust institution, those who are worse off in the society have no right, no standing, to complain that they are being treated unjustly. For Cavell, this response is a way of avoiding the claims (the pain, the suffering, the sense of injustice) of another by pointing to a rule (a just distributive scheme) that justifies—makes morally unproblematic—the state of affairs that prompts a sense of injustice in the less fortunate. This response is troubling to Cavell because an individual "may not know to which institutions" they can point, to "persons who have done" some specific injury to them; nor may they even "contemplate asking anyone" to do something about this. Yet the sense of injustice may not be confused, or childish, or irrational, an instance of someone not understanding what it is to be treated unjustly (Cavell 2004, 180).

Cavell's way of understanding the injury or wrong done when one claims one's actions to be above reproach by way of pointing to a rule that justifies those actions is to say that such a response "makes me the judge of my obligations, but in a way that removes me from the consequences my verdicts have upon others, as if I were acting from the recognized office or station of a judge" (Cavell 2004, 179). Taking this idea perhaps too literally, I think one can say that the justification of one's actions by reference to an "institutional" role and institutional rules institutionalizes the one to whom I am responding, the one who is claiming an injustice. Rather than responding to the individual human being standing there, acknowledging the suffering and pain of another, I point to a rule as if I am a judge, the very first rules being those that determine the role of having standing, in the legal sense: does this individual before me have standing, have the right to be in this court, to make a claim to which I must respond responsibly? Rules of standing determine whether this individual is one to whom I must respond responsibly. To the extent that I find that this individual does not have standing, cannot meet the requirements of being a complainant, I have no responsibilities, no need to address or respond to their concerns. I am blind to—I blind myself to—the other as suffering being by transforming my relation to the other through a set of rules that justify why the other lacks standing to claim what they claim.

Here we have an instance where a justification justifies dismissing an individual's moral standing because the justification avoids an individual by denying that individual, by demanding that we be blind, like justice, to that individual. The justification demands that the individual, as it were, declare not only their suffering or their sense of injustice but their standing to claim suffering or injustice. The justification demands that I, as judge, take on a role that is not unique to me (because open to all), and it demands that the individual before me take on a role that is not unique to them (because open to all who have standing under a set of general rules for having standing). The justification demands and produces this blindness to the individual before me. If in Kant what is necessarily wrong— the punishment of homo phaenomenon who cannot be responsible for his actions—is transformed into an act of justice by repressing through a justification the possibility that a wrong has occurred, in Cavell we see how a justification renders morally acceptable—and even demands—that we be blind to, that we avoid, the standing of an individual to raise a claim by denying on the basis of rules that such an individual has standing at all. If in Kant the injury is that an undeniable wrong is repressed through justification, in Cavell the injury is that an undeniable suffering is avoided or denied through a justification that can only respond to a suffering that satisfies procedural criteria for claiming anything at all.

THE IMPOSSIBILITY OF JUSTIFYING STATE VIOLENCE

Of course I do not pretend that these examples can do all the work I want them to do. Much more would need to be shown to fully demonstrate that within Kant's system only homo phaenomenon could be a singular being in Nancy's sense of the term. Homo noumenon, insofar as by definition it exceeds all empirical determination, bears some characteristics of the singular being, and perhaps it is unsurprising that Nancy, through a Heideggerian reading of Kantian dignity, ascribes to ek-sisting Dasein the absolute value and dignity that Kant reserves for homo noumenon, which cannot ek-sist at all (see Nancy 2003, 178–86). But homo noumenon may simply be one manifestation of a persistent blindness to singularity in Kant's moral philosophy. On the other hand, the Cavellian example does not morally justify physical acts of violence, and thus I do not think of it as violence (although Cavell does).

My hope is that the two examples do get at the way justifications can themselves injure when they avoid, deny, or repress the being before us by either repressing the existence of a wrong as such, or by avoiding the being before us by demanding that they take on a predetermined "role" of complainant with standing. In both cases, I would argue, the singular being is missed, intentionally or otherwise. If Nancy, Adorno, Levinas, Derrida, and a host of others are right to think that we always miss the singularity of a singular being, we often injure those beings by missing them. Of course not all injuries are physical, and if we maintain a physicalist concept of violence, then the mere fact of injury is not enough to call justificatory injury "violence." Moreover, when we "injure" another being "merely" by conceptually determining it and denying its singularity, it is fair to say that we are doing wrong to it in a sense even further removed from violence in the physical sense and even in the wider sense of injury (except, as it were, etymologically).

It is worth dwelling on the etymological relationship between justification and injury. Both terms, with their Latin roots in *jus*, centrally concern the notion of justice, of doing justice or failing to do justice to something. It would be quite paradoxical to claim that a justification itself can injure, because a justification is precisely that which denies that an injury has been done, and where there is injury there can be no justification (although there might be excuse). My own sense of justification in cases where actions go awry follows the difference drawn by J. L. Austin in "A Plea for Excuses." When we defend conduct that has gone wrong in some way, Austin argues, for the most part we try to excuse or to justify that action. To offer an excuse is to admit responsibility for doing something wrong and to provide mitigating reasons for our action. For example, if I rear-end your car because the car behind me hit my car, pushing my car into your car, there is I am very likely responsible (legally) for hitting your car. I should have been more careful. But I didn't intend or try to hit your car, and but for the car behind me hitting my car, I would not have hit your car at all, no matter how dangerously close to you I might have been. I can try to excuse my actions without denying responsibility, and you might very well accept my reasons while still reasonably and rightfully demanding compensation from me for any damages (Austin 1961, 176)

To justify my action, on the other hand, is to admit full responsibility for something but deny that what I have done is wrong (Austin 1961, 176). Justifications are the kinds of things we employ all the time when, for example, we answer a question about what makes imprisoning someone or invading a country something we have a right to do. We may even admit in some cases (although Austin seems less inclined to examine these cases) that what we are doing is, taken in itself, quite bad (how many people would actually claim that the killing involved in capital punishment, by itself, is a good thing?). But we deny that such an action is wrong, and thus our justification denies the possibility of there being any injury.

Again, it would seem exceedingly paradoxical, both etymologically and commonsensically, to say that a justification is capable of causing injury. I think a good case can be made that some justifications do in fact injure, precisely because justifications and injury cannot coexist. In other words, justification rules out injury, thus rules out violence. Any justification of an action is a denial of injury. But a justification that injures is the perfect crime, for the very injuriousness of the justification is hidden in the justification: how can I have injured you, given that injury and justification can never be in the same place at the same time? Injurious justification is a uniquely pernicious form of injury because it is a strange speech act: it makes the injury it is disappear, like a bizarre magician placing a rabbit in a hat before our very eyes.

Let me provide another example of what I mean, this one not from a book of philosophy. A common feature of human relationships of all kinds is a conflict over whether what one person does to another is injurious or justified. Criticism of all kinds often provokes such conflicts (often under the disputed name of "tough love"), and where the claim to injury wins out over a justification, the action is shown to be unjustified. But are there cases in everyday human relationships that reveal justifications that injure? I think there are. These are cases in which someone's justification of what they do shows such insensitivity to the person who feels wronged, such blindness to who they are and what they need or desire, that the justification itself proves as or more hurtful than the act being justified. For example, I describe people who watch too much (bad) television as lazy, contemptible individuals wasting away their lives and weakening their already deficient intellect. My friend, whose television-watching habits I am aware of, takes offense, in part because that remark hits home a bit too much (he is already anxious about his intellectual capacities, something I am also aware of), and explains why such a remark is hurtful. I justify my remark with something along the lines of "if the shoe fits … ," and knowing my friend as I do, I know that they know that the shoe does sort of fit. But what I am denying or neglecting in the justification is something I also know: that my friend already has doubts and anxieties about precisely this issue, and I know that because, after all, I am their friend (and a close one at that). However right my statement may be, and however successful the justification of it, the justification itself injures precisely because it depends on denying something about my friend that I can and ought to know. What my justification does is call into question my friendship, my desire to be friends with this friend of mine, to perform the role of a friend, and it does so precisely by manifesting my indifference (or blindness) to their sense of self, their anxieties and worries.

I am not sure what, if anything, to call the wrong of denial or avoidance. It may seem too subjective to be called a wrong, for it depends so intimately on the idea that one can and ought to have not missed or denied or avoided something, and this is something that seems so difficult to "prove." If my friend were to point out that I know all about their anxieties and that this knowledge should have forced me to be more careful in my words (or just to say nothing at all), I think it is reasonable for me to say, "Really? Do you keep in mind everything you know about me when you talk to me?" Yet my own sense again is that just the one thing that I did not keep in mind ought to have been kept in mind in that situation, not when I was saying it but when I was justifying it. My failure to take seriously your sense of injury, to deny your injury, is to deny, as it were, you; at the very least, it is to deny your mattering to me in ways that I have let you matter to me (for I know your anxieties and how they shape your life). These situations in everyday life seem to me if not quite as common as other forms of injury, common enough to be reasonably claimed as prevalent injuries in human encounter.

I have already argued, though, that I am wary of calling violence just any appropriation, denial, avoidance, or repression of the singular being. The addition to the definition of violence I have been struggling to articulate is explicitly linked to physical violence. My burden was to show that justifications themselves can injure. I hope to have at least made such a suggestion plausible. If we are always avoiding, denying, or repressing singular beings, thus doing some sort of injury to them, treating them wrongly, then in at least those cases where we try to justify those actions and those justifications injure by avoiding, denying, or repressing the singular being who is the object of those actions, we can say that sometimes justifications that avoid, deny, or repress a singular being to justify an action against that singular being are injurious.

I want to use the word *violence* for those cases where we injure a singular being by avoiding, denying, or repressing the singularity of that being in the course of morally justifying physical violence. I have been striving to show that my addition to the ordinary definition of violence is linked to everyday conceptions of physical violence and injury so as not to appear arbitrary. Justifications serving the end of morally justifying physical violence are obviously closely linked to physical violence. The whole point of morally justifying violence is to deny that some forceful physical practices are violent at all, that is, are wrong.

If the justification of physical violence that avoids, denies, or represses the singular being is rightly called violent, then the singular being whose treatment is morally justified—hence not violent—is caught in a circle of violence. The injury done by the justification is the repression of the injuriousness of the physical act, the transformation of what is wrong into what is right by an act that is itself wrong. If the justification itself is violent, then how can a violent action justify another violent action, the justness or rightness of which is precisely what is in question, hence requiring justification? The violent act requires justification because it might be wrong, but the justification of that questionable act is wrong because violent. The violent justification needs justification. By the very logic that makes such a justification violent, so must the justification of the justification be violent. And so on.

Acts that avoid, deny, or repress the singular being to morally justify physical acts of violence are themselves violent because they injure in order to justify physical violence that is necessarily injurious because incapable of a justified justification. Moral justification injures the singular being physical violence injures, too.

We repress, and must repress, the singularity of the singular being to morally justify physical violence because the singular being, like homo noumenon, cannot be reached save through a distortive proxy (homo phaenomenon) that, as Kant insists, is "another person." We are always missing the proper object of violence, always acting violently against "another person" than the being we "ought" to be acting violently against, and in so doing, we are always acting wrongly.

Rather than singular beings, prisoners. Rather than singular beings, enemies. Rather than singular beings, rights-bearing subjects. Rather than singular beings, collateral damage. Rather than singular beings, murderers. Yet, in each case, in each justification of violence, or in each identification of the singular being as some determinate thing so that we can do just violence to that identifiable entity, the singular being does not disappear. There it is, there it is in prison, or dead, or maimed, or starved. We justify punishing the criminal, but here is a singular being (if we expose ourselves to it). We justify killing the enemy, but that dead body is a singular being (if we expose ourselves to it). We justify the accidental deaths of civilians, but there is a pile of bones and a pool of blood, all singular beings (if we expose ourselves to them). Our justifications miss the singular being by avoiding, repressing, and denying their singularity, but our violence does not miss. If our justifications miss the singular being, then they cannot justify the violence that does not miss.

That acts that avoid, deny, or repress singular beings to morally justify physical violence are themselves violent means that there is an abyssal logic in place, an infinite regress that entails that physical violence is morally unjustifiable. As a subset of physically violent acts, state violence cannot be morally legitimized and justified. There is no possible moral justification of state violence if my argument here is correct. To be sure, there is much that is contestable in my argument, a great deal of ontological commitment and some contentious definition. But to be impressed by the singularity of beings and what this entails for some of our relations to singular beings leads or has led me to the impossibility of morally justifying violence against those beings, and thus leads or has led me to the impossibility of morally justifying state violence.

Before ending this chapter, I would like to use one more example—this time less philosophical than political—to show how justifications of state violence deny the singularity of the beings that are the victims of that violence.

THIRD EXAMPLE: THE PROBLEM OF DIRTY HANDS

The political problem of dirty hands is a subset of the problem of moral dilemmas, and in many respects my argument in chapter 5 can be seen as a response to the same political problem. By looking at the problem of dirty hands, I can exemplify how the singular being is ignored in a complicated justification of state violence and begin to distinguish my claims about moral horror from this problem.

Doubts about the existence of moral dilemmas have been raised from various standpoints, but my conclusion is that there really are moral dilemmas (even if I will not and cannot argue for that now). More important, the political problem of dirty hands might be real even if moral dilemmas don't exist because dirty hands implies a conflict not (just) within morality but between an institutional role (the politician) with duties attached to that role (many of which are legally required) justified not by morality but by the purpose and rules that define the role and, on the other side, the person who, as a person, also has moral duties. At any rate this seems to be the way the conflict is seen in Michael Walzer's "Political Action: The Problem of Dirty Hands," still the classic essay on the subject.[9] That the problem of dirty hands is as relevant today as it was in 1973 can be seen from Walzer's central example: a politician has to decide whether to torture a rebel leader to discover the location of bombs set to go off throughout a city in twenty minutes. This "ticking time bomb" scenario is the basis for the extensive contemporary literature on the legal and ethical responses to and justifications and criticisms of the very real torture that has been (and surely continues to be) used by the United States and other nations.

Walzer's essay, though, was a response to a set of papers published a year before in a symposium on morality and the rules of war. Thomas Nagel, R. B. Brandt, and R. M. Hare engaged in a debate in which, as Walzer notes, the real issue turns out to be the problem of dirty hands. By first examining the prehistory of Walzer's essay, especially Nagel's contribution, I can better show why I find Walzer's position and the problem of dirty hands more generally to be flawed by its inattention to the singular being in its justifications of (the tragic fact of) political violence.

Nagel's essay, responded to by Brandt and Hare, argues for the existence of real moral dilemmas faced by the politician who must decide in some cases between an "absolutist" position in which certain actions are unjustifiable (e.g., murdering innocents) and the maximization of good outcomes that might be achieved by murdering innocents. Nagel's absolutist position depends on a respect for persons. When restricting actions we may justifiably perform, there is a single principle:

> that hostility or aggression should be directed at its true object. This means both that it should be directed at the person or persons who provoke it and that it should aim more specifically at what is provocative about them ... Whatever one does to another person intentionally must be aimed at him as a subject, with the intention that he receive it as a subject. It should manifest an attitude to him rather than just to the situation, and he should be able to recognize it and identify himself as its object. (Nagel 1972, 135–36)

In other words, in war one can justifiably kill an enemy combatant but not kill their family standing nearby so as to distract the real enemy and make killing him or her easier. Likewise, one can justifiably kill those who are driving munitions to the front line, but not those driving food, for the former is intimately linked to the war effort and the latter is linked to a condition of human existence (and one is not at war with the human being on the opposite side but with that human being insofar as they are the enemy combatant). This is surely a riff on Kantian respect for humanity, which justifies not only not lying to another person or breaking a promise made to them but also killing them provided one kills them in such a way as to respect them as ends in themselves.

For Nagel, although absolutism implies that, say, carpet-bombing a city to force a truly terrible enemy to submit (e.g., Germany in World War II), is never justified, reasons of utility might render the absolutist position "untenable." But "even in such cases absolutism retains its force in that one cannot claim justification for the violation. It does not become all right" (Nagel 1972, 137). Hence, the moral dilemma. Key to Nagel's position is a laudable recourse to the perspective of the object of violence, the victim, something conspicuously absent in Brandt's, Hare's, Walzer's, and many other discussions of the problem of dirty hands (and how to understand contemporary practices of torture). In Adriana Cavarero's language, Nagel downplays the "warrior-criterion" for thinking about violence and adopts the position of the "defenseless" (Cavarero 2009, 73–74). For Nagel, the absolutist position is made sense of by asking how one might justify, say, torturing another person to that specific other person as they are being tortured. Brandt's contractual rule utilitarianism, for example, asks us to justify rules of war (including such things as torture) by asking what rational, self-interested actors behind a veil of ignorance would choose as rules of war (Brandt 1972, 150). The absurdity of this position is made clear by Nagel:

> If one abandons a person in the course of rescuing several others from a fire or a sinking ship, one could say to him, "You understand, I have to leave you to save the others" … One could even say, as one bayonets an enemy soldier, "It's either you or me." But one cannot really say while torturing a prisoner, "You understand, I have to pull out your fingernails because it is absolutely essential that we have the names of your confederates." (Nagel 1972, 137)

Once the specific person is taken seriously as the one to whom a justification is being given, the idea that one could appeal in any way to what they would have rationally understood or agreed to in a situation where they are not being tortured denies that treating "someone else horribly puts you in a special relation to him, which may have to be defended in terms of other features of your relation to him" (Nagel 1972, 137). Brandt's insistence that we distinguish between justifying an act to the specific person and justifying an act behind a veil of ignorance (in which we choose rules rather than the application of those rules in a particular case) repeats the flaw of Rawls's position pointed out by Cavell: to appeal to a rule requires one to ignore the other person, the specific, unique person in front of you (Brandt 1972, 151). Imagine if, for some reason, rational people agreed on rule utilitarian grounds that torture could be used in war (for it has been proven to be useful for procuring information and ending wars more quickly and with less bloodshed). Are we really to demand, once the veil has been lifted and the tortured person finds out just what he had agreed to accept behind a veil of ignorance, that that person being tortured is simply out of order if he should change his mind about the rightness of torture? It is not enough to claim, as Brandt does, that there is a difference between justifying a prison sentence to a condemned man in a way that persuades that prisoner (something unlikely to happen) and justifying imprisonment to that prisoner if he were to be a rational chooser behind the veil of ignorance. Although I see less of a difference between imprisonment and torture than most, I assume most everyone else would see a quite radical difference between the two (for starters, torture is not punishment; see Scarre 2003, 297–98).

The failure to take seriously Nagel's "victim viewpoint" and whether we owe anything in the way of justification to the specific human being we are attacking undermines Brandt's (1972) and Hare's (1972) responses to Nagel.[10] The failure to take the victim viewpoint is also a pervasive feature of Walzer's essay, in spite of his obvious, although not unreserved, sympathy for Nagel's position. Walzer's concern—along with contemporary theorists interested in how we should politically and legally respond to torture— is the politician with dirty hands, the one choosing to torture, rather than the tortured. Walzer does agree with Nagel that the politician faces a real moral dilemma and he also agrees that moral rules are such that "when rules are overridden, we do not talk or act as if they had been set aside, canceled, or annulled. They still stand and have this much effect at least: that we know we have done something wrong even if what we have done was also the best thing to do on the whole in the circumstances" (Walzer 1973, 171). Thus, it really is true that the torture of the rebel leader Walzer describes is wrong, even if it was the best thing to do on the whole, and thus the most appropriate response to that action is in fact to punish the politician (Walzer 1973, 180).

However, for all of the genuine pathos Walzer legitimately feels for the politician who must dirty his hands, there is no pathos or attention reserved for the tortured rebel leader. Walzer does not enlarge his thinking so as to see the question of dirty hands from the perspective of the tortured. That the torture is wrong is merely claimed, and perhaps torture is in fact so terrible an act that the action needs no explanation of its wrongness (alternatively, that wrongness can be explained by several different moral principles). Of course, if it is so terrible, then how can it be overridden by utilitarian reasons? This is where the political problem of dirty hands reveals itself: the politician acts "for us," we citizens who will be potentially blown up by the bombs in the city, and in so doing, he has at his disposal the means of violence (Walzer 1973, 163). Thus on one hand the politician is not (just) out for himself but out for all of us, and thus has a political obligation to us (say, to our protection from terrorist acts); on the other hand, because politicians have the means of legitimate violence in their possession, they have a moral obligation not to become "killers," that is, to use their political power for immoral ends (Walzer 1973, 164). So the politician has a political obligation to take "us" into account when deciding what to do against "them" with the means of illegitimate violence; yet he has a moral obligation as a human being to take into account what he is doing to "them" with the means of illegitimate violence, albeit it a moral obligation that we, those he represents, should punish politically. None of this seems to really matter—that is, there is no problem of dirty hands— until what is at issue is not legitimate violence but illegitimate violence, such as torture. For even if we feel a "half-conscious dislike and unease" when we think about the politician's control of the means of violence, there is no real dilemma until the possibility of an illegitimate, hence immoral, violence is made real and present (Walzer 1973, 164). Thus, one difference between my position and Walzer's—a difference that has ethical and political consequences that will become clear in the next chapter—is that I am arguing that there is no legitimate state violence at all (hence the problem of dirty hands is far worse than Walzer sees).

To be fair, Walzer does not strictly divide the moral from the political in the way I am attributing to him, for at many points in his argument the moral and the political bleed into each other or compensate for each other. As just mentioned, a moral failing (such as torture) is to be punished politically and legally, and for precisely political reasons a politician "with dirty hands needs a soul, and it is best for us all if he has some hope of personal salvation, however that is conceived" (Walzer 1973, 178). Thus, a sense of moral obligation is important not only for the politician but for political reasons relevant to the citizenry as well: we citizens want a politician with a soul, if not for the sake of "them" then certainly for our own sake. But this overlap of morality and politics hurts Walzer's position, for it forces us to ask: why shouldn't the politician respond morally to the rebel to be tortured? The answer seems to be that the politician, as a politician, works "for us," and thus has political obligations to us that outweigh (at least in some cases) his moral obligation to the rebel. But the political overwhelms the moral not just because there is a clash of obligations the politician must negotiate. It does so because the political, in Walzer's argument, requires the rebel to be tortured precisely by denying the singularity of that being: the being to be tortured is a "rebel," a "terrorist," both of which are politico-legal terms. This is to deny the singularity of the one being tortured, and thus to justify (state) violence by denying, avoiding, or repressing the singularity of a singular being. The "moral" person who happens to be a politician is not confronting a singular being, for the politician has already defined, appropriated, the singular being.

The appellation "rebel" is obviously not normatively neutral from a political point of view, just as the use of terrorist means of violence is not normatively neutral from a political and legal point of view. By modifying the scenario Walzer describes, one might imagine whether torture would be the best thing to do, all things considered, if the "rebel" were a uniformed soldier in another army who had set up bombs in various parts of the city. Or, one might wonder whether it would be morally and legally acceptable to torture such a solider because we knew that he knew the location of a munitions factory that, if destroyed, would end the war quickly and with a minimum of casualties. The problem is that the name "rebel" and the means of violence feared by Walzer's politician has, in a sense, already decided the issue in advance. The singular being as "rebel terrorist" is already outside the legal and political order, and now the only question is whether it is better on the whole to torture this rebel, that is, to exceed the legal, political, and moral limitations on the politician. The only real obstacle left on Walzer's account of the situation is a moral obstacle, an obstacle for the human being who is also a politician.

Walzer has already politicized the moral dilemma faced by his politician by confronting the politician not with a singular being but with a rebel terrorist. Even if the politician thinks that torture is always wrong, always unjust, and thus that torture is never deserved, the question he is asking in the specific case is whether this rebel who knows about bombs that are set to go off is to be tortured despite the injustice, for the sake of the lives of those the politician represents. The object of potential torture is understood solely in political terms and the dilemma is between a just political end and, in spite of all the talk of torture always being wrong, an unjust violent means to that just political end. We are thus back with Benjamin, but with a twist: the dilemma is between a use of violence that is justified in reference to a just end and that same violence, taken in and of itself, as unjust regardless of the ends it serves. But this only becomes a dilemma if the singular being is a "rebel who knows about bombs about to go off." There is certainly no question here about whether torture is always unjust, for we know that it is. If the singular being to be tortured were not a "rebel who knows ..." then there would be no dilemma at all. The dilemma only appears because the singular being is appropriated in a particular way and not because, as it might at first seem, there are, in fact, bombs about to go off. In other words, the dilemma Walzer describes and negotiates is constituted by the denial of the singular being, the naming of the singular being as rebel terrorist, and not at all by the fact that citizens may die from a set of bombs about to go off in the city. One need only ask whether on Walzer's account the torture that has been committed becomes immediately unjustified if, during the torture, the bombs do go off and people die, thus having eliminated the need for the torture. I am fairly confident that Walzer would maintain that the torture, however wrong, was justifiable (or, more precisely perhaps, excusable) because of the political obligations of the politician. In that case, whether the bombs go off or not, whether citizens die or not, is not the crucial factor in constituting the dilemma. Nor is it the case that the mere possibility of bombs going off is enough to justify the torture, on Walzer's broader account of war. For in war, especially modern war, there are always bombs about to go off, often in heavily populated cities (as Walzer well knows; see Walzer 2006), if not always bombs planted by terrorists. But if that is so, we are forced to ask: should Walzer's politician punish a soldier in an opposing army who knows about a planned aerial attack? If we are to trust Walzer's later distinction, in *Just and Unjust Wars*, between guerrillas and terrorists, where the former have rights (if they have the support of the people) and the latter have violated both the war convention and the political code and thus stand outside the field of rights, then the determination of the singular being as a rebel who seems to be using terroristic means, and whose imminent torture is in question, is crucial to his argument (Walzer 2006, 176–206). One cannot torture a guerrilla, but one can torture a terrorist. Insofar as this deter-mination is crucial, it is clear that the moral assessment of the situation is fatefully shaped by this determination: once a "rebel who knows ..." is applied, the singular being is pushed beyond the protections of law and left in the no-man's-land of the politician's no-longer-all-that-tragic dilemma. After all, it is a terrorist we are torturing; the politician who must be punished might, if his deeds are glorious enough, still receive the admiration of those he served (Walzer 1973, 180). After all, and again, it is a rebel terrorist he is torturing.

What if one were to begin from the position of the singular being, to think the same situation without reference to the "warrior criterion?" Depending on the particular situation, perhaps very little would change. As one might imagine based on my argument here (although it does not follow from my argument at all), I do think torture should never be used, no matter how useful it might be. But what if it is a matter of, say, conducting drone strikes in violation of international law within the territorial bound-aries of a state against which war has not been declared? There are no doubt many utilitarian calculations one might make, and many politicians would surely decide to conduct those strikes. Perhaps many of those politicians would have a soul and thus feel the dilemma Walzer poses. But one would not, if one is viewing the situation from the position of the defenseless, the singular being, leave open the possibility that glory might attach itself to the politician who chooses the immoral, unjustifiable option of using illegitimate violence. One might also endorse the legal punishment of the politician without assuming that such punishment is enough to clean the politician's hands, as Walzer sometimes suggests. For both options—glori-fying the deed and punishing it to cleanse—continue to ignore the singular being whose existence was destroyed or attacked by the violent action.

Both glorification and punishment ignore the singular being because they are actions that remain insular, as if the politician's criminality was a crime like any other, one "against" the political community he represented, and as if his glorification was a "decision" made by that community to recognize that their representative's deeds were, however personally diffi-cult, deserving of appreciation. From the perspective of the singular beings destroyed or injured by state violence, such responses to the politician seem beside the point. It is difficult to even imagine a Pakistani or Afghani whose family and village have been destroyed by a drone strike glorifying the Bush or Obama administrations' decision to bomb their village. But punishment, too, seems not quite enough, for punishment is for the living. No matter how great the punishment, the singular being who is killed remains killed. Perhaps all one can hope for is forgiveness. But that, too, is for the living.

Although Walzer recognizes the moral unjustifiability of certain political acts, he tends to mitigate the seriousness of those acts, perhaps because he feels that such acts are sometimes necessary and that we therefore need people willing to act in dirty ways who are yet good enough not to want to perform such actions. But these acts are, by his admission, absolutely wrong, and they seem to be absolutely wrong because of what they do to the object of those actions. If so, we should begin from the perspective of that object: the singular being. From the perspective of the singular being, the unjustifiable violence we find in politics is not tragic, as Walzer, following Weber, acknowledges (although he thinks such acknowledgment must be supplemented by punishment): it is horrifying.

Or it is tragically horrifying, akin to the horror Oedipus sees at the end of *Oedipus the King*. Oedipus, upon learning the truth, rushes in to see his wife/mother Jocasta hanging. He pulls her down:

> When he saw her, he cried out fearfully
> and cut the dangling noose. Then, as she lay,
> poor woman, on the ground, what happened after,
> was terrible to see. He tore the brooches—
> the gold chased brooches fastening her robe—
> away from her and lifting them up high
> dashed them on his own eyeballs, shrieking out
> such things as: they will never see the crime
> I have committed or had done upon me! (Sophocles 1991, 66)

This, I would suggest, is a better figure for thinking about unjustifiable state violence than what we find in the problem of dirty hands. Oedipus, ripping open his mother/wife's robe, exposing her dead and naked body, thrusts into his eyes the brooches that conceal and thus reveal the singular origin of his singularly miserable life and the site of one of his horrible deeds. Witnessing the violence he has brought to pass however unknowingly, Oedipus punishes himself. This scene of horror, inside the palace, is unbearable. It is almost, but not quite, unlivable, for Oedipus does not kill himself, after all, although he might have. He puts his life into the hands of fate and asks Creon for permission to leave Thebes.

I am certainly not calling for us to blind ourselves in the face of the horror of unjustifiable state violence. On the contrary, I argue in the next chapter that we should keep our eyes firmly fixed on that violence, more specifically on the singular beings that are the objects of unjustifiable violence. I also argue that the horror of a political life in which we allow unjustifiable violence to continue should not be understood (only) in aesthetic terms. So in some ways, the example of Oedipus is inapt. What remains, for me, powerful about the image of Oedipus blinding himself is that rather than turn away from the scene of his dead wife/mother, he reveals it even more fully. He exposes himself to the exposed dead and naked body. He exposes himself to horror. And the sight is unbearable. The knowledge of that horror can be lived, but not borne. Oedipus is a sort of "proof" of what our lives would be like if we could in fact overcome what Slavoj Žižek describes as the "fetishist disavowal" at the heart of any ethics: " 'I know, but I don't want to know that I know, so I don't know.' I know it, but I refuse to fully assume the consequences of this knowledge, so that I can continue acting as if I don't know it" (Žižek 2008, 46). Oedipus, and perhaps only Oedipus, can live this unbearable horror. But if we cannot bear it or live it, then we must seek to lessen the horror.

5 MORAL HORROR

ALTHOUGH IN SOME WAYS INAPT, the image of Oedipus exposing himself to the horror of his wife/mother's dead, naked body is one that I take to be a plausible representation of the horror provoked by state violence. The experience of horror, specifically what I call moral horror, is how I would like to describe the condition citizens (should) live in given the unjustifiable violence of the state that most of us acquiesce to (and many of us support, to varying degrees). The image of Oedipus is perhaps misleading for another reason, for moral horror is not, I want to argue here, the same as what I call aesthetic horror.

Horror is an affect, the etymology of which stems from the Latin for bristling or shuddering. As an affect, it is unsurprising that most uses of the word *horror*—and most discussions of horror in modern aesthetics and political and philosophical thought—refer to an object of horror, often (but not always) visual or to be imagined (as in literature), that horrifies us. Noel Carroll, referring to what he calls "art-horror," that is, the horror produced by the horror genre of art, defines *horror* as follows:

> I am occurently art-horrified by some monster X, say Dracula, if and only if 1) I am in some state of abnormal, physically felt agitation (shuddering, tingling, screaming, etc.) which 2) has been caused by a) the thought: that Dracula is a possible being; and by the evaluative thoughts: that b) said Dracula has the property of being physically (and perhaps morally and socially) threatening in the ways portrayed in the fiction and that c) said Dracula has the property of being impure, where 3) such thoughts are usually

accompanied by the desire to avoid the touch of things like Dracula. (Carroll 1990, 27)

For Carroll, horror is an occurrent emotional state with bodily components such as shuddering and bristling caused by connected thoughts and desires of a particular being that horrifies us either in person (as happens to characters in a Dracula story) or to readers and viewers. In short, horror is an aesthetic experience (in the full sense of aesthetic), but it is a horror caused by the thought of something horrifying.

I do not agree with Carroll that the affect of art-horror must always be caused by a thought or set of thoughts because I am not convinced that his account of the relation of emotions, which involve cognitive elements, to bodily affects (such as shuddering or bristling in horror) must be so unidirectional. Affects and emotions and thoughts, neuroscience is showing, are related in complex relations of causality that may preclude the kind of causality assumed in Carroll's account (Carroll 1990, 26). But I think that thoughts can sometimes cause (art and nonart) horror. The horror I feel at the sight, say, of the many photographs of lynchings in the United States seems, phenomenologically, to precede either the thought that this is possible/real or that this is bad or good or threatening. Of course, I already think lynching is horrifying and have seen such pictures before, so I definitely come to any photograph with a set of predispositions and prejudices, but this only proves the complexity of the encounter. To be sure, a photograph of a "real" lynching may be other than the art-horror Carroll describes. On the other hand, memory can produce the affect of horror and memory, if not necessarily thought alone, is certainly an experience that emerges in consciousness. This point is central for my argument because later I claim that moral horror is a "product" of thinking and perception.

Stanley Cavell gives the name "horror" "to the perception of the precariousness of human identity, to the perception that it may be lost or invaded, that we may be, or may become, something other than we are, or take ourselves for; that our origins as human beings need accounting for, and are unaccountable" (Cavell 1999, 418). For him, the object I am horrified by is the inhuman, the monstrous, but if no monsters of the right sort exist—if there are no vampires—then the only candidate for the horrifying, he claims, is the human. When Cavell defines *horror* in terms of the precariousness of human identity, he does not refer to (the sometimes frightening) fact that who I am today may not be who I am tomorrow.

Rather, he refers to the fact that my very status as a human being might come into question or be violated. Thus, he speculates, "if only humans feel horror (if the capacity to feel horror is a development of the specifically human biological inheritance), then maybe it is a response specifically to being human" (Cavell 1999, 418). After all, he continues, that human beings are (biologically) what they are is a matter of evolutionary chance, and we know that the human being, as a natural being, will surely evolve into something else (which may expand or exceed the concept of the human). Thus, it is not only that one's "status as a human being" may come into question or be invaded when, say, a political party claims that a minority group is not human so as to violently exploit, dominate, and kill them. Rather, one's human status is threatened by the very fact of being, biologically, a human. To be a member of a (self-conscious) species of natural being is to live the instability of one's membership in that species. It is key to note here that Cavell defines horror as a perception, which entails or at least implies aesthesis. But what is it a perception of? I suggest later that we can understand what I am calling moral horror as the perception not only (or not at all) of some object that is horrifying, but of oneself, of a fundamental incongruity between what one understands oneself to be and to be justified in doing and what one sees when what is seen is seen as an object of unjustifiable violence.

Adriana Cavarero retains the aesthetic conception of horror even though she describes horror quite differently. For her, the affective shuddering of horror and the repugnance horrifying objects produce is linked to the singularity of the human being. When horrorist acts such as suicide bombings or drone attacks occur, what appears as a result of such violence is not only death but dismemberment, such that the body does not preserve its "figural unity." When this happens, "what is unwatchable above all, for the being that knows itself irremediably singular, is the spectacle of disfigurement, which the singular body cannot bear" (Cavarero 2009, 8). Cavarero's argument, in detailing the deep connection between horror, violence, and singularity, traces many of the same lines of argument I have been following. But where she employs a notion of horror that is, at bottom, aesthetic, based on the vision of something horrifying—where what is horrifying is so in part because of the loss of "figural unity"—I want to extend the notion of horror beyond the aesthetic, for I want to argue that if state violence is morally unjustifiable. yet we will, for nonmoral reasons, continue to use state violence, then the experience of an unjustifiable violence we allow to take place is moral horror rather than the aesthesis of a distorted or destroyed singular body.

Moral horror is the experience of horror produced by the thought of the contradiction between the unjustifiable violence of the state enacted on individuals and my willingness to let that violence continue. I use the adjective *moral* to distinguish moral horror from aesthetic horror, by which I mean horror caused by the sense experience of some horrifying object. In this chapter I want to elaborate as completely as I can the idea of moral horror, how it is different from aesthetic horror, how and why moral horror arises and finally what kind of ethics and politics acknowledging and living with moral horror furthers.

MORAL HORROR AND AESTHETIC HORROR

The academic interest in aesthetic horror has taken, so far as I can see, two major forms. The first is the study of the horror genre throughout the arts, especially film and literature. Psychoanalysis is often chosen as the means through which to understand the peculiar fact—not unique to the horror genre—of why many people are drawn to images and stories that disgust and revolt. The horror genre is also often understood in political and ideological terms—for example, the 1950s horror movies that were clear allegories for the Cold War—whether art-horror is read as ultimately in service of, or in defiance of, the status quo. However, accounts of aesthetic horror most obviously relevant to my concerns here are to be found in discussions of photographic representations of horrific events: the Holocaust; lynching; genocides in the Balkans, Rwanda, Sudan, Cambodia, and so on; as well as in Cavarero's *Horrorism*. I would like to focus a bit on these debates, especially on the contentious discussion of whether photographic images of "real" horror can be relied on to produce "proper" ethical and political responses. There are two main issues I explore: first, Susan Sontag's argument that photographs of atrocity are unreliable vehicles for determining individuals to respond in such a way as to produce ethical and political judgments and actions that reduce the likelihood of such horror reappearing in the world; second, Cavarero's philosophical account of horrorism. My goal is to demonstrate the limits of aesthetic horror as a ground for challenging an unjustifiable state violence, thereby setting the stage for my discussion or moral horror.

Sontag's *Regarding the Pain of Others*—despite her well-known res-
ervations about photography—ends on a somewhat ambivalent note.
Throughout the text she offers compelling reasons for the conclusion that
photographs of atrocity, of real horror, are incapable of guaranteeing—
although they are more than capable of generating—ethical and political
responses to represented horror that seek to end the horror, to do something
about it. Is it true, Sontag asks in reference to photographs of slaughtered
innocents in the Spanish Civil War, "that these photographs, document-
ing the slaughter of noncombatants rather than the clash of armies, could
only stimulate the repudiation of war? Surely they could also foster greater
militancy on behalf of the Republic" (Sontag 2003, 8). She adds a few
pages later: "In fact, there are many uses of the innumerable opportunities
a modern life supplies for regarding—at a distance, through the medium
of photography—other people's pain. Photographs of an atrocity may give
rise to opposing responses. A call for peace. A cry for revenge. Or simply
the bemused awareness, continually restocked by photographic information, that terrible things happen" (Sontag 2003, 13). The insufficiency
of photographs—or painted images—to guarantee antiviolence ethical and
political responses is almost too obvious. Karen Halttunen shows that long
before the photograph, the eighteenth-century literature and art intended
to provoke the sentimental sympathy of readers and viewers to the suffering of others "from the outset lent itself to an aggressive kind of voyeurism
in which the spectator identified not just with the sufferings of the virtuous
victim but with the cruelty of his or her tormentor" (Halttunen 1995, 309).
Infamously, images of lynchings were often sold as souvenir postcards, and
national exhibitions of lynching photographs from 2000 to 2002 along with
the publication of *Without Sanctuary* in 2000 provoked feelings of outrage,
shame, horror, and an interesting debate over whether such photographs
should even be displayed (Apel 2003).[1] Images from the Holocaust have provoked similar sets of responses (Friedlander 1992; Hirsch 2001; Dean 2003).
In short, for Sontag and many others, the ethical and political effects of viewing
photographic or painted (or reading literary) representations of horror are
utterly ambivalent. For this reason, aesthetic horror is limited in its ethical
and political capacities to put an end to the horror the photograph represents.

A second reason photographs fail to guarantee antiviolence responses,
Sontag argues, is that people become indifferent to them for lack of meaning-
ful connection to the victims of violence (or they feel no threat of the violence striking themselves). Alternatively, observers are often so overwhelmed

by the magnitude of the violence and the impossibility of bringing that violence to an end that they affectively (and thus effectively) shut down (Sontag 2003, 99–103). Left with either an outrage with no outlet or the loss of affect, photographs lack the capacity to link the fact that human life is filled with horror to the desire to end that horror.

Sontag offers other reasons for the limitations of photography, but she eventually reevaluates the photograph because it has the power to "haunt" us. Whatever photographs lack,

> it still seems a good in itself to acknowledge, to have enlarged, one's sense of how much suffering caused by human wickedness there is in the world we share with others ... There now exists a vast repository of images that make it harder to maintain this kind of moral defectiveness. Let the atrocious images haunt us. Even if they are only tokens, and cannot possibly encompass most of the reality to which they refer, they still perform a vital function. The images say: This is what human beings are capable of doing— may volunteer to do, enthusiastically, self-righteously. Don't forget. (Sontag 2003, 115)

That photographs can prick us and inform us of the fact of horror in the world as well as inspire the thought necessary to make of that fact something more than just another addition to the ceaseless violence within human history becomes the ethical and political purpose of the photograph of horror. Of course, none of this entails that the thinking undertaken by the observer will lead to the "proper," that is, hoped-for ethical and political response. But that may be asking too much of the photograph (or of anything, I suppose). Thus, I agree with Sontag that for any number of reasons nothing guarantees the link between the representation of horror and atrocity and the politics that strives to put an end to such horror. This is a central reason an understanding of the horror of political violence that is grounded in aesthetic horror will always remain ambivalent.

There is a second and far more important limitation of the reliance on aesthetic horror for challenging political violence, particularly the violence of the state. The problem is simple: the vast majority of acts of state violence are not aesthetically horrifying at all. If my argument in the previous two chapters is correct, then all acts of state violence are unjustifiable. I am claiming in this chapter that this should lead us to the experience of moral horror. Below I make an argument for how this experience emerges. The whole reason I am making such an argument is that if all state violence is unjustifiable and should lead to an experience of moral horror, then I have to account not only for the obviously horrifying acts of dismemberment, killing, rape, starvation, and so on that we see in war or in modern penal systems. I also cannot rest my argument on the horrors of state killing through the use of capital punishment for even there the contemporary means of killing, particularly the use of lethal injection, makes the aesthetic horror of the scene difficult to imagine. The scene is far more likely to appear clinical, and unless one has a terrible repugnance toward needles, the lethal injection of a prisoner—paralyzed by drugs that supposedly eliminate pain but also eliminate the ability to move and speak—isn't horrifying at all. Most acts of state violence— imprisonment and detention for various lengths of time—are simply not aesthetically horrifying. A focus on aesthetic horror is neither a necessary nor a sufficient condition for thinking about and responding to the violence of the state.

To these limits on aesthetic horror one can also add the limits of Cavarero's powerful argument in *Horrorism*. For her, modern life is characterized not only by terror and the terrifying but by horror and the horrifying, i.e., "the peculiarly repugnant character of so many scenes of contemporary violence" (Cavarero 2009, 29). Bodies are not simply killed in contemporary life: bodies are dismembered and dismembering weapons, exploding and ripping apart the intact human body. The intactness of the body that is dismembered is a crucial, but unargued for, premise of Cavarero's argument. Cavarero links singularity—the singularity I discussed earlier—to the intactness of a body. What horrifies in horrorist acts, Cavarero argues, is an "offence to corporeal unity" that "actually extends even to the outer surface that is the expression of a unique existence: the face, the physiognomy" (Cavarero 2009, 12). If the intact body expresses the singularity of the singular being then the destruction of that body, its being ripped apart, is a fate worse than death. It is a killing "that overshoots the elementary goal of taking a life and dedicates itself instead to destroying the living being as singular body, such that repugnance, as a symptom of spontaneous rebellion of the body, is, in a certain sense, nothing other than an organic repulsion with respect to the violent act that deforms it" (Cavarero 2009, 12). Although largely in agreement with Cavarero, I find her aesthetic horrorism limiting. The problem here is twofold.

First, that the singularity of a body as the outward expression of singularity must take the form of the corporeal unity of that body is, as I have already noted, a premise for which no argument is given. What is the necessary link between singularity and corporeal unity? Cavarero, as we saw just a moment ago, also refers to the "figural unity" of the singular body that is destroyed in horrorist acts. The figure of the body, its form or delineation, becomes in the argument itself a figure in the rhetorical sense: it figures singularity as unity, as the intactness of a unit vulnerable to destruction, of a "singularity not yet offended, that reveals itself in physiognomic features" (Cavarero 2009, 20). Why must the figure of singularity—in the sense of a form—form a unity that must be offended to be horrifyingly breached, destroyed to come into horrifying contact or touch with another being? For Nancy, as we have seen, there is no unitary singular being awaiting contact or touch with another being; rather, the singular being is always already exposed to other beings, appearing with or alongside other beings, constituted by being singular plural. The claim to the unity of the corporeal figure of the singular being appears, in Cavarero's text, as, I take it, an aesthetic premise (or preference?) rather than an ontological necessity.

More than just naming and describing horror aesthetically, Cavarero's argument also appears to rely on (again unargued for) aesthetic norms: the norm of unity and of naturalness. The aesthetic desire for or requirement of unity—for example, the unity of form and content, of theme and expression—seems at play in Cavarero's text in unacknowledged ways, the importance of which becomes manifest in the definition of what is horrifying in horrorist violence. Specifically, the condition of possibility of horrorist acts is the aesthetic, figural, corporeal unity of the singular body, the dismemberment of which engenders a "spontaneous rebellion of the body," an "organic repulsion." Thus, in the face of the destruction of the corporeal unity of the singular living body, the still living, presumably still singular (intact, figured) witness of and to horror undergoes an organic, natural affective convulsion. Just as the Kantian aesthetic judgment relies on the (subjective yet universal, i.e., "as if") principle that the purposiveness of beautiful objects presupposes that the object is formed so as to put the imagination and understanding into play, the idea of an organic, spontaneous, and natural response of the singular witness to horrorist violence seems to imply a similar principle of horrorist aesthesis: the dismembered body is, as it were, predeformed to disgust and repulse me (see, e.g., Kant 2000, 5:245). I am wary of the link between singularity and corporeal and figural unity for (Nancyean) ontological reasons, and I am even more worried by what I take to be the positing of an implicit connection between corporeal unity and a spontaneous organic revulsion. The suggestion of an unmediated affective experience of horror—for I take it that "spontaneous" and "organic" refer to the force of embodied affect prior to the constitutive activities of consciousness—denies the ways even affect, for all of its preconscious power, is importantly shaped over time by cultural and individual repetitions and experimentations (Connolly 2003, 85). That affect is influenced by culture is presumably a major reason representations of atrocity provoke such different affective responses and judgments. Thus, I am not convinced that the affect of horror is, in the case of contemporary violence, a spontaneous organic revulsion to the dismemberment of the singular body. However, even if Cavarero is correct, she cannot account for the horror of state violence when it leaves the singular body almost entirely untouched (say, when it punctures the vein with a needle). Then again, she may not think such an act is horrifying. But I do, and my burden is to show how that can be.

Aesthetic horror is a powerful, if limited, concept for understanding contemporary violence just as it is an important, if limited and unreliable, impetus to ethical and political action against the existence of horrifying violence in the world. It requires supplementation of all kinds—as all things do—and moral horror, as I will now argue, may offer its own contribution to understanding and responding to, at the very least, the unjustifiable violence of the state.

VIOLENCE, THE ANIMAL, AND THE HUMAN

Aristotle, in *The Politics*, claims that man is a political animal with and because of speech, and in politics what we speak of is the just and the unjust, the useful and the harmful, good and evil. The political animal lives (or should or needs to live) in a state, and this distinguishes humans from both animals and the gods, who are either too dumb for or too self-sufficient to need politics (Aristotle 1992, 1253a1–29). The exclusion of the animal from reason, speech, and politics in Aristotle and the relegation of the animal to a lower mode of being—a persistent feature of Western philosophy—is challenged, at least in part, by Adorno at the end of his chapter on freedom in *Negative Dialectics*. Adorno asserts, against Kant, a new kind of ethics: "to try to live so that one may believe himself to have been a good animal" (Adorno 1973, 299). This is linked to the new "categorical imperative" forced on humankind by Auschwitz, to

> arrange their thoughts and actions so that Auschwitz will not repeat itself, so that nothing similar will happen. When we want to find reasons for it, this imperative is as refractory as the given one of Kant was once upon a time. Dealing discursively with it would be an outrage, for the new imperative gives us a bodily sensation of the moral addendum—bodily, because it is now the practical abhorrence of the unbearable physical agony to which individuals are exposed. (Adorno 1973, 365)

More recently, of course, Foucault and, partially following him, Agamben, have examined and in their own ways challenged the (politics of the) distinction in Aristotle and Greek thought more generally between *bios* and *zoe*, the specifically human life and the animal life that man nonetheless is (Foucault 1978, 135–59; Agamben 1998) The distinction between human and animal—a distinction affirmed and denied in the very idea of a political animal—is, I argue, what is at stake as a consequence of the unjustifiability of state violence, and the putting into question, the rendering indiscernible of this distinction in our everyday lives, is the cause of moral horror. To live moral horror, I will argue, is to learn to live, as Adorno exhorts us to live, as a better animal. But first I must account for the claim that moral horror arises from the undoing of the difference between the human and the animal that the realization of the unjustifiability of state violence sets in motion.

The distinction between the human and the animal has often been philosophically drawn on the basis of the human possession of speech and reason. As one sees in Aristotle, this possession is not without political consequences, for the possession of speech and reason—as well as the insufficiency of the human—is in part why man is a political animal. Because the human being can speak about the just and the unjust, he can also decide on which acts of violence are just and unjust. This distinction seems uniquely human or, at the very least, is only applied to human actions by human beings. Human beings can make and uphold distinctions between acts of violence, some of which are justified and some of which are not. Where lions, spiders, eagles, and bears use physical force and intelligence to satisfy the necessities of survival, human beings are capable of not only finding alternatives to violence but also justifying those acts of violence to which no alternatives have been (perhaps can be) found. We do not ascribe to lions, or ticks, or pitcher plants for that matter, the adjectives *just* and *unjust* when, for example, lions attack zebras, or ticks transmit Lyme disease to humans, or pitcher plants trap various bugs. Presumably this is because the violence in question—even calling it "violence" seems wrong—doesn't imply the other concepts and/or capacities that are assumed in distinguishing human acts of violence (e.g., self-consciousness, conscience, responsibility, intention). This difference between human and animal acts of force may be prejudicial, flatly wrong, impossible to sustain and so on, but as a matter of ordinary language such a distinction does, as far as I can see, continue to structure our everyday thinking about (this aspect of) human and animal life.

However, the distinction between legitimate and illegitimate violence is not just restricted to human beings, for that conceptual distinction is a key component of the broad distinction drawn between humans and animals. Cora Diamond argues in her essay "Eating Meat and Eating People" that one of the ways we learn the difference between the human and the animal is that we human beings sit around a table eating them, whereas we humans do not sit around tables, or anywhere else, eating other humans (except in prescribed, or very contingent but specific situations; see Diamond 1978). The distinction between the human and the animal—which takes many different forms in different cultures—is learned not only (or rarely) through explicit teaching but through practices to which we are socialized and in which we learn just what humans are and are not (e.g., in biology classes, nature documentaries, punishments for pulling the dog's tail too hard, and punishments for pulling one's sister's hair too hard).

I would suggest that just as we learn about ourselves and (our relations to) animals from our practices of eating, the capacity to distinguish between legitimate and illegitimate violence and the actualization of that capacity in particular cases in part constitutes (our sense of) the difference between the human and the animal. When this capacity is lost, or where the distinction between kinds of violence cannot be sustained, the distinction of the human from the animal is threatened. In other words, the capacity to make these distinctions in acts of violence is conditioned by the capacity for reason and speech and is intimately linked to the human/animal difference for which reason and speech is often cited as the essential differentiating factor. Part of what it means to be a political animal, that is, a human being as opposed to all other animals, is to be capable of justifying acts of violence and judging other acts of violence as wrong or unjust. To find out that we cannot justify (at the very least) acts of state violence would mean that a significant number of violent acts within human life are, in a sense, no different than the acts of the animal that the human nonetheless is. That horror can emerge from the (re)discovery that the human being is an animal—more precisely, that one's identity as a human being (as opposed to an animal or living being) is unstable, liable to be undermined, as Cavell argues—is something I show in a moment. First, I offer some examples of how the human/animal distinction links to the capacity to distinguish justified and unjustified acts of violence.

One "negative" example comes from Adorno's *Minima Moralia*. Adorno argues that

> Indignation over cruelty diminishes in proportion as the victims are less like normal readers, the more they are swarthy, "dirty," dago-like ... Perhaps the social schematization of perception in anti-Semites is such that they do not see Jews as human beings at all. The constantly encountered assertion that savages, blacks, Japanese are like animals, monkeys for example, is the key to the pogrom. The possibility of the pogroms is decided in the moment when the gaze of a fatally-wounded animal falls on a human being. The defiance with which he repels this gaze—"after all, it's only an animal"—reappears irresistibly in cruelties done to human beings, the perpetrators having again and again to reassure themselves that it is "only an animal," because they could never fully believe this even of animals ... what was not seen as human and yet is human, is made a thing, so that its stirrings can no longer refute the manic gaze. (Adorno 2005, §68)

This is not an isolated perception. Richard Rorty explains atrocious acts of violence in human history committed by people who profess the inherent dignity of all human beings—from the Crusaders to Thomas Jefferson to the Serbs in the early 1990s—by the fact that these individuals assume that "there are animals walking about in humanoid form," that is, that it is not that human beings don't have inherent dignity but that some humans are "humans," mere animals without dignity (Rorty 1998, 168). Although Cavell does not accept the idea that slaveowners, for example, denied the humanity of their slaves, he does show how those owners might have denied that slaves are "purely human," an interpretation of the relation between owner and slave that relies on the slave being both not an animal and yet not a (pure) human either (Cavell 1999, 372–78).

What we learn from the persistent and prominent "animalization" of those against whom violence is committed is that once a human being is placed outside the realm of the human, either definitively or partially, the violence one does against that human/animal no longer falls under the moral rules that regulate our violent acts against other humans. Legitimate violence is for humans, and against humans, alone. Adorno's fragment implicitly emphasizes this conclusion through its attention to the compulsive repetition of "it's only an animal" on the part of the violent actor. This repetition is necessary not merely because the supposed animal is, nonetheless, a human (and thus we need to delude ourselves), but precisely because—and here I am moving beyond Adorno's analysis but I think he would agree—the human is an animal. The animalization of the human is only possible—the images of monkeys only have their horrific, violent effect—because the human being is, in fact, an animal, specifically a mammal, specifically a primate. The delusion produced by the repetition works only because it is based on a real perception that in the bonobo's eyes we do see ourselves, just as in those human eyes we also see the bonobo. In this indecision between the human and animal, the legitimacy of violence hangs in the balance. Adorno gives—along with many others—one indication of the constitutive function of the legitimate/illegitimate violence distinction for our conception of the human being.

A second example comes from social contract theory. Biological, ethological, and philosophical investigations of moral behavior in nonhuman animals has shown that it is probably inaccurate to ascribe to humans alone certain moral capacities or desires, such as cooperation, fairness, and trust (Bekoff 2004). But it is unclear to me how the capacity for such practices can possibly lead to a moral distinction between just and unjust uses of force: say, for example, when it comes to hunting animals for food. It is important to remember that human beings have debated the practice of killing animals for food for a very long time, just as they have also debated whether killing someone to punish them for wrongdoing is fair and just. These debates are, of course, concerned with cooperation, trust, and perhaps most important, fairness. But they are not centrally concerned with these issues. The distinction between legitimate and illegitimate violence in social contract theory concerns not what it is fair to do but, as it were, the grounds of what it is fair and not fair to do in the case of acts of violence within an artificial community constituted by consent. That this community is artificial doesn't necessarily deny that there are "natural" communities. Rather, only the naturalness of the political community must be denied. With the generation of the polis, however, comes a (not absolute) distinction between "kinds" of violence: the state becomes the (almost always exclusive) wielder of legitimate violence. Even if there is no state of nature, the point is simple: there is, in many political philosophical accounts of the polis, a recursive, deliberative, and volitional component to the distinction between legitimate and illegitimate violence. Human beings found the political distinction between legitimate and illegitimate violence (with the notable exception of political theologies of various kinds, including perhaps Locke's account of punishment in the state of nature).

Take Hobbes for example. Hobbes claims that covenants with beasts are impossible because "not understanding our speech, they understand not, nor accept of any translation of Right; nor can translate any Right to another; and without mutual acceptation, there is no covenant" (Hobbes 1997, XIV). That this incapacity is due solely to the (often reflexive) power of language is clear because animals, at a first order of mental life, share much with human beings. Animals, Hobbes claims, can recognize similar images, but they cannot distinguish between true and false images (e.g., between a man and an image of a man in a mirror) for true and false are properties of a speech that only humans possess (Hobbes 2005, I, 3, §8). The same goes for syllogistic reasoning (Hobbes 2005, I, 4, §8). Yet animals, like human beings and even inanimate objects, can contract habits; animals have sense and the memory sense requires; animals have "discourse of the mind," for phantasms arise in animal minds; and, finally, animals can deliberate (in the Hobbesian sense of alternating appetitive and aversive thoughts) and will (again in the Hobbesian sense of will as the last act of deliberation) (Hobbes 2005, 22, §20, 25, §5, 25, 8, 25, §13). What animals lack especially is what Hobbes calls "names of the second intention," that is, names of names (Hobbes 2005, 2, §10).

More telling is first that Hobbes denies the possibility of a political life to animals, largely (but not solely) because they lack language and because their communal existence is natural, not (as in the case of humans) artificial (Hobbes 1997, XVII). Lacking language, animals cannot deceive about what is good or evil or distinguish between injury and damage, and because their social existence is a product of natural sociality—for Hobbes, man is not naturally political—animals have no need of the artificial structures of politics. Second, Hobbes sees the relation of human beings to animals as falling under the regime of the right of nature, "forasmuch therefore as it proceeds from the right of nature, that a beast may kill a man, it is also by the same right that a man may slay a beast" (Hobbes 1991, XII, §10). Insofar as animals cannot be covenanted with and positive law only exists (and thereby actualizes and makes enforceable the laws of nature) through the artifice of the sovereign, animal violence against man—as well as man's violence against the animal—never constitutes injury or injustice. Animals live, one must assume, in a perpetual state of nature under the regime of the right of nature. There is no justice or injustice in such a state, no law, no sovereignty, no right, no politics. As Derrida claims in *The Beast and the Sovereign*, the animal, like the sovereign, "seem to have in common their being-outside-the-law" (Derrida 2009, 17).[2]

For Hobbes, then, the distinctions between just and unjust, legitimate and illegitimate, are human, and only human, distinctions. Moreover, they are distinctions human beings must create through covenanting, for such distinctions themselves are not natural to the human. It is no surprise that Hobbes describes life in the state of nature as brutish: the term should be taken mostly as the description of an animal life defined not by its lack of reasoning or speech—for such things exist in the state of nature and are, in fact, partly responsible for the state of war—but by its lack of law, of justice and injustice, legitimacy and illegitimacy. To lose these distinctions, or to never attain them, is to remain an animal among animals, actors for whom no distinction between legitimate and illegitimate violence exists. One can see similar gestures in, for example, Locke's *Second Treatise* (e.g., Locke 1988, §§16, 172, 181).

The difference introduced by human beings between legitimate and illegitimate uses of force, between animal force and human violence, makes and marks a difference between the human and the animal. Using illegitimate violence when the law is in place or ignoring the distinction altogether "reduces" the human being to an animal. Although the distinction between legitimate and illegitimate violence is not often taken—unlike the possession of speech and reason—as the specific difference that marks man, a good case can be made that this distinction is just as internal to our conception of the human being. For if the distinction depends on the kinds of speech and reason assumed to be unique to human beings, this does not mean that—rhetorically and conceptually in the Western tradition—the human being can remain human with only speech and reason. To be human it is necessary, but not sufficient, to have the use of reason and speech. It is also necessary to distinguish between justifiable and unjustifiable violence.

MORAL HORROR

If I am right to argue that the distinction between just and unjust violence is internal to our conception of the human being and is linked to the difference of the human being from the animal, if my argument in previous chapters that there is no possible moral justification of state violence is correct, and if state violence nonetheless takes place, often with the approval or at least acquiescence of great numbers of citizens, then the distinction between humans and animals is under threat as a result of this interconnection of arguments. The source of moral horror is the loss—more precisely the threat of the loss—of the distinction between humans and animals that accompanies the threatened loss of the legitimacy/illegitimacy distinction. But why describe this loss as threatened rather than actual?

The loss is threatened rather than actual because the temptation to conclude that if state violence cannot be legitimized then we lose the legitimacy/illegitimate violence distinction altogether is just that: a temptation. Robert Paul Wolff succumbs to this temptation in his essay "On Violence" and to show why we should resist this temptation—and thus accept that there is a distinction between legitimate and illegitimate violence—at the same time that we accept that state violence is always illegitimate I want to look at his argument in more detail. I will show that moral horror emerges in part from the appearance of this temptation and our resistance to it, and thus it emerges from our exposure to our own animality rather than our "collapse" into it.

Wolff's argument for the loss of the legitimate/illegitimate distinction is straightforward enough and should be familiar to anyone who has read *In Defense of Anarchism*. He draws a distinction between force and violence. The former is the "ability to work some change in the world by the expenditure of physical effort" (Wolff 1969, 604). Violence is "the illegitimate or unauthorized use of force to effect decisions against the will of others" (Wolff 1969, 606). Violence, then, depends on a distinction between legitimate and illegitimate authority and if there is no such distinction—Wolff's main anarchist claim—then we cannot distinguish between legitimate and illegitimate force, that is, force and violence. The conclusion drawn by Wolff is not that all force is violence but the distinction between the two should simply be discarded and in place of the distinction we should rely on more basic moral rules for justifying our actions, for example, the rule that our actions should do more good than harm. He offers two explanations for why we cling to the force/violence distinction (in addition to the obvious rhetorical and political reasons for calling one act force and another violence). One "subjective" reason is that we distinguish between regular and irregular uses of force. In different societies at different times, certain conflicts are habitually dealt with by physical force and others are not (Wolff 1969, 612). The second, "objective" reason is that some of our interests are central to our lives and others are peripheral. In the latter case physical force is not to be used because the interest just doesn't matter enough for the benefits of physical force to outweigh the risks; the opposite is true for central interests. Of course, one person's central interest is another's peripheral interest, which explains many of our disputes (Wolff 1969, 613).

Wolff's argument debunks the force/violence distinction to show that it is simply prejudicial, given the a priori impossibility of legitimate authority, to call one thing violence and another force. For Wolff, the legitimate/illegitimate violence distinction disappears. I think his argument for the a priori impossibility of legitimate authority is wrong, but I am more interested in his argument for getting rid of the force/violence distinction such that we cannot properly use the term *violence*, and hence illegitimate violence, at all. Why do we cling to the legitimate/illegitimate violence distinction if it cannot be sustained?

My own answer should be obvious at this point: it is part of our self-understanding as human beings that some violent acts are legitimate and others are illegitimate (the force/violence distinction is unhelpful and unnecessary). It may be true that what any particular society names legitimate and illegitimate violence is customary, and it may also be true that we draw distinctions between central and peripheral interests on which we call certain violence acts legitimate and others illegitimate. But the distinction itself, I am arguing, is not "customary" or "conventional" if by that we mean "merely" conventional or customary. What explains the fact that nearly every society we know about draws a distinction between violent acts that are legitimate and violent acts that are not? One needn't rely here on any concept of human nature, but simply on a concept of convention as natural to the human being to show that what is conventional may be so deeply embedded as to acquire a quasi-transcendental status in human life (see Cavell 1989, 40–52, 1999, 86–125; Das 2007, 88–89). I agree with Coady's description of Wolff's self-assured acceptance of the consequences of his position (including the claim that a sit-in may be more violent than a beating and if the former is justified so might the latter) as "no more than schoolboy bravado" (Coady 2008, 37). Philosophically coherent or not, the legitimate/illegitimate violence distinction is central to the self-conception of many individuals and to nearly all cultures of which we are aware.

The consequences drawn by Wolff are tempting, but succumbing to the temptation threatens our identity as human. There is nothing wrong with losing our identity as human per se, but I do not see any argument here as likely to convince anyone or any culture, nor do I think it should. I also do not think we should ignore the temptation or deny its presence, because the collapse of the legitimate/illegitimate violence distinction as a result of philosophical argumentation is a genuine threat. If state violence is always wrong but we persist in employing it, then it is hard not to come to the conclusion that we are no different than those animals for whom there is no distinction. But it is also hard (extremely hard, like cutting off the branch we are sitting on) to deny a distinction between legitimate and illegitimate acts of violence that enables us to argue that some acts of violence—or all acts of (state) violence—are illegitimate. We need this distinction, and yet the impossibility of actually justifying state violence threatens the distinction and, with it, the human/animal distinction. This is one reason we find ourselves in moral horror. Why describe this threatened loss as moral horror?

To help answer this question, I return to Cavell's brief account of horror in *The Claim of Reason*. Cavell identifies horror as the perhaps biologically inherited perception of the precariousness of human identity. By this he means the knowledge that to be a human being, and even what we understand to be a human being, needs "accounting for, and [is] unaccountable" for the human being, like all natural beings, has evolved (Cavell 1999, 419). The experience of horror, he claims, might very well be a way of interpreting tragedy (as against the ideas of fear and pity), and in that horror what we see is that "not merely human law but human nature itself can be abrogated" (Cavell 1999, 419). Although Cavell only suggests, without much argumentation, that horror can be a response to the perception of the animality of the human being, I think there is much to be said for such an interpretation.

Both the experience of horror and the capacity to experience horror, Cavell argues, emerge from the contingency of the human's biological status as the human animal. But why is the realization that one is an animal, with all of its consequences, so horrifying? Cavell's argument—that monsters horrify us and since there are no real monsters only the human is left as an object of horror—isn't very convincing because the real argumentative burden is not to show that the human is the only candidate for the horrifying, hence something about the human being must be horrifying. Rather, the real burden is to show more specifically why and how the human being's precarious identity as human becomes an object of horror when the human being reveals its animality, hence its groundlessness, its contingency, its finitude, its embodiment. Why is a groundless, contingent, finite, embodied animality horrifying?

More specifically, how and why is moral horror produced when one realizes that state violence is unjustifiable and yet one will (in whatever way) let it continue? The "how" is fairly straightforward. As I argued in previous chapters, judging that an act of state violence is legitimate is always undermined by the reception and "recognition" of the singular being that is the object of that judgment. Moral horror is produced when the recognition of the necessary failure of any moral justification of state violence is not enough to compel us to no longer acquiesce in state violence, that is, when we are not compelled to stop that violence. In short, moral horror results from a cognitive contradiction or dissonance, as it were. It is distinguished from aesthetic horror precisely in this respect: moral horror doesn't emerge from the aesthesis of a horrifying "object" but is produced as an affect by a contradiction in our thinking and/or between our knowledge and our action. This contradiction within what we "know" or between what we "know" and what we "do" produces horror insofar as it transforms our vision of the object of state violence: it horrifies (in an active, transitive sense) us, makes us horrifying to ourselves. Let me give an example.

A UC Berkeley web page (which unfortunately seems to have disappeared) contained a story headlined "The Joy of Learning ... at San Quentin" (the original web address was http://ls.berkeley.edu/?q=node/757). The page contains a picture of several prisoners and a teacher, and most of the men are smiling and happily posing.[3] (One can easily find a number of similar images of prisoners with smiles on their faces, any one of which will serve the purposes of this example.) I assume that the joy is mostly obvious and real. Nothing horrifying here. This picture may exaggerate, but there are any number of images of prisoners going about their lives in prison, images one would be hard-pressed to describe as "horrifying." Recall, for a moment, that the *OED* defines violence in part as a physical impairment of one's freedom. Imprisonment, then, is undoubtedly violent. What justifies this violence? I have argued: nothing does or can justify this violence. So why are these individuals being violently treated without moral justification? The answers here may vary, but my own answer would be (pending further knowledge about what crimes these individuals have committed and the fairness of their trials) if, say, one person had murdered several innocent people: "because he or she has shown that they are a threat to other people and we, as a society, simply cannot take the risk, for now anyway, of their killing again." My answer is plausibly acceptable, but, I would suggest, it is in no way a moral justification of the violence being done to the individual (I deal with obvious objections to this claim in the next chapter). If my answer cannot morally justify this violence—and nothing else can—then what does this say about me, about us, about our practices of state violence?

As a prediction, of course, I cannot claim that other people will feel moral horror when confronted with the disjunction between the moral unjustifiability of state violence and our continuing acquiescence (or militant support) of it. But they should. I would suggest—although I cannot argue for this point on strictly Kantian grounds—that the experience of moral horror (say, the "judgment" that something is morally horrifying) has the same modality as Kantian judgments of the beautiful: it is subjectively necessary and universal, that is, it demands that others should also be morally horrified when I am morally horrified, although the morally horrified individual cannot presume or even expect that others will be morally horrified (Kant 2000, 5:237–40). I suppose the real analogue here would not be judgments of the beautiful but of the sublime insofar as the feeling of sublimity is produced by thoughts rather than the form of the object (for sublime objects are formless); I already cede the dubiousness of providing strictly Kantian support for my sense that I can demand that others be morally horrified as well. What I take from Kant is the sense that something about the experience of moral horror, once it is provoked by the cognitive contradictions detailed above, feels compelled in me, rather than dependent on me, and thus I can demand of others that they should be morally horrified when faced with this cognitive contradiction.

My sense that I can demand that others be morally horrified finds further support in the political nature of what morally horrifies me. For if state violence is necessarily unjust and state violence is unjustly authorized by us—that is, we members of the polis—then we are all far more unjustly and illegitimately violent than we claim, or unknowingly assume, or unthinkingly fail to realize. Of course, we are not all violent in the act but in the moral justification (or indifference to moral justification) of the act. If it is violent to deny the singularity of a singular being in the service of morally justifying a physical act of violence, then those who morally justify state violence are violent. Those of us who don't morally justify state violence but find reasons to support such violence (even passively) may not be violent, but we are horrifying, as horrifying as those who are violent in their justifications of state violence.

The disjunction between what we know about the justifiability of state violence and what we do with that knowledge is morally horrifying because it transforms the "objects" of state violence into victims of state violence and acknowledges that we who allow state violence to continue or violently legitimize it are unjust participants in acts of violence. This victimization is constant, continuous, and pervasive. Where there is state violence there are only victims of state violence. By this I don't mean to imply that objects of state violence are helpless to resist (this, thankfully and because of the courage and political genius of many prisoners around the world, is not always true) nor that being a victim of state violence expiates the guilt of anyone. The besotted frat boy in the drunk tank and the mass murderer on death row, however, have at least this much in common: they are victims of an unjustifiable state violence. We members of the various political communities around the world: we are horrifying, horrible, as we either violently justify or passively allow this violence to continue.

The "how" of moral horror, then, is this process of first realizing the impossibility of justifying state violence and then comparing this realization to one's justifications of state violence or to one's actions in the face of this knowledge. Moral horror must be produced by acts of thought or it will not emerge.

Why moral horror is produced when one thinks one's way toward the disjunction between what one knows and what one does vis-à-vis state violence is a more difficult question to answer. It is not immediately obvious why horror should be what we experience when we experience this disjunction. But I would like to suggest the answer may lie in precisely the threat to one's identity as human that the experience of this particular disjunction provokes. For if, as we saw above, many philosophers and political theorists have noted that the animal falls outside the law, hence outside the legitimate/illegitimate violence distinction, and if, as I have argued, such a distinction is just as internal to our concept of the human being as the capacity of speech and reason, then to discover that the human being must but cannot distinguish between a legitimate and illegitimate violence and that state violence, however illegitimate, is accepted, even justified (in nonmoral terms), is to discover the threat of a "slide" into animality. In short, if state violence cannot be legitimized and yet we continue to practice state violence, then either the human is not so distinct from the animal or the concept of the human must be broadened to include the capacity to legitimize, but the impossibility of legitimizing, state violence. The disjunction causes moral horror because of this threat to the identity of (and/or the concept of) the human.[4]

Furthermore, this failure calls into question not the capacity for reason and speech, hence for justifications of all kinds, but the capacity of reason and speech to conceptually distinguish human violence from nonhuman violence. This limitation on reason and speech entails a great number of political theoretical consequences for, as so many philosophers have argued, reason and speech are necessary conditions of man as a political animal and the distinction between just and unjust is internal to the political (though not exclusive to it), specifically the distinction between just and unjust violence. To find out that reason is limited is not or need not be horrifying at all. One may find the arguments of *The Critique of Pure Reason* to be many things, but I'm not sure why anyone would (or more precisely could demand that others) find it horrifying. However, when limitations on reason and speech entail the consequence that a defining difference between the human and the animal cannot be sustained, this may engender a (limited) horror, specifically moral horror.

I have still not offered an answer to the question of why realizing one's exposure to one's animality vis-à-vis state violence should be horrifying (morally or aesthetically) at all. Why is horror the result of acknowledging that with regard to violence human beings can justify certain pervasive forms of it no more than any other animal? One answer might be to follow Carroll (who follows Mary Douglas) by emphasizing the experience of impurity as central to the experience of (art-) horror. Impure objects, Carroll writes are "categorically interstitial, categorically contradictory, incomplete, or formless" (Carroll 1990, 32). In other words, objects of horror confound our expected—and often desired—conceptual distinctions, and thus they cause horror because the objects challenge both our descriptive and normative categories for making sense of experience. Impurity is not enough, according to Carroll, to produce art-horror. But it may be enough to produce moral horror.

Impurity in moral horror would lie not in the object (the victim of state violence) but in ourselves: we are impure. Our impurity is a consequence of the (partial) breakdown of the distinction between the human and the animal. When we realize that we cannot justify the state violence we nonetheless either endorse or passively acquiesce to, the sense of responsibility for a no-longer-justifiable violence creates categorical confusion: am I human or animal? Human beings are not only capable of but actually distinguish between legitimate and illegitimate violence, whereas animals do not. But given the (a priori) failure to actualize the capacity to justify state violence, it is unclear what status, human or animal, I have. That the animality of human beings can cause, at the very least, disgust at that animality is a common enough, much reported experience. For many philosophers and theologians, the body is the source of all that is wrong in human existence. Even in ordinary contexts the body can be a source of horror and, perhaps because of this, fascination. The bedroom and the doctor's office are only two spaces in which the animal body—with its liquids; its differing layers of skin, fat, and tendon; its smells, grunts, howls, shrieks, spontaneous utterances, and so on—is brought to the forefront of consciousness and can become horrifying. Thus, it may not be implausible to suppose that the loss of the human/animal difference can be a source of moral horror. If, after all, I am responsible in some way for unjustifiable acts of violence, or I let them continue and even benefit from them, then it seems entirely plausible to see myself as a horrifying creature. I am complicit in killing. I am complicit in what can only, now, be described as torture. By the millions. I am the monster.

Although I am attracted by the impurity argument (in Carroll and in moral horror), it seems insufficient to explain what is horrifying in horror because it identifies horror too quickly with disgust (for Carroll, one must also feel threatened by the object). Moreover, without a corresponding account of why disgusting objects also seem to be attractive—Carroll's explanation explicitly sidesteps this point—one is left wondering why purity and impurity are so important for the experience of horror, for if I am attracted by the impure, why am I horrified by it (and why am I hor-rified sometimes by pure things?). But more important, impurity alone doesn't account for what I take to be a further feature of moral horror.

What seems key to moral horror as the horrifying experience of realizing one's animality vis-à-vis unjustifiable state violence is, as I would like to put it, the feeling "this is (not) me." In Cavell's analysis of horror, he links horror to the necessity of but impossibility of performing an "accounting" of the human being's origins: "our origins as human beings need accounting for, and are unaccountable" (Cavell 1999, 419). Linked to the biological fact that humans are evolved and evolving human animals, our unaccountable origins reveal pervasive contingency in human existence. Yet the human being must understand: "experience must, sub specie humanitatis, make sense," but the problem is that "the field of sense, over which explanations range from 'I just don't know' to 'It's a freak of nature,' is broader than any a priori bargain knows" (Cavell 1999, 62). The necessity that human experi-ence must make sense exists alongside the contingency of human experience and the human, the fact that the human is itself a product of evolutionary factors and thus is subject to disappearance, is finite. To understand things sub specie humanitatis is to understand that there is no assured understand-ing sub specie humanitatis because to be human, as Wallace Stevens writes in "Sunday Morning," is to live "unsponsored, free." Any pleasure we might take in this freedom, however, is countered by the difficult, never complete, yet necessary process of self- and others- and world-understanding.

When I realize, in moral horror, that I am undecidably human/animal and try to make sense of that experience, I am struck by the shifting move-ments of mis(recognition) of myself. For I am, on one hand and still, the one who can justify state violence, a human being, the being that strives to be moral, that unlike all other beings can distinguish between just and unjust violence; on the other hand, I cannot justify state violence, I am no different than other beings in this respect. Yet I allow this violence to continue without justification and without excuse. Being incapable of actually jus-tifying violence is no excuse for allowing that violence to continue. This is not a reason to continue trying to justify violence either, in the hopes that one day I will succeed. The impossibility of success is no reason to deny that I nonetheless have the capacity to make moral distinctions and that I can see the difference I cannot justify. And so on.

The movement back and forth between two identities in both of which I (fail to) recognize myself is part of moral horror. It is the horror, once again, of Oedipus as he moves between the intellectual recognition of who he is through the process of interrogating various characters and the hope, sustained almost until the moment before his blinding, that he is not, after all, what he (still) knows he really is. That Oedipus finds himself impure is not enough to completely horrify him, as we find out in *Oedipus at Colonus*. For in that late Sophoclean play Oedipus, while still a miserable man, often refuses to accept responsibility for what he had done: "Indeed, what I have done / is suffering rather than doing, if I were to tell you / the story of both my parents, which makes you dread me. / That I know well. How can my nature be evil, / when all I did was matching others' actions? Even had I done what I did full consciously, / even so, I would not have been evil" (Sophocles 1991, 91). Leaving aside the possible effects of years of ambulatory misery and exile and the possibility of self-delusion, Oedipus has clearly changed his understanding of himself: he is a horrible victim rather than a horrifying agent. Such is not the case in *Oedipus the King*, at least at the apex of the narrative when Oedipus blinds himself, yelling such things as "they will never see the crime / I have committed or had done upon me" (Sophocles 1991, 66). Here Oedipus has not—I would suggest that at this point he cannot have—"decided" whether he is responsible, and this is part of the horror, part of the reason "they" (i.e., his eyes) must be ruined.

I don't want to rest my whole argument on Oedipus, tempting as that is, but I hope the example illustrates the importance of (mis)recognition in the experience of moral horror. Gathering the various lines of thought I have been following: I experience moral horror when I think my way to the unjustifiability of state violence alongside my continuing acquiescence in and perhaps support of its existence because I am exposed to the animality of the human in such a way that I (mis)recognize myself as human/animal. A less definitional, more intuitive account of moral horror in the face of unjustifiable state violence is simply as follows: I am a monster. Experiencing moral horror is unpleasant, to say the least. It puts one in the position of having to live with the knowledge that the life one leads is partially predicated on the existence of a state violence without justification, that is, on pervasive and continuous suffering from an unjustifiable violence. To remain cognizant of this fact and to continue to live with and in moral horror is difficult, if not impossible. The question then becomes how to live moral horror, which can be rephrased as: what are the ethical and political stakes of my argument in this book?

THE ETHICS AND POLITICS OF MORAL HORROR

George Kateb, in his essay "Punishment and the Spirit of Democracy," expresses many of the same worries about state violence (confined mainly to punishment within constitutional democracies) that I have elaborated in this book. In response to these worries he proposes a unique justification of punishment as a necessary and lesser evil based on the "spirit of constitutional democracy," specifically, for the United States, the US Constitution. Briefly engaging Kateb's argument will help me elaborate my reasons for thinking that moral horror is a key aspect of an (nonpacifist) ethics and politics that wants to challenge state violence.

Kateb's essay begins by emphasizing, against our usual indifference, the curious moral puzzle that even "justified" punishment poses: "The core of punishment is the deliberate infliction of pain on a human being. Should there be no puzzlement in the very fact of deliberate infliction of pain, even when the pain is not corporal, and even when the criminal has acted violently and perhaps odiously, though often without deliberation?" (Kateb 2007, 269). The answer for Kateb is that we should be puzzled. A further motivation to puzzlement is the long, continuing, and unresolved debates between theories of punishment that complicate the moral puzzle of not only the justification of punishment itself but more important of the fact that punishment continues to be affirmed and practiced in societies around the world. Kateb's justification of punishment is based on the principles of constitutional democracy, especially on those articles of the US Constitution that clearly protect the accused and (less clearly) call for restraints on punishing. Based on these principles, he argues that the "democratic sentiment that should accompany inflicting punishment should be reluctance. From reluctance should come leniency, and provided there is a commitment to leniency, deterrence seems to follow as the principal justification of punishment" (Kateb 2007, 272). Furthermore, Kateb asserts that punishing is not an act of justice and that the necessary evil of punishment should not be justified by pointing to any social benefits to be gained (rather, we should justify it by pointing only to the greater evils that would exist without a system of punishment) (Kateb 2007, 302–3).

I am sympathetic to Kateb's conclusions although I am one of the many who, as he admits would probably be the case, disagrees with his reading of the US Constitution as providing a reluctant, lenient principle of punishment. However, his argument relies too much on an account of human dignity that, as he recognizes, is just as much a ground for retributive punishment as it is a reason to prevent certain kinds of punishment or to punish reluctantly and leniently (this emerges in his discussion of Herbert Morris). The problem is that Kateb's response to this possibility is only that "democratic sentiment would still incline to the infliction of less suffering as the superior value" (Kateb 2007, 301). This claim, however, elides the real ethico-political problem with Kateb's argument: (constitutional) democracy. Democracy itself is, especially within democracies, subject to political contestation, not only at the polls but in its meaning. The "would" of Kateb's claim presumes a predictive status for the assertion when, in fact, it is a normative, political claim. Much of the essay rightly takes for granted the punitive nature of US culture, and yet unless one is willing to deny that anyone who justifies punishment in stronger terms than Kateb is undemocratic, then one's claims about what is and is not properly (constitutionally) democratic are political rather than theoretical, normative rather than descriptive. I don't think Kateb would necessarily deny any of this, but what such a response throws into relief is that if democracy and its adjectival modifications of concepts and practices such as "punishment," "sentiment," or "rationality" are always contestable, then basing a response to the moral puzzle of punishment on such contestable grounds risks undermining the political goal of claiming such a ground, that is, to make punishment more reluctantly and leniently administered.

In addition to the contestability of these claims—all political claims are contestable, so this is, immediately, no major criticism—and perhaps because of the nature of those claims, Kateb's argument does not, I suggest, provide a sufficient ethico-political motivation to challenging punishment (and state violence more generally) because it stops short of exploring what it is like to live in an unjustifiably punitive political society when one knows that such violence is unjustifiable, but one is (in some sense) responsible for that violence (if not by consent, then by some other means of support). To be clear, the problem I am identifying is not that the grounds of Kateb's argument are contestable—the same is true of my argument, or almost any argument—but that a more powerful motivation to challenging state violence comes from an analysis of what it means to live with unjustifiable state violence (rather than only providing, as I do as well, arguments against state violence as such or as currently practiced). The position I am articulating in this book is more than just an experience of contradiction; as I have tried to argue, it is one that should lead us to an experience of moral horror. Unjustifiable violence for which I am (again in some sense) responsible or to which I am acquiescing makes me responsible for suffering and pain in a real and unjust way. To acknowledge not only that my society is betraying its principles but also that the unjustifiable physical and psychological suffering of others is something that I am connected to, is to live with an immense burden on oneself. It is livable, but only with great difficulty.

The experience of moral horror, then, may do more to motivate ethico-political responses to state violence then appeals to human dignity, constitutional principles, or democratic sentiments. It may do so not because the motivation is "self-interested" in the sense of "selfish," but self-interested in the meaning given by Arendt to Thoreauvian and Socratic conscience, where an interest in the self, a care of the self, is a prerequisite of avoiding evil (Arendt 1972, 60–68). Unjustifiable state violence attacks not only the singular being but the self of the one who allows that violence to continue. These two consequences are not the same, nor is the putting into question of the self "equivalent" to or just as violent as what is done to the singular being. But to be undone by the moral horror of what is done to others in my name or for me is to begin to transform one's relation to the victim of state violence. If one acknowledges and doesn't shrink from the knowledge of one's own horrifying acts, this may be a motivation to stop state violence or at least greatly limit it. It may create a link between the self and the victim of state violence by recognizing that state violence causes suffering even if (or especially when) that suffering is not aesthetically horrifying at all. I would like to conclude this chapter, then, by suggesting that an ethico-politics that begins from moral horror finds its further impulse in a response to the physical suffering of others and aims for a "better animality" that does not avoid but seeks to continuously acknowledge the suffering of others. If moral horror arises because of the threat of the slide of the human into the animal, then I argue that it is in affirming that human animality, rather than denying it, that we best enable challenges to state violence.

I cited Adorno's claim in *Negative Dialectics* that humans should live so that they can believe that they had lived as better animals. For Adorno, this ethical position is tied to his arguments for the necessity in moral life of what he calls the "addendum" or the "impulse." Without such an impulse, he claims, an impulse that escapes or precedes the rational subject, freedom would be impossible for it would then only be domination (the autonomous domination of the self by the self). The impulse or addendum is the spontaneous, heteronomously experienced jolt or shock of a force that precedes the dualism between mind and matter, or will and nature, the I and the Other (Adorno 1973, 221–23, 226–30). Neither purely mental nor purely material, the impulse/addendum is nonetheless, it seems, "natural":

> The addendum has an aspect which under rationalistic rules is irrational. It denies the Cartesian dualism of res extensa and res cogitans, in which the addendum, as mental, is lumped with the res cogitans, regardless of the difference that separates it from thought. The addendum is an impulse, the rudiment of a phase in which the dualism of extramental and intramental was not thoroughly consolidated yet, neither volitively bridgeable nor an ontological ulti-mate … The impulse, intramental and somatic in one, drives beyond the conscious sphere to which it belongs just same … The adden-dum is the name for that which was eliminated in this abstraction [the abstraction of pure practical reason in Kant]; without it, there would be no real will at all. It is a flash of light between the poles of something long past, something grown all but unrecognizable, and that which some day might come to be. (Adorno 1973, 228–29)

The addendum is the spontaneous impulse of nature in man, but not nature as understood by Enlightenment reason, that is, nature as a reified, control-lable, mathematically comprehensible object. The impulse refers back to "something long past" and also something not yet: the impulse is that jolt of nonidentical, nonreified nature in the human that enables "truly" free action and thus gestures toward a life without domination, in which the dom-inating/dominated subject and the dominated/nonidentical object would finally be reconciled. However, Adorno is also quick to note that freedom without the "I," without the subject and its reason, is just as false as the freedom of the autonomous Kantian "I" (whose freedom is just rule, domi-nation, of the self by the self). Thus there is an aporia here, typical of negative dialectics: freedom requires both the synthesizing transcendental "I" and an impulse that surges into the subject and escapes the transcendental "I."

The jolt of the addendum must be distinguished from Cavarero's spon-taneous response to horror because, in typical dialectical fashion, Adorno is (usually) skeptical of immediacy and, as just noted, he insists that free action also requires the unifying power of the "I" (albeit, again in dialectical fashion, a transcendental "I" that cannot be ontologically distinct from its genesis in an empirical, historical context). Yet once again in typical dialectical fashion, the addendum that conditions our freedom is a force from beneath or beyond the "I," a jolt that resists (perhaps even conditions) the spontaneity of the Kantian transcendental subject (see Jütten 2012, 554–59). What these dialectical twists and turns lead to, though, is not a recognition or acknowledgment of the "good" of nature, or something beautiful (or sublime). J. M. Bernstein goes as far as identifying the addendum/impulse with the horror provoked by suffering bodies (in context, the suffering bodies in Auschwitz): "Appropriately contextualized within the history of reason, our horror at the suffering of the drowned and the saved is itself the moral addendum implied by the new imperative. Hence the rational force of the imperative is just the acknowledgment of the suffering itself" (Bernstein 2006, 32). The suffering physical body, the animal agony of corporeal pain, is (or more precisely can be) horrifying. Yet as many attest, bodily pleasure can equally horrify. That living as a better animal is a maxim for ethics and politics in a world of physical suffering does not relieve the horror that human animality can inspire in human beings; to the contrary, it may even mean intensifying that horror.

My interest in Adorno at this point is—as mentioned earlier—that he links the addendum to the basis of ethics (especially after Auschwitz), an ethics grounded in the "unvarnished materialistic motive" of responding to and preventing physical suffering. As Christian Gerhardt has shown, animality appears as a trope in Adorno's work that signifies nonidentity, the "inhuman," materiality, the other; in short, animality figures that which the human as the "rational animal" has conceptually subsumed and ethically and politically dominated (Gerhardt 2006). To live as a better animal, then, is to acknowledge those aspects of the human that reveal themselves most clearly—but not always immediately—in the suffering of physical bodies, that is, in their animality. One does this by acknowledging that the condition of free action and response, and the "object" of the ethical and political project in a world of physical suffering, is the animality that inhabits the human being.

If we are to live as better animals, then we must respond thoughtfully to the somatic suffering of other beings in the world (not just human, but I remain focused on human beings), and we do so by recalling ourselves to our own animality, our sentient materiality, to, among other things, the impulse or addendum that sparks our free activity. The somatic, intra-mental impulse responds to the "somatic, unmeaningful stratum of life," which is "the state of suffering, of the suffering which in the camps, without any consolation, burned every soothing feature out of the mind, and out of culture, the mind's objectification" (Adorno 1973, 365). Although the concentration camp is the explosive and definitive event of the twentieth century (for Adorno and many other thinkers), the somatic element of suffering and the physicality of death is that to which our ethical and political lives should be attuned in general. Suffering may not be the condition of truth, as Adorno claims. But to point out the suffering within life would be trivial if not for the ease with which such suffering is forgotten, avoided, or (perhaps most important) justified. Suffering is what States cause whenever they act violently, and thus suffering, unjustifiable and pervasive throughout our political worlds, is to be responded to and alleviated by living as a better animal.

To live as a better animal requires—in the context of my argument—our responsiveness to the material suffering of the singular being and to the animality that threatens our identity as human and welcomes another possibility of being human, one in which we are better precisely as animals. The gloomy negativity that the thought of embracing moral horror may inspire is not the whole story. The philosopher, Adorno insinuates—and I also count this as a task for the citizen—should be childlike in their interest in the material realm of suffering and death:

> Children sense some of this in the fascination that issues from the flayer's zone, from carcasses, from the repulsively sweet odor of putrefaction, and from the opprobrious terms used for that zone ... An unconscious knowledge whispers to the child what is repressed by civilized education: this is what matters, says the whispering voice. And the wretched physical existence strikes a spark in the supreme interest that is scarcely less repressed: it kinds a "What is that?" and "Where is it going?" (Adorno 1973, 366)

To become childlike in one's relation to physical suffering is to become, as we saw in Nancy, curious about the suffering body, interested in it, and potentially, hopefully, motivated to stop the suffering. But as many of us know, have seen, or have read about, that childlike fascination with death and decay reveals a pleasure in materiality, an attraction, that is attested in the "paradox of horror" recognized by Carroll: many people who we have no reason to assume are psychopaths, enjoy art-horror.

I am not suggesting, of course, that we take pleasure in suffering bodies, that is, that we indulge in horror as a pleasing spectacle. Lest my argument in this book seem unrelentingly negative, I think it is important to recall that Adorno—the thinker of relentless negativity—finds in a moment of pleasure taken in animality something like redemption in response to nihilism, a response to the wish for nothingness:

> People to whom despair is not a technical term may ask whether it would be better for nothing at all to be than something. Not even to this is there a general answer. For a man in a concentration camp it would be better not to have been born—if one who escaped in time is permitted to venture any judgment about this. And yet the lighting up of an eye, indeed the feeble tail-wagging of a dog one gave a tidbit it promptly forgets, would make the ideal of nothingness evaporate. A thinking man's true answer to the question whether he is a nihilist would probably be "Not enough"—out of callousness perhaps, because of insufficient sympathy with anything that suffers." (Adorno 1973, 380)

The tail-wagging dog is, I take it, to be responded to in the same way we respond to the suffering body: as a body, as a sentient, somatic creature capable of suffering but also, as Bernstein shows, as a sentient, somatic, suffering body the being of which testifies to the possible pleasures and sweetness of natural, embodied, animal life (Bernstein 2004, 8–10). Part of the point of emphasizing moral horror and the singular being to which we should respond in its material suffering is that the singular being need not suffer and, to be sure, we need not suffer from horror either. As I argued in the introduction, state violence is a temptation, one we can resist. The image of that happy dog, happy to be eating, to be fed, to be in relation to someone who cares for it and takes its existence seriously, seems a paltry example for a world in which we relate to the suffering of the singular being differently, less violently. But the paltriness is precisely the point: as Adorno prophesied, the redeemed world looks just like this one, only slightly different. What I am calling for in this book is not a utopian fantasy but a refusal to justify our practices of state violence so that more individuals might happily eat dinner at home with friends and family. Nothing more, but nothing less. Moral horror is a means to such an end, or so I hope.

This goal requires a child's fascination with the material world of death and suffering. On the other hand, to be fascinated like a child by the suffering or dead body is (hopefully) not to take pleasure in it, but to be inter-ested in it, to share a "between" with that body, thus to share in that body's world (I explore how to create a link with suffering or dead bodies in Arnold 2011). Childlike curiosity toward the physicality of the body in its suffering is perhaps too immediate for an ethics or politics, but that childlike impulse to look, touch, see—especially in light of the usual adult prohibitions placed on these bodies—is one mode of the addendum's jolt. That one can link oneself to that body through an acknowledged horror that takes an interest in that body by way of one's animality may open up the sphere of the animal human to possibilities beside horror. These possibili-ties—including new or renewed forms of joy, of pleasure, of happiness, and of friendship and love—may be sparked by thinking and living through the experience of moral horror.

To live as a better animal vis-à-vis state violence is to live our moral horror, to expose ourselves to our own undecidable humanity/animal-ity, and to do so to see and respond to physical suffering. Moral horror compels us to see the object of state violence as a singular suffering being even when the suffering is not immediately obvious or visible. Moral horror may open a realm of experience and relation in and within the materiality of our lives that was hitherto closed off. But this last point is speculation or hope. What concerns me more than our possible joy is my (I hope our) horror, horror at what states do to bodies and the horror we legitimize when we justify the violent practices of states.

(IN)CONCLUSION

IF YOU HAVE MADE IT THIS FAR, then you have surely experienced moments of confusion, distrust, distaste, angry rejection, and a variety of other dissatisfactions with my argument; but I have withheld commenting on what I take to be its limitations. Although I cannot address all of the problems that remain—many of which are internal to my interpretations of the authors I am criticizing or appropriating—I have been struggling with two significant objections since I first started to articulate the ideas that eventually formed the basis of this book. I must admit that I have still not come to any firm conclusions or resolutions about or for these problems, hence the (now out of fashion) punnery in the title of this final chapter. The two objections I focus on here concern the potential consequences to be drawn from my argument rather than any particular moment of argumentation.

The first objection is the worry that in denying moral legitimacy to state violence and yet refusing to make the further argument that this requires pacifism, my position leaves arguments for and against state violence entirely to what is called—used here in a very broad sense—instrumental reason. The problems this raises are numerous, but perhaps most important the worry is that instrumental reason has, according to most of the thinkers I have cited, contributed greatly to the denial of singularity and consequent practices of domination and violence, consequences that my argument is clearly trying to avoid. Thus, my position may very well reinforce, rather than undermine or prevent, the very conditions and thus the very consequences I am worried about.

The second objection is that I have deprived us of any criteria—at least any moral criteria—by which we might distinguish between "better" and "worse" practices of state violence and, more broadly, "better" and "worse" states vis-à-vis state violence. Given the absoluteness of my position and crucially my reliance on a concept of singularity that bars calculation, identity, measure, and so on to claim that a state that only imprisons, say, a hundred people rather than a million is "better" becomes a problematic (if not incoherent) judgment. I will handle these objections in turn although again, I am not entirely satisfied with my responses. They are subjects of future work for me and, I hope, for those who find themselves in agreement with the argument here.

INSTRUMENTAL REASON

I have argued that there is no possible moral justification of state violence, and any attempt to justify state violence, including and especially moral justification, engages in justificatory violence by denying the singularity of the being on whom that violence is to be enacted. One conclusion that might be drawn is that if practices of state violence are nonetheless to continue—with our acquiescence or through active support—then the only kinds of argument left for and against particular practices or acts of state violence are "instrumental" arguments, that is, arguments that employ instrumental reason. What other criteria for the use of state violence might there be? It is telling that the two famous "approaches" in modern moral philosophy to justifying punishment—deontology and various consequentialisms—either prioritize the Right vis-à-vis efficacy or else "moralize" efficacy by claiming that practices of state violence are necessary to achieve ultimate moral ends such as pleasure, happiness, and satisfaction (and the diminishment or elimination of pain, unhappiness, dissatisfaction, etc., with all the variations and complications in particular theories). What this shows, I take it, is that in thinking about state violence—and this applies equally to just war theory, for example—we almost always take into account morality and utility. We sense that a purely moral justification of, say, punishing someone, does not mean utility cannot be taken into account at the same time (or later, as even Kant thinks), while we also recognize that a purely instrumental view of punishment denies to the punished a moral standing that they surely have (e.g., Bentham's claim that punishment is evil).

Insofar as my argument settles the moral question of state violence in advance of any particular case of its use—and barring a pacifist conclusion—then the only arguments left for the use of state violence in particular cases are instrumental in nature. I have left us with only one side of the Right/Consequence approach to state violence. However, this is highly problematic.

First, instrumental reason has been an object of criticism for a number of important nineteenth- and twentieth-century thinkers, including many I have drawn on or referred to in this book (although the main modern source for the narrative about the rise of instrumental rationality is Weber). For these thinkers, instrumental reason is not only a particular way of thinking about, choosing, and justifying particular types of action but, as Heidegger argued of technology (in what is largely but not solely a critique of instrumental rationality), a way of revealing the world, of encountering beings. For Heidegger, the age of technology is that age in which beings are revealed in a "challenging" [*Herausfordern*] "which puts to nature the unreasonable demand that it supply energy that can be extracted and stored as such" (Heidegger 1977, 14). Beings are revealed, in the age of technology, as storable, manipulable, transferable, extractable—in short, usable—things. Beings are no longer even "objects," they are "standing-reserve," things that are nearby so that they may be used in various ways. Thus "whatever stands by in the sense of standing-reserve no longer stands over against us as object" (Heidegger 1977, 17). It is precisely because beings are no longer revealed as objects that we can say that we have entered a new age; it is also for this reason that Heidegger's critique is of instrumental reason as that understanding of Being that sees beings as means to various ends.

Despite obvious differences in genealogical historicization and philosophical commitment, Adorno in his own work and with Horkheimer in *Dialectic of Enlightenment* shares with Heidegger the view that contemporary Western Reason is (and/or has become) instrumental to the core, for the essence of Western Reason, of Western enlightenment is technology: "technology is the essence of this knowledge. It aims to produce neither concepts, nor images, nor the joy of understanding, but method, exploitation of the labor of others, capital" (Horkheimer and Adorno 2002, 2). Technological, instrumental reason works by identifying, quantifying, systematizing, and using everything, thereby "amputating the incommensurable" (Horkheimer and Adorno 2002, 9). Again, instrumental reason is not only one particular mode of cognition but, in the Heideggerian language Adorno would reject, a way of revealing the world.

A significant impulse in the work of Hannah Arendt is the recognition and critique of the domination of instrumental reason, especially as it emerges out of the activities of homo faber. The human who makes must be instrumental in their reasoning, argues Arendt, for "the process of making is entirely determined by the category of means and end" (Arendt 1998, 143). The problem is that instrumental reason and its fabricated products becomes in a laboring society merely another means of subjecting human beings to the rhythms of a nonhuman force (see Arendt 1998, 145–46). On the other hand, instrumental reason is, by its very nature, incapable of securing for any end its finality, that is, of rationally putting to a stop the process by which an end becomes a means for another end. To judge everything by instrumental reason, by utility, is, Arendt argues, to "generate meaninglessness" because no particular end is stable enough, permanent enough, to take on stable meaning (Arendt 1998, 154–55). This process reaches its paradoxical conclusion in the Kantian attempt to make man a "final end" or "end-in-itself," for although Kant was trying to escape the meaninglessness of instrumental reason, he remained stuck in its conceptual framework with the idea of man as the highest end on Earth (Arendt 1998, 156). More broadly, as Dana Villa has shown, Arendt's *The Human Condition* is a consistent critical engagement with the philosophical dream of a politics of making, of fabrication, and hence of instrumental rationality (see Villa 1996).

Lest one think that only twentieth-century Germans recognize the dangers of instrumental reason, Michael Oakeshott's characterization and criticism of the "rationalist" and of the place of "rationalism" in politics also identifies the limits and dangers of instrumental rationality. Oakeshott's rationalist "stands (he always stands) for independence of mind on all occasions, for thought free from obligation to any authority save the authority of reason." Like Adorno's figures of enlightenment, the rationalist is both deeply skeptical and "optimistic" that reason can assess the proper value, truth, and propriety of all things and actions (Oakeshott 1991, 6). The rationalist, in politics, is a problem solver, an engineer, and "what he cannot imagine is politics which do not consist in solving problems, or a political problem of which there is no 'rational' solution at all. Such a problem must be counterfeit" (Oakeshott 1991, 10). For the rationalist, all knowledge is "technical knowledge."

One could list more writers and philosophers (especially Foucault and Habermas), but what all these thinkers share is not the position that instrumental reason is bad in itself; rather, they argue that the dominance of instrumental reason in modernity—its position as the exclusive or nearly exclusive type of rationality—and its elimination of other modes of rationally knowing, experiencing, and encountering the world (or redescription of those modes as "irrational") is a chief (if not sole) reason our modern politics and history is so violent, so endangering, and so terrifying. Hence the import of the objection I am raising to my view: if state violence is left to the domain of instrumental reason, then won't that lend paradoxical support to the very practices I argue are morally wrong? Furthermore, isn't it possible, perhaps likely, that removing moral argumentation from political discussions of state violence will lead to a "nihilism" in which the moral illegitimacy of state violence becomes so assumed that it lacks motivational force?

My response, perverse and counterintuitive, is that if justifications of state violence are left solely to the domain of instrumental reason then we have good reasons for thinking that this is better than any other alternative. Why?

First, the worry that instrumental reason denies, represses, or avoids the singular being, as I argued in chapters 3 and 4, is real, yet this repression is unavoidable. We cannot know or act in the world without subsuming singular beings under concepts or reducing their singularity to a set of traits or features that allow for successful epistemic and pragmatic encounters with them. This does not mean that there are not other modes of access, brief or limited as they might be, in which singularity is "experienced." But it does mean that, as Nancy claimed, we always appropriate the singular being. However, as I noted already, the problem with instrumental reason according to its most prominent critics is not that instrumental reason exists but that it has become the central way in which we know, encounter, and deal with other beings in the world. The particular ways instrumental reason knows, thinks, and encounters beings becomes problematic when generalized or totalized, when they become the way of revealing beings in a particular age. Yet for Heidegger, as we know from *Being and Time*, the use of "objects" within a set of practices oriented within and toward various human ends is the primary way human beings encounter "objects." The hammer used by the carpenter to build the house so he can have a home for the sake of being a parent and partner is enmeshed in various levels of "instrumental rationality" to the extent that we understand this form of rationality, with Heidegger, on the Aristotelian model of practical (rather than theoretical) knowing. Likewise, Arendt's homo faber is not wrong to use instrumental reason when building the table; there is no alternative. In both Heidegger and Arendt's figures of the hammerer and homo faber instrumental reason is given its proper due and the singular being is encountered not as singular but as, for example, wood to be planed and then nailed.

That state violence would be argued about solely in instrumental terms does not, in itself, further the denial of the singular being or uncontrollably expand the domain of instrumental rationality beyond the world of hammers and carpenters. If so, then nearly all pragmatic domains of human life would be subject to the charge of furthering the domination of instrumental rationality, and this seems untrue to the spirit, arguments, and intent of critics of instrumental rationality. Adorno, Heidegger, Arendt, Oakeshott, Foucault, Habermas, and others do not and would not deny that instrumental reason is essential for various human activities. Thus, the sheer fact that practices of state violence would be left to instrumental reason has as a consequence (so far as I can see it) only that of delimiting the areas of human life in which questions of state violence are discussed as pragmatic domains, ones in which questions of efficacy and goal achievement have their place. Moreover, in claiming that state violence should only be discussed and justified in instrumental terms, there is no danger of instrumental reason expanding its hold over the rational practices of modernity. State violence is already and with good reason a sphere of human life in which questions of efficacy and goal achievement have their place.

Second, and more important, one might object that the real problem here isn't that state violence becomes a matter of instrumental reason as such but that the abandonment of moral arguments is tantamount to a kind of "nihilism" in which the argument against the moral legitimacy of state violence loses its motivational and political force. After all, I have placed the motivational force in a cognitive-affective experience—moral horror—that can just as easily be ignored, or never undergone, rather than maintained. If the moral question of state violence is already decided, then the danger is that without the experience of moral horror, the illegitimacy of state violence will become just another moral platitude lacking political effect. This is how instrumental reason will "run amok" without the check of moral argument: a more plausible possibility is that morality will be forgotten or trotted out ritualistically ("as we know, of course, this war is wrong; however ...") just as moral arguments are often used in politics, just as ideologically or ritualistically, to justify state violence. In spite of the risks, the objection might continue, the benefits of deontological and utilitarian arguments in thinking about punishment, for example, is that they provide internal moral checks on practices of punishment. Although it may be the case that Kant denies the singular being to justify the death penalty and punishment more broadly, the same basic principle—the moral requirement to treat rational human beings as ends and never merely means—checks what we can do and how we can do what we do when we punish. Similarly, utilitarian justifications of punishment have the merits of taking the interests of all into account, including the punished. Thus, even in the violence of moral justifications of state violence, the form of or appeal to morality is left, which can be actualized in other ways. This recognition of the punished would be lost if we "de-moralize" consequentialist arguments for acts of state violence, and rather than respecting the singular being, we are left with mere human objects to be used in the course of pursuing our ends. This, anyway, seems more plausible, goes the objection.

As I see it, my suggestion that a politics in which state violence is "instrumentalized" would be better than what we have now really hinges on my response to this objection, specifically to the political world the objection imagines (one in which moral horror fails to check state violence; worse, it becomes mere ritual incantation). As speculation, both the objection and my response lack a firm foothold in reality, or only selectively draw on the present and past to imagine the future. This compromises the argument from the start. Nonetheless ...

That discussions of state violence would lack a moral component performs a positive service: it disables the kinds of justificatory violence that we saw in Kant, Rawls (as read by Cavell), Walzer, and Simmons. In the objection, one key point is that morality checks our actions toward various individuals, for example, the punished, so that we treat morally even those against whom we are acting violently. I have already argued against the morality of this view in chapter 4. But I have not argued against the related idea that getting rid of morality in justifying state violence would be likely to increase the number of acts of state violence by getting rid of the checks moral arguments place on the use of state violence. The objection imagines that these acts would increase in number as the checks disappear. But I don't have to prove that the singular being would magically "appear" once we get rid of moral justifications of state violence to show why the objection is very likely mistaken in its prediction. What I would like to suggest now is that the use of state violence is likely to diminish if we remove moral justification from arguments over state violence.

Let's imagine a world in which moral justifications of state violence, if not entirely rejected by all citizens, are at least rejected by enough that, within a particular democratic system, they could form on their own or in coalition with others a majority of the population. What would such a state look like vis-à-vis state violence? The objection I have raised imagines that world as one in which moral arguments, beliefs, desires, knowledge, and so on disappears from public discussions of state violence entirely or, perhaps, one in which the rejection of the legitimacy of state violence becomes empty ritual.

However, I think we have good reasons to assume that a political future in which the rejection of moral justifications for state violence is a politically powerful (if not dominant) position within public discourse would look very different. As I noted already, discussions of state violence often turn on moral and utilitarian or instrumental reasons. Even Kant allowed for utilitarian considerations as long as the moral requirement of treating an individual as an end rather than a means was satisfied. But what political role does morality or claims to morality play in justifying state violence? To answer this question we don't need speculation, for we have so many examples from present and past polities that the response has become a platitude.

Whether genuine or ideological, moral claims, beliefs, desires, characterizations, and so on play a powerful rhetorical role in the politics of justifying (and criticizing) state violence. Publicly proclaiming the moral failings of the enemy, or convict, is such a recurrent feature of public political justification that for many of us, we are shocked that people still appear to actually believe that there is an "axis of evil" or that Jews are running the world from a bunker, and so on. Let's imagine a world in which recourse to such claims, to the moralizing demonization of those against whom we use violence, was not publicly available, or was constantly, and publicly, contested? How would state violence be justified to a public?

If I am correct, then in instrumental terms. But what would a supporter of a particular practice of state violence say to convince others? Imagine if George W. Bush had said: "We are invading Iraq because there is money to be made by people I know; because it will give us another foothold in a strategically vital, but unstable, part of the world; because Dave Chappelle is right to remind us that Saddam Hussein tried to kill my father; because of peak oil problems," that is, for all the nonmoral economic, political, strategic, and military reasons that many have offered as explanations for the invasion. There would be no mention of the rights of citizens or of freedom, of moral duties (rather than positional duties, i.e., duties of office) to protect the homeland, of the justice of punishment, and so on. What we would have in the public discourse is truly naked, and presumably unabashed, instrumentality. It would not be a world in which moral ideas like rights and freedoms were absent either in the public discourse or in legal and political documents, but such moral ideas could not be invoked when arguing for state violence. How likely would it be that practices of state violence would gain wide approval?

My answer, speculative as it may be, is that many (if not most) practices of state violence would not be widely accepted by a citizenry precisely because they could not be morally justified, no matter what ideological use morality is put toward. I base this claim on the long-standing and widespread ideological and rhetorical use of moral discourse within political justifications of state violence, not on any presumption that human beings are deeply moral or immune to self-interested arguments. Even if we take the use of moral discourse to be mere ideology masking the real causes and intentions of interstate violence—to take one example—the point remains: such moral discourse has its place precisely to justify the instrumental reasons that apparently cannot justify state violence on their own. Why else would moral discourse play such a continuous role in political justifications of violence if not for the fact that instrumental reasons alone are not sufficient?

Take an old example. The famous Athenian point in Thucydides's account (or construction) of the Melian dialogue—the "strong do what they have the power to do and the weak accept what they have to accept"—is a truism of realism in the study of international relations, the moral being that the moral has no place, or only an ideological place, in the practice of international relations. But it is important to remember that the Melians and the Athenians (at the request of the Melians) met behind closed doors rather than in front of the whole population (Thucydides 1972, 400–402). Behind closed doors the Athenians explicitly dispense with (and ban the use of) claims to right and justice, thereby admitting that these concepts have their (clearly ideological) place in public, for the people. What if the dialogue had been held in public? Would the Athenians, as they suspect, have easily won over the population with their clear military advantage supporting every word? Would the Melian recourse to justice and fair play make more sense, and have a more powerful rhetorical effect, if the appeal had taken place in public? Could the Athenians have banned moral arguments from the start if they were forced to account for their actions before a citizenry? My suggestion, of course, is that if the Athenians were to speak in public, they might have been surprised to find that in spite of their military might their appeals to self-interest might not have gone down as easily, or they might have decided to return to the language of morality to make the bitter pill of slavery easier to swallow. Whatever one makes of this alternative scenario the point is simple: from Thucydides to the 2003 invasion of Iraq, moral discourse has a very public role in the justification of practices of state violence, and the most plausible explanation of that role is that without it the state would have greater difficulty in gaining acceptance for its actions. The overwhelming evidence of the present and past is that moral justification is crucial to public justification of state violence. Take that away, I would suggest, and the likelihood of instrumental rationality leading to an increased use of state violence is slim.

However, the objector might respond, this leaves out a crucial characteristic of public discussions of state violence: the power of affects such as fear, resentment, terror, and so on within justifications of state violence from the standpoint of security. If there is a figure that organizes modern discussions of state violence, it is the figure of security, and such discussions need not rely on any particular moral argument or position at all. Unless one wants to make the argument that survival itself is a moral end—something I find rather difficult to do—then the obvious conclusion is that practices of state violence do not need the cover of morality to gain wide acceptance from a citizenry: all a government need do is raise the threat of existential annihilation. What can potentially stop the dangers of a securitized debate over practices of state violence is morality, and thus the objection now is that without moral discourse checking state violence (even as it justifies it some of the time), state violence will increase or intensify in the security climate of modern states. This undermines my claim that state violence would diminish if we were to leave justifications of it to instrumental reason.

A first response to this objection is that my earlier responses have tended to neglect the fact that when I claim that only instrumental reason will be left to justify practices of state violence, this doesn't mean that morality plays no role in such discussions; it simply plays no role in justifying state violence. Its role is entirely critical. Thus, it is not as if there would be no moral check on security arguments for state violence.

However, the real heart of the objection is that security justifications of state violence that draw from and amplify fear, resentment, anger, and so on, are so powerful that they will overwhelm any "external" critical role my argument might play. Only an internal moral check—even an ideological or "false" check—that leaves at least the form or trace of morality within practices of state violence can slow or stop the intensification of such practices. For example, only a moral distinction between torture and interrogation—and not just a legal or technical distinction—can prevent security justifications from leading, as they have, to the use of torture. Such a distinction can be maintained on deontological and utilitarian grounds, whereas my argument leaves us only with the response "They are both wrong." Moreover, legal distinctions are not enough, as we have learned, because they rely in part on technical distinctions that are just too open to self-serving interpretation (this was revealed yet again in the most recent Bush administration's "torture memos"). The moral distinction can draw on the "spirit" of the law more easily than the law itself, and thus it may be the only bulwark against unrestrained instrumentality. My argument leaves no internal moral check, and this is the problem with it. When it comes to influencing decision making in the detailed, conditioned, contingent, and often fast-paced world of politics and policy, the absoluteness of my position, its way of taking morality off the table, robs us of a moral measure that can help us decide between alternative political and policy paths. Although my position cannot leave me morally pure, it does leave me unable to say anything other than "No!" to every possible practice of state violence while nonetheless acquiescing to such practices. Surely some practices are morally better than others, and in the compromised world of conditioned politics, to deprive oneself of a capacity to measure better and worse in the name not of moral purity but of an inescapable moral horror is politically disastrous.

This further objection, then, is in many ways the second objection to my argument that I outlined above, so I postpone my response to the objection for a moment. It is important to note that my argument is in no worse a position vis-à-vis the security argument than any other moral argument, at least insofar as one is imagining the political power and persuasiveness of justifications of state violence. Security is a basic political end, even if it is far from being the only goal of political organization. Security will always come into conflict with other moral, legal, and political ends for reasons that I will briefly adduce later. Thus, insofar as the first objection to my argument claims that there will be more of and more intense state violence if we exclude moral justification from discussions of state violence, I think this is wrong for the reasons I have outlined.

THE MISSING MEASURE

The second objection to my argument is that insofar as it relies on a concept of singularity that makes identification, comparison, commensuration, or measuring the plurality of singular beings in the world a "violent" act, judging whether one State is morally better than another vis-à-vis state violence—or judging whether one violent practice is morally better than another practice of state violence—is seemingly impossible or wrong. The focus on singularity is one reason thinkers such as Derrida, Levinas, and indeed Nancy turn to figures of the incalculable, undecidable, immeasurable, impossible, unconditional, and so on to "conceptualize" justice, responsibility, decision, and more broadly, ethics and politics. This way of approaching the problem created by an affirmation of singularity is problematic because it requires each thinker to provide an account of the relation between what, in Derridean language, could be called "unconditional politics" and "conditional politics." For Derrida, a constant tension exists between the unconditional (whether it is forgiveness, hospitality, responsibility, justice itself) and the calculations, measurements, judgments, rules, and laws in which all conditional and conditioned ethics and politics must deal. This tension, as I have noted in chapter 2, is in many ways the motor of ethical and political life for Derrida. However, I am unconvinced by the residual Kantianism of this view (despite Derrida's distancing of his argument from Kant's) as well as the desire—first revealed to me in some comments about Derrida by Stanley Cavell—for an absolute that however impossible to experience remains a desire for something beyond the finite existence of humans, hence a skeptical desire. The Derridean "solution" remains, for me, unavailable.

How, then, can my position give proper due to the intuition that one death is morally "better" than one hundred; that imprisonment is morally "better" than the death penalty; that some means of warfare, to the extent that they reduce death and suffering for all involved, may be (but about this I am far less sure) morally "better" than, say, nuclear war, or a full-scale ground war; that torture is worse than other interrogation practices? One doesn't need tired examples of station masters diverting trains or lifeboats with too few life vests or terrorists in a torture chamber with bombs about to go off to accept that there is something morally powerful about the calculation that if there is to be death, then fewer rather than more; if there is to be punishment, then less physically and psychologically destructive punishment, and so on. Most important, how can one give this claim its due while nonetheless affirming the position in this book that morally speaking one death is just as wrong as one million, seen from the perspective and affirmation of the singular being?

So there are two claims, both of which I find compelling. Yet they demand different, even opposed moral judgments. These moral judgments only meet up when no violence is chosen, but this is a rare occurrence. This is not only a philosophical problem but a political, even policy problem.

One mode of response that has attracted me is Lyotard's concept of the differend. For Lyotard—drawing on various philosophers, especially Wittgenstein—a differend occurs when "the plaintiff is divested of the means to argue and becomes for that reason a victim" (Lyotard 1988, 9). Lyotard is describing a situation in which a claim to having suffered some damages is inarticulable in the language of the other party. One of his clearest examples refers to the worker in a capitalist society. When the worker complains of exploitation, he is told that he has contracted to sell his labor, that his labor is a commodity he possesses and can sell on an open market. That is the language of capitalism; what if the worker thinks—what if it is the case—that one's labor is not a commodity at all? In the bourgeois capitalist court of law, the laborer's complaint cannot be heard, he has no standing, because in that court of law he has already lost the case by appearing in that court, by accepting its terms—the most important term being that labor power is a commodity for sale. There is a differend between the language of bourgeois capitalist labor law and the non- or anti- or postcapitalist language of an uncommodifiable labor power. We saw something similar in the discussion of Cavell and Rawls, where a justification of a society being "above reproach" denies or avoids the complainant by denying the competency of the speaker to make claims. When a complainant cannot articulate their claims in the language of the other party, the complainant becomes a "victim" (Lyotard 1988, 9–10). Not only has the worker suffered damages by having his labor exploited, he has also been denied the power to assert those damages by and in the language of the defendant. A differend occurs when two incompatible language games meet and an individual cannot express the damage done to them in the other language game. For Lyotard, what the differend demands in each situation where it arises is a new phrase, new listeners, new hearers, new rules of speech because not only is language amenable to these transformations and creations but "every wrong ought to be able to put into phrases" (Lyotard 1988, 13).

I would like to suggest that between the two moral claims I have been examining—that drawn from the affirmation of the singular being and that drawn from the "utilitarian" calculation of more or less violence—there is a differend. For the singular being, or from the perspective of the singular being, to calculate, to measure, to say that one death is morally "better" than one hundred, or that one person's imprisonment for robbery is "better" than the pain and deprivation of ten victims of robbery is to wrong the singular being, the being in jail or dead. In my classes, when these sorts of issues arise, I ask my students to imagine what they would say to the tortured prisoner, or to the victims, living or dead, of a drone attack in Pakistan. How would they justify what their country has done, the violence committed? This thought experiment for me and in general for my students (I imagine for Thomas Nagel as well) often causes an uncomfortable silence. It seems a bit hollow to say "well, in general drone attacks cause less death and destruction than ground assaults, and although you were the unfortunate victim of it, you must understand that taking all the numbers into account, this is the best way of achieving a peaceful world." If one thinks that only applies to innocent victims of state violence, then I imagine you to have a far firmer sense of moral righteousness than I do. To be told that one's suffering at the hands of the State is justified by the moral calculations of (loosely speaking) utilitarian reasoning is to employ a language game in which the singular being is wronged again. In fact, in many respects this is merely a repetition of the argument of this book.

However, if the language of calculation wrongs the singular being, then it also seems to be intuitively plausible that the language of singularity and the argument of this book make inarticulable the claims of those who create policies and choose practices of violence that reduce the number of victims of state violence as well as the severity of that violence. Granted that these individuals are not victims but practitioners or designers of state violence, nonetheless it seems unfair to those who work within States to reduce violence to deny that their efforts fail to lessen the immorality of state violence, if not in each particular act then on the whole. Further and more important than the feelings and moral descriptions of bureaucrats, the politics of reducing state violence seem to require the kinds of calculations, measurements, commensurabilities, and so on that the singularity argument forbids, or allows only as a concession to the inevitability of everyday politics. As a matter of political tactics and strategies, where compromise is often inevitable (and occasionally desirable), even those of us who would defend the "absolutist" position of this book would have to accept, even welcome, significant reductions in state violence even though such policy changes would only reinforce the legal and administrative "legitimacy" of state violence. Thus, to deny that there is a moral element to these calculations and, furthermore, to deny their place in any morally inflected political action and argument is wrongheaded.

There is a differend here. So what? This doesn't really take us anywhere. Lyotard's point is not (merely) to identify differends but to create new phrases, languages, speakers, and listeners to allow those wronged to articulate that wrong. I suppose I may have been trying to do that for the singular being in this book, but now I've allowed that the language I have offered itself forecloses certain linguistic possibilities for articulating damages. Unless I have a way of negotiating between these two languages—and I have rejected the Derridean approach—what are we to do?

One way to resolve the issue is to lexically order the two claims, that is, to prioritize one claim. One clue to which moral claim is "more important" or perhaps "deeper" is to ask "who are the victims of each language game?" Within the language of calculation and measure the victim is the singular being; within the language game of the singular being the victim is … who exactly? I suggested that the victims were bureaucrats, policy makers. The reason I point to this group of people is that they are the ones whose decisions and determinations are denied moral legitimacy, moral weight, by the singularity position, and thus one might expect that they are "damaged" in some way. I am at a loss to find any other victims of the singularity language game insofar as that position seeks to deny the moral legitimacy of all state violence, hence take into account every victim of state violence. Even if one accepts or supports a policy change that reduces the number of victims of state violence, this does not legitimize the policy and thus violently deny the singular beings victimized by the policy, precisely because of the argument from singularity. Those individuals who make up the machinery of the State are the ones who cannot defend themselves in the language game of singularity: is this something about which we should worry?

No. It is clear to me that the deeper moral position, the position that has priority to the calculative utilitarianism that chooses one death over a hundred, is the position I have argued for in this book. The singular being is exposed to violence twice over by the language of calculation: first, the physical violence of the State; second, the justificatory violence that legitimizes, putatively, the physical violence. The bureaucrat is exposed to no physical violence, and it is unclear what damage is done to the bureaucrat at all by the "unfair" characterization of their policy decisions by the singularity language game (perhaps their reputation suffers? Their sense of self? The sting of conscience?).

The position I have argued for in this book issues in the judgment: there ought not to be any state violence, it is always wrong, it is always morally illegitimate. But if there will be state violence, there ought to be as little as possible, and the particular practices chosen ought to be the least violent, do the least damage possible to obtain the ends we desire even as we know that what we are doing is morally wrong.

My responses to the two objections are not entirely satisfying to me, and I expect they are not (entirely) satisfying to you. I see this as, in part (perhaps in large part), a function of the deep difficulties the fact of state violence creates for those of us who study politics and/or act politically. Drawn in opposite directions by the political ends of justice, security, freedom, stability, solidarity, cosmopolitanism, and a host of other goals, the rope that ties and draws these ends together—and at the same time threatens to quarter us and everyone else—is state violence. If there is a desire to reconcile these various ends by morally justifying state violence and thereby legitimizing the pursuit of security, stability justice, and freedom, my argument suggests that these ends are in irreconcilable conflict precisely because of the impossibility of any moral justification. If security requires violence, then pursuing security will require injustice; if individual freedom require security, then enhancing individual freedom will require injustice; and so on. I admitted the power of the security argument in public discourse, the way it can so easily trump other arguments, especially ethical, legal, and moral arguments. This only makes the task of challenging state violence more important.

As that violence becomes ever more hidden, insidious, distanced, and hence ever more intimate for its victims—drone attacks, lethal injection, torture, indefinite detention, to name a few—it becomes more important to expose that violence to a critique and challenge that refuses it the legitimacy that States demand for it. Within democracies, where legitimacy is putatively placed in the People, the moral horror of our acceptance of state violence is more acute: within democracies, the horror of a wrong political life that cannot be lived rightly is even more apparent for citizens have nowhere else to turn but to themselves, to each other. The hope of this book is that the horror that forces us to question and doubt ourselves and our fellow citizens brings us to turn ourselves toward the victim of state violence, toward that singular being against whom we act violently, always without right. Wrong violence cannot be employed rightly.

NOTES

INTRODUCTION

1. Yet the "Kantian" approach, in its own way, also neglects, unfortunately, the violence the state claims a moral right to enact, deflecting the issue of violence toward a discussion of the right to punish. On the idea of deflection, see Diamond (2003, 11–13).

2. Of course, the reference here is to Habermas. I do not deal with Habermas in this text for a few reasons. First, I am unconvinced that he has really shown that the possibility of communicative action is guaranteed by universal formal-pragmatic structures of communication such as three basic world concepts to which three kinds of validity claims correspond, and so on. Largely on the basis of these structures Habermas can dispense with the objections of Adorno and Horkheimer—for they are stuck in the paradigm of the philosophy of consciousness and thus cannot see rationality other than in instrumental terms—as well as the French poststructuralists and take up a certain kind of critical theory. The problem, as I and others see it, is that Habermas cannot really ground his claims for these formal structures because to offer a transcendental deduction would be to lapse into metaphysics; at the same time, he can't assume anything less for these formal structures than a "peculiar half-transcendence" (Habermas 1987, 125). By doing this, Habermas thinks he can "take up questions that have previously been dealt with in the framework of transcendental philosophy" and thus ground the possibility of there being universally valid claims to truth, rightness, and sincerity (Habermas 1987, 119). Yet as Hent de Vries has shown, Habermas can be postmetaphysical only by consistently

referring the formal structures of linguistic communication to (the trace of or as the) ab-solute, some "thing" that escapes the transcendental and the empirical, "grounding" the universality of language without itself being either (wholly) transcendent or (wholly) immanent (de Vries 2005, especially chapters 1 and 2). Habermas recognizes this:

> We have, by way of anticipation, characterized the rational internal structure of processes of reaching understanding in terms of (a) the three world-relations of actors and the corresponding concepts of the objective, social, and subjective worlds; (b) the validity claims of propositional truth, normative rightness, and sincerity or authenticity; (c) the concept of a rationally motivated agreement, that is, one based on the intersubjective recognition of criticizable validity claims; and (d) the concept of reaching understanding as the cooperative negotiation of common definitions of the situation. If the requirement of objectivity is to be satisfied, this structure would have to be shown to be universally valid in a specific sense. This is a strong requirement for someone who is operating without metaphysical support and is also no longer confident that a rigorous transcendental-pragmatic program, claiming to provide ultimate grounds, can be carried out. (Habermas 1984, 138)

As far as I can see, Habermas never carries through on this requirement for grounding objectivity (in *The Theory of Communicative Action* he opts for another task), but his entire philosophical, sociological, moral, and political thought is based on it. As he notes, "The moral point of view from which we can judge practical questions impartially is indeed open to different interpretations. But because it is grounded in the communicative structure of rational discourse as such, we cannot simply dispose of it at will. It forces itself intuitively on anyone who is at all open to this reflective form of communicative action. With this fundamental assumption" (Habermas 1994, 1).

Second, I don't deal with Habermas for reasons I mention below; that is, I don't deal with any thinkers who argue for the possibility or actuality of state legitimacy. But his own account of what it would take for the law to be legitimate, from my perspective, is particularly problematic because of its reference to procedures dependent on the idealizing, counterfactual presuppositions of communicative action. As Habermas claims early in *Between Facts and Norms*—and he repeats this ambiguity again and again—the legitimacy of law and its statutes "is measured against the discursive redeemability of their normative validity claim—in the final analysis, according to whether they have come about through a rational legislative process, *or at least could have been* justified from pragmatic, ethical and moral points of view" (Habermas 1998, 31, emphasis added). The question is: is the legitimacy of the law and its statutes a result of actual deliberation processes that are, more rather than less, akin to the ideal speech situations presupposed by the theory of communicative action? Or is the legitimacy of law a function of a hypothetical reconstruction in which a law, assessed from pragmatic, ethical and moral points of view, is determined to be valid, legitimate? Finally, if hypothetical reconstructions can legitimize law, then is the reconstruction undertaken, or must it be undertaken, from the first-person standpoint of a participant or from the third-person standpoint of an observer? In other words, is Habermas arguing for a democratic procedural account of legitimacy (as seems to be case) or is he allowing that law can be justified not democratically through actual procedures between citizens, but cognitively through reconstructions? Much hinges on this decision, and I'm not sure where Habermas ultimately stands. Insofar as he oscillates between these two positions, his theory of legitimacy through democratic procedures that actualize the discourse principle appears less than capable of reconciling private and public autonomy in a way that avoids the potential dangers of voluntarist individualism on the one hand and the potential tyranny of rationality on the other.

Finally, and most important for my purposes, Habermas consistently elides the problem of state violence by placing the sanctioning, enforcing power of the legitimate law on the side of facticity rather than validity. Insofar as law mediates between facts and norms—it is itself a self-referential nexus of facts and norms—law can and should compel through factual, instrumental, strategic, or pragmatic reasons (of which the threat of force is one) and through the normative validity of law on the basis of which actors can obey the law not strategically but because the law is legitimate because of, for, and to them. Insofar as law is a means of social integration, both the facticity and the validity of law is required. However, Habermas consistently places the actual practices of enforcing law, that is, state violence, on the side of a specific facticity of law that is legitimized by the discourse principle's application to democratic procedures of lawmaking (Habermas 1998, 31, 33, 124). This becomes clearer in chapter 4, where Habermas discusses the relation between law and political power. Law, Habermas claims, pre-supposes, implies, political power because, as Derrida would agree, there is no law without force (Habermas 1998, 132–35). Thus there is an internal connection between law and the power that law requires. The justification of political power—of which state violence is one manifestation—comes not from the legal form the state employs but from the legitimacy of the law, which is a result of democratic lawmaking procedures and a legitimate con-stitution. In noting the internal connection between law and state violence, Habermas reiterates an analytical point about law; but in legitimizing state violence through the legitimacy of law he repeats a mistake Benjamin—as we will see in the first chapter—identified in "Critique of Violence": seeing violence as justified either by the justice of ends (as in natural law) or by the justness of procedures (as in positive law and in Habermas) is to justify violence as a means, not violence itself, irrespective of its use as a means. In other words, Habermas places state violence on the side of a facticity that makes of violence an instrumental force and thus elides the question of whether violence is ever justified no matter what procedures of legitimacy are available or engaged. For this reason, Habermas, like many thinkers of legitimacy, does not make an independent case for the rightness of state violence, and thus his work, however interesting it is, also elides the problem of legitimizing state violence (he does briefly refer to "Critique of Violence" in Habermas 1979, 54–56).

3. Thus, I have learned a great deal from, and I am usually in full agreement with, the scholars who have written in, for example, the edited collection *The Killing State* (Sarat 1999). My argument, however, concerns all acts of state violence, not just state killing.

CHAPTER 1

1. Throughout this chapter, and this book, I sometimes use the terms *legitimacy* and *authority* as if they are synonymous when the particular issue allows for that identification. However, the interrelated concepts of political legitimacy, political authority, and the political obedience that follow from either are not always interchangeable. As Allen Buchanan has argued, an entity has political legitimacy "if and only if it is morally justified in wielding political power, where to wield political power is to attempt to exercise a monopoly, within a jurisdiction, in the making, application, and

enforcement of laws" (Buchanan 2002, 680). On the other hand, he defines political authority as follows: "an entity has political authority if and only if, in addition to (1) possessing political legitimacy it (2) has the right to obeyed by those who are within the scope of its rules; in other words, if those upon whom it attempts to impose rules have an obligation to that entity to obey it. To say that X has a right to be obeyed by P implies that if P does not comply with X's rules P wrongs X" (Buchanan 2002, 691). Buchanan's real aim in distinguishing the two is to argue that we don't really need an account of or justification for political authority—a preoccupation of a great number of political philosophers—if we are interested in justifying the legitimacy of the state. Recall that legitimacy consists in a morally justified monopoly on making, applying, and enforcing laws.

2. The debate over philosophical anarchism continues to be lively and interesting. Garthoff (2010) argues that the normative authority of law arises from its capacity to solve "moral coordination problems" for duties that are extra-legal moral requirements; thus political authority or legitimacy is not necessary to give normative, obligatory force to the law, blunting the anarchist conclusion. Klosko (2004) defends a "multiple principle" theory of obligation that grounds obligation in various natural duties, the principle of fairness, a "common good" principle, and so on (a position that Simmons might be sympathetic to given his own "ethical pluralism"; but see his response to Gans 1992 in Simmons 2001, 112–17). Christiano argues that anarchists like Simmons underestimate the moral necessity of the state, for they assume that prepolitical duties can, in principle anyway, provide the assurance necessary for the establishment of justice in society. For Christiano, the state is morally necessary for social justice to be established (see Christiano 2008, 237–39). Edmundson argues against the "correlativity thesis," according to which legitimate political authority necessarily entails political obligations on the part of those subject to that authority. Instead, he argues that although there may be no prima facie duty to obey the law, legitimate authority only requires a "prima facie duty not to interfere with the administration of a just (or at least reasonably just) state's law" (Edmundson 1998, 49). A central feature of his argument is the denial of what he calls the "warranty thesis," that is, the claim that if being an authority entails claiming to create political obligations, then being a legitimate authority entails truly claiming to create political obligations, that is, actually generating in political subjects political obligations (Edmundson 1998, 39). This thesis largely leads to philosophical

anarchism, so its denial is crucial to his argument. For a sympathetic but still critical response to Edmundson, see Dagger (2000). These texts are only a small percentage of the existing literature.

3. For more on Benjamin's criticism of the means–ends in "Critique of Violence" as well as a historical contextualization of the essay see Hanssen (1997, esp. 240–45).

4. Geoffrey Sayre-McCord's helpful mapping of the moral realism debate, although a bit dated in some respects, nonetheless usefully abstracts from specific positions within realism so as to show that all realisms, including moral realism must hold "(1) the claims in question, when literally construed, are literally true or false (cognitivism), and (2) some are literally true" (Sayre-McCord 1988, 5). Simmons, it seems clear to me, does make or imply his commitment to both claims. But first, as far as I can see, he is also committed to further realist claims, for example, that there are (objectively valid) natural laws. The abstract claims are already controversial, and this further claim requires more than just a defense of cognitivism and a refutation of some "error theory"; it also requires some account of the "ontological" status of natural laws, that is, what they are. I assume that Simmons would not claim that natural laws have the same mode of being as rocks, or human beings, or tools, or animals (to use some Heideggerian distinctions). Are they like scientific laws? Are natural laws "observable?" Do they require a special kind of intuition to apprehend? I raise these questions only to suggest that if one thinks, as I do, that Simmons's account of the state's right to punish (and use other violence?) really rests on a commitment to a certain version of moral realism, then the defense of that position requires sustained engagement with these live questions in moral philosophy.

5. The balance-of-reasons view largely mirrors Habermas's distinction between justification and application, where the former provides reasons for the validity of norms but cannot itself directly apply the norm to a concrete situation or, solely by itself, motivate an actor to act according to the norm. See Habermas (1994).

6. I should note that commitment to a Heideggerian understanding of Dasein that criticizes Cartesian dualism does not entail that one reject as well the possibility of grounding a set of moral ideas and an understanding of moral community quite in line with the moral duties and conception of the moral life that one finds in Simmons (or any number of other moral philosophers). For example, Frederick Olafson grounds an understanding of ethics and ethical duties—including a responsibility to treat other human

beings as individuals whose own interests and cares must be taken into account—on an extension of Heideggerian *Mitsein* (which we return to in chapter 3). Olafson's disagreement with a philosopher such as Rawls is not, as I understand it, the particular moral obligations and duties he emphasizes. Rather, it is that such duties are not properly grounded in a correct ontological account of human sociality or not given any ground at all. The ethical principles Olafson proposes are not very different from what we find in many moral philosophers, but the grounding of those principles in an explicit ontology of human being that is critical of the (not so explicit) ontology assumed, for example, in Simmons, does distinguishes his position from other moral philosophers. See Olafson (1998, esp. chapter 2).

CHAPTER 2

1. Derrida's point is better understood—as is the paradox of founding in general—when thought together with Derrida's interest in Husserl's *The Origin of Geometry*. As Paola Marrati describes the problem:

> For Derrida, the originality of Husserl's transcendental project lies in the intuition that truth has to have an origin in time, even if its value does not depend on time. Truth has to be born, otherwise it could be the product of a subject, however transcendental that subject may be. And yet, this birth can in no way affect the sense of the being of truth. Were it to do so, truth would not be truth. (Marrati 2005, 45)

In other words, unless we are to rely on a false quasi-Platonism to guarantee the truth of, say, the Pythagorean theorem, we must grant that a mathematical truth is produced by a subject existing in a specific time and place. In admitting this, we seem to undermine the universality and a-temporality of a mathematical truth, for it is tied to history, to time, and to the contingency of an empirical act of thought and speech. Similarly, the paradox of founding arises because unless we assume some doubtful eternal ground for political communities—God, natural law, and so on—then we must understand how a political community can be born in time and exist through time without undermining the legitimacy of the birth and existence of the community. The place of truth in geometry is occupied by legitimacy in politics. What makes the political problem more dangerous is that the politics of maintaining the legitimacy of a political community despite its "bastard" birth always seems to tend toward violence.

2. Although partially in disagreement with Honig and Connolly, Chantal Mouffe describes and affirms a paradox of liberal democracy that opens up an adversarial "agonistic pluralism" that can and must negotiate the paradox that democratic sovereignty and liberal freedom are impossibly combined in liberal democracy. See Mouffe (2009). Honig's thinking has pursued the disclosure and affirmation of paradox not only through the "paradox of founding" but within politics more broadly, for example in the emergence of new rights and political movements (such as the slow food movement). See Honig (2009). Sofia Näsström argues that there is not only a paradox of founding vis-à-vis the government but also a paradox inherent to the constitution of the people, a paradox sidestepped by many contemporary theorists (but also Rousseau, I would add), by claiming that the foundation of the people is a matter of historical contingency. See Näsström (2007).

3. That there is a paradox of founding that implicates all states, not just democratic states (as I suggest later) can be seen by addressing one criticism of the paradox of founding position by Hans Agné. He argues that the paradox of founding within democracies is a matter of inclusion/exclusion, that is, that we seemingly cannot decide democratically the question of who is part of the democratic community (in this he follows Näsström 2007). Agné's response is that if humanity as a whole has a right to decide on the founding of particular states, then we can solve this problem. Whatever the merits of that solution, it does not avoid the paradox of founding. For the paradox of founding as Arendt, Schmitt, Derrida, and in their own ways Hobbes, Locke, and Rousseau have shown, concerns not who decides but what legitimizes the decision. Even if everyone decides, this doesn't solve the paradox, for we can ask "on the basis of what right can each individual legitimately found legal and political authority?," and the only answer can be something like an appeal to natural rights of one kind or another, that is, some prepolitical set of rights and powers. Agné's solution simply sidesteps the issue by neglecting to provide a justification of such a right/power to institute the political ex nihilo, as it were. (In particular, the normative justification of presuppositions of democratic procedures and of democracy itself, e.g., equality are assumed. This wouldn't be a problem except for the fact that the argument turns precisely on those justifications, not

the theoretical coherence of the idea that everyone in the world has a right to decide within the foundations of particular states.) See Agné (2010).

4. In this Rousseau is in full agreement with Schmitt. Schmitt argues that forming a constitution presupposes the existence of a political unity that decides on the specific form of its political unity through the constitution. It is a common mistake, he claims, that a constitution "always founds a new state, an error, moreover, which derives from the confusion of a 'social contract' (founding the political unity) with the constitution" (Schmitt 2008a, 75–76).

5. The paradox of founding becomes particularly acute in Rousseau because he seems aware of it and because he largely ignores, or relies only minimally on, natural rights theories in *On the Social Contract*—unlike Hobbes and Locke. Natural rights theories can be used to attempt a solution (however unsuccessfully) to the paradox of founding. For example, in the *Second Treatise*, after having demolished arguments for state legitimacy and political obligation from divinity, Locke's task is to find another origin of political power (Locke 1988, §1). That power comes, of course, from the express (or tacit) consent of the citizenry. But what, Derrida might ask, makes such consent legitimate, what authorizes the consenter's consent? The answer is presumably the natural freedom they have to order their lives within the boundaries of natural law, and both natural rights and natural law are founded in God. But God as the ultimate ground of the legitimacy of political power was precisely what Locke had just rejected, so we are forced either to accept divinity once again (and solve the paradox) or find other ways of denying the existence of the paradox.

Rousseau's version of the paradox of founding is also more pressing because unlike Hobbes, the sovereign is not necessarily distinct from a people that authorize but are subject to that sovereign: in Rousseau the people are sovereign and subject at the same time. For Hobbes, the sovereign remains in the state of nature vis-à-vis his subjects, and because he is the authoritative ground of civil Law, hence above it and not subject to it, the attempt to combine autonomy and law, force and freedom, is not even desirable, much less necessary. The sovereign's right of nature is the prepolitical ground of his right to do whatever is necessary to preserve the lives and encourage the felicitous possibilities of his subjects. But this is not the case for Rousseau, for whom the sovereign people are also subjects of the law. Rousseau must find a way to think and found together the absolute autonomy of the sovereign people and the absolute subjection of those people to themselves as sovereign.

6. A further problem with Rousseau's response—one that implicates his paradox of founding with the legitimacy of state violence—is that it ignores what he argues in *Political Fragments*, number 11: "*On that basis, one should be careful not to confuse the essence of civil society with that of sovereignty.* For the social body is the result of a single act of will, and its entire existence is only the sequel and the effect of a prior engagement whose force does not cease to act until this body is dissolved. But *sovereignty, which is only the exercise of the general will is, like it, free, and is not subject to any kind of engagement. Every act of sovereignty, like every instance of its existence, is absolute, independent of the one that precedes it; and the sovereign never acts because it wanted, but because it wants*" (Rousseau 1994, 24, emphasis added). This fragment is revealing because it acknowledges that the historical origin of a political community, as historical, is of another temporal duration then sovereignty, which exists in a sort of perpetual present, not subject to any engagement or obligation, even to time's passing. If each community can be "split" between, on the one hand, its historical, contingent, and finite existence as civil society and, on the other hand, its immortal, unchanging, always present existence as sovereign, then on which side are we to locate the legitimacy of state violence?

7. It is tempting and politically useful to sacralize foundings, to ground contingent origins in something necessary, to gloss over the facticity of the body politic. Arendt shows how this need to found the unfoundable by deifying the Nation during the French Revolution was in part responsible for the horrific violence that ensued (Arendt 1965 153–64). She also shows how the American revolutionaries almost escaped the same mistake, until they founded their claims to authority on the self-evidence of Truth (Arendt 1965, 189–95). Honig has shown how Arendt's reading of the Declaration of Independence denies a fundamental undecidability that undermines the possible authority and legitimacy of any performative ground for political authority and legitimacy (Honig 1991).

8. A claim such as this must have led John McCormick to base an entire reading of this section of "Force of Law" on the idea that Derrida couldn't possibly have meant what he said about Benjamin and thus must have been performing a nonviolent defense of Benjamin in the very spirit of Benjaminian nonviolence (McCormick 2001, 407). McCormick's essay, the goal of which is to defend "Force of Law," depends on what can well be

described, despite his protestations, as an "esoteric" reading of the text, one in which the first half of "Force of Law" is a restaging of the trial of Socrates and the second half is the performance mentioned above. McCormick's reading of Derrida, to my mind, is unsuccessful for a variety of reasons, most obviously because I simply cannot accept—see no reason to accept—the hermeneutical framework he erects. For a response to McCormick, see Ben Corson (2001).

9. The philosophical error is that Benjamin's account of a sphere of nonviolence characterized by the sphere of language is based on a conception of proper or pure language as a manifestation rather than a communication of information via the sign. Those familiar with Derrida's earlier texts will immediately see how this conception of a "pure" language which can, as it were, dispense with the sign, with mediation, and so on, is one Derrida cannot accept.

10. To be perfectly clear, I am not questioning the Derridean claim that a structural law governs the contamination of justice *by* law in each attempted instantiation of justice *in* law. Rather, the much more mundane question I ask is why legal institutions are the privileged site for justice. I was compelled to add this note after reading Hent de Vries (2002).

11. It is interesting to note, however, that the same cannot be said for Ricoeur's "foundational" discussion of the paradox of politics. The paradox of politics, Ricoeur argues, is that on his Aristotelian/Rousseauian/Hegelian conception of the State, the State represents an autonomous domain of polity that institutionalizes human rationality; at the same time, this rationality fosters specifically political evils, for the empirical practice of polity—politics—introduces violence into human affairs (Ricoeur 1992, 248). Thus, the paradox is that an increase and manifestation of human rationality coincides with the introduction into human life of an evil that is the "closest approximation of radical evil" (Ricoeur 1992, 261). Within the context of elaborating this paradox Ricoeur identifies what Connolly creatively and productively *mis*reads as the paradox of founding. My concern with Connolly's misreading is not pedantic, but political: it tends to elide the specific fact of violence that Ricoeur repeatedly refers to in his essay.

For Ricoeur, the origin of the state is consent, but this original consent is "virtual," that is, it "is not an historical event, but one which only comes out in reflection" (Ricoeur 1992, 251). Thus, in a passage quoted by Connolly, "it is of the nature of political consent, which gives rise to the unity of the human community organized and oriented by the State, to be able to be recovered only in an act which has not taken place, in a contract which has not been contracted, in an implicit and tacit pact which appears only in political awareness, in retrospection, and in reflection" (Ricoeur 1992, 252). In line with his focus on the paradox of lawmaking in Rousseau, Connolly reads this passage as the claim that every political act lacks full legitimacy because it relies on justifications and criteria that are only incompletely understood and consented to (because the act of consent has never "actually," i.e., transparently and completely and without remainders) taken place (Connolly 1995, 139). Moreover, Connolly argues, the "retrospective" character of appeals to founding moments reveals the inescapability of temporality in politics, the fact that time is always out of joint in political life such that legitimacy is always retrospected or prospected without ever achieving a fully present reality now.

However, Ricoeur goes on to argue that the virtuality of the social contract, its "ideality," its existence only in reflection, must be understood to found a "real community," just as the ideality of a universal law must be understood in relation to its perversion (my term) by, for example, the bourgeois class (Ricoeur 1992, 253). In short, the tension seems to be between a necessarily virtual, rational, ideal act of consent that is the truth of political community and the actual acts of politics that will necessarily distort this truth. This makes of the relation between political acts and their conditions of legitimacy a relation of perversion, perversion of the ideal by the real, of thought by empirical action. It is not that political acts are not fully legitimized by a necessarily a-legitimate historical founding; rather, it is always a matter of

> a pact which is a virtual act and which founds a real community; an ideality of law which legitimizes the reality of force; a ready-made fiction to clothe the hypocrisy of a ruling class, but which, before giving rise to falsehood, founds the freedom of citizens, a freedom which ignores particular cases, the real differences of power, and the real conditions of persons, but which is nevertheless valuable because of its very abstraction—such is the labyrinth of polity. (Ricoeur 1992, 253)

Rather than questioning the origin of polity, the manifestation of polity in politics is what is problematic. I read Ricoeur as repeating Rousseau rather than—as I take Connolly to be claiming—diagnosing but not solving the paradox of politics.

My reading and Connolly's reading of Ricoeur are both contestable. But whatever one makes of the relation between an ideal, virtual social contract and its empirical manifestations, it allows Ricoeur to remain focused on state violence and the violence that founds empirical political communities. He can attend to the fact that even fully legitimate violence is still violence, still domination, and he at least suggests, to my mind, that even legitimate violence is evil (Ricoeur 1992, 255). Ricoeur also notes, in his reading of Machiavelli in the same essay, the violence of inception, of founding violence, and the ways a contingent, hence a-legitimate, founding violence is "resorbed" into the legitimate state (Ricoeur 1992, 258). Although I disagree both philosophically and politically with Ricoeur's reading of the social contract (it is too Aristotelian and, perhaps unsurprisingly, Husserlian), I appreciate his attention to the connection between problems of state legitimacy and state violence, something I find only occasionally attended to in Honig, Connolly, and Derrida.

CHAPTER 3

1. I don't mean to suggest, of course, that the arguments, or even the proximate reasons or motivations for the formulation of arguments about the proper name and the "singular" being or object are the same in all of these thinkers. For Kripke and Searle—despite their opposing views—proper names become problematic in the context of responding to Frege and Russell, specifically the former's distinction between sense and reference (where the latter depends on the former). However, Kripke's *Naming and Necessity* (1980) relies consistently on intuition, and one of the unstated intuitions I suspect in Kripke's argument is that a description theory of proper names fails to account for some seemingly obvious facts about singular objects, for example, that although I can imagine many statements/facts about Richard Nixon as not being true of Nixon in other possible worlds, it is hard (perhaps impossible) to imagine Nixon not being Nixon (in the sense of not being born to Nixon's parents; in the sense of this particular, singular lump of material). This comes out clearly when Kripke turns to the "origin" and "substance" of a particular wooden table to help us understand the necessity properties of the table (what makes it *this* table

and not any other table). For Derrida, the proper name has a more obvious relation to singularity, but his concern is to show that the proper name can only name the singular other in its singularity insofar as the name, as a signifier, opens itself to the loss of its uniqueness and its unique relation to the singular "signified" by the name. What is nonetheless striking to me is that in all of these cases there is an initial, prephilosophical (as it were) perception at play: how do we respond to, identify, name, conceive, conceptualize, and so on *this* being in front of me, and what ontological, metaphysical, logical, epistemological, and/or ethical conclusions follow from this encounter with the singular being? See Strawson (1959), Searle (1958), Kripke (1980), and Derrida (1988).

2. Such a reading is reinforced by the centrality of "nonrelationality" to resolute anticipation of one's death. No one can die for me, and I cannot die for another; in this way, death is truly my ownmost possibility, one that makes possible my answering the "who?" of Dasein without (sole) reference to das Man (Heidegger 1962, 308).

3. Deleuze is a thinker I have yet to fully understand, just as the analytic tradition in which the problem of individuals emerges is one that I feel incapable of commenting on (now, at any rate). Thus, in addition to positive reasons to focus on Nancy as opposed to anyone else—reasons that will become clearer below, often in footnotes—there is the humbling fact that I just don't know enough to comment competently on any number of other philosophical texts and traditions. I feel more competent and confident—though not unreservedly so—in discussing Nancy.

4. I will not be providing an exegesis of Nancy's extremely complex and varied philosophical works as whole. Nancy's writings range across ethics, aesthetics, ontology, psychoanalysis, poetics, political philosophy, and more. Although I consider "Of Being Singular Plural" his most important work—certainly it is the most explicit account of the ontological "ground" of all of his philosophical work—one cannot really grasp the singular plural, for reasons internal to Nancy's claims about the singular plural, without attending to the diverse fields of philosophy, art, politics, and indeed "human experience" generally.

5. I will not be dealing with Nancy's work on community, the centerpiece of which is Nancy (1991). This book is also the focus of much of the political theory responses to Nancy, at least in English. For one important early response see Norris (2000). Andreas Wagner, drawing more heavily on *Being Singular Plural* and other "ontological" texts responds

in part to Norris in Wagner (2006). Fred Dallmayr draws *The Inoperative Community* into dialogue with international relations theory, specifically Samuel Huntington's work, in Dallmayr (1997). For an attempt to critically appropriate Nancy's *Inoperative Community* for a defense of a republican model of political community, see Schwarzmantel (2007). As other scholars have shown, however, the link between "Of Being Singular Plural" and *The Inoperative Community* is clear. See Devisch (2002, 239–43).

On the other hand, several responses to Nancy's ontological work have appeared, many of which are expository in nature and, for the most part, share my sense and exposition of his ontological work. See Raffoul (1999), Devisch (2002), and James (2006).

6. For a response to the Dreyfus/Olafson debate, see Boedecker (2001). The most important critical response to and appropriation of *Mitsein*—albeit one that is entirely implicit—can be found in Hannah Arendt. For Arendt, of course, the fact that men, and not man, inhabit the Earth—that is, plurality—is one of the human conditions and the condition of all political life (Arendt 1998, 7, 2005, 93). Given Arendt's complex but obvious indebtedness to Heidegger, it is difficult not to see, as Jacques Taminiaux (1997), Richard Bernstein (1997), Dana Villa (1996), and other (more hostile) critics have shown, that Arendt's conception of human plurality, the rise of the social, authentic and inauthentic ways of answering the question "who are you?" are responses, often harsh ones, to Heidegger. What readers of Arendt often neglect is that toward the end of her life—specifically in the opening chapters of *The Life of the Mind*—many of the conditions and elements of the political—hence only human conditions—such as appearance, display, expressiveness, and disclosure began to be attributed to Being per se, or at least to all animate creatures (Arendt 1978). The relationship between *The Life of the Mind* and the rest of Arendt's more explicitly political texts is complicated, but I think it is fair to say that when she let herself—which was not very often—speak in a more distinctly philosophical voice (in her sense of the term philosophy), her ontological tendencies pushed her to see in Being what previously only held for human beings. This is yet another way, I would argue, in which one can understand Nancy's ontology as a (mostly implicit) elaboration and deepening of Arendt. For other engagements with Mitsein in *Being and Time* and Nancy's response to Mitsein see Dallmayr (1980), Figal (2005), Rubenstein (2008, 99–111).

7. The debate turns on the plausibility of Dreyfus's Wittgensteinian interpretation of Heidegger generally, and of das Man in particular. Olafson

argues that das Man and all of its conformism "is at bottom a deforma-
tion of Mitsein," that is, it is just one way in which our being-with-others
can be actualized. From Olafson's perspective, though, Dreyfus almost
"exalts" das Man and turns what is an undesirable actualization of our
being-with-others into "the repository of the whole stock of accumulated
know-how of a given society" (Olafson 1994, 59). This makes of Dasein,
on Olafson's account, a mere product of its culture, depriving Dasein of
any real capacity to choose or interpret those norms that undoubtedly
exist in any given society.

Dreyfus responds by admitting that there is textual evidence for both
his view and Olafson's, but that Olafson's position "locks" Heidegger into
"the deviation into subjectivity that he says ultimately led him to abandon
Being and Time" (Dreyfus 1995, 428). Against this, Dreyfus tries "to help
Heidegger remain true to his goal of writing an ontological interpretation
of Dasein in which its essential structures are laid out and show to account
for the fact that human beings are able to disclose entities. This amounts
to taking one aspect of Heidegger's task to be to develop a phenomenology
of the role of social norms in forming the background of intelligibility, even
though he finds such norms degrading and dangerous" (Dreyfus 1995, 428).
Of course, there are many more details within this debate—including the role
of Division II in interpreting Being and Time as well as the concept of "presence"
in Heideggerian ontology—but there is no need to go any further into this debate.

8. "A singular being does not emerge or rise up against the background of a chaotic, undifferentiated identity of beings, or against the
background of their unitary assumption, or that of a becoming, or that of
a will" (Nancy 1991, 27).

9. For Heidegger, authentic existence—what might be called the
achievement of singularity (what he calls "authenticity" or the proper)
comes in the mode of nonrelationality: being-toward-death. It is in resolutely anticipating one's death, a death that is the figure of one's "mineness,"
of one's most proper possibility, that Dasein frees itself from the domination of das Man and achieves an authentic singular existence. Thus, even
if being-with is an essential structure of Dasein's being-in-the-world, it
is nonetheless the case that it is only through death—through a mode of
nonrelation—that singularity can be achieved and, further, an "authentic"
relation to others can come into being. On the other hand, Levinas begins
from the death of the Other as that which singularizes "me." If for Heidegger
it is through responsibility for my singular, irreplaceable death—what he

calls resolute anticipation—that Dasein achieves singularity, for Levinas it is in responsibility for the Other's death—a responsibility untransferable as well—that the "I" becomes itself. This responsibility for the Other, paradoxically, undoes the ego's self-interestedness, decomposes that ego, but at the same time singularizes it as a self called toward a responsibility it cannot escape and cannot delegate to others (just as for Heidegger my death cannot be delegated or transferred to another). For Levinas, even if there is a "relation" at play out of which emerges singularity, that relation is restricted to the face-to-face encounter with the Other. The ethical relationship "stands out" against the backdrop of the third party, of the other Others to whom and for whom one must inevitably compromise one's responsibility without thereby mitigating or undoing that responsibility. See Heidegger (1962, §§46–53) and Levinas (2002, 12, 43). For a discussion, and defense, of Nancy in relation to Levinas, see Watkin (2007).

10. The genealogy of these ideas about time and space begins, as I see it, with Derrida's "Ousia and Gramme" (Derrida 1982, esp. 53–57), and in some ways through, in other ways past, Derrida towards Heidegger, Hegel, Kant, and Aristotle.

11. See Nancy (2000, 10). If my reading of Nancy on the themes of strangeness and, later, curiosity, are correct, then it puts into question what I take to be Simon Critchley's insightful misreading of Nancy (Critchley 1999a, 239–53). Although a longer discussion would be needed, the same goes for Robert Bernasconi's criticism, written before the publication of "Being Singular Plural," that "from a Levinasian perspective, Nancy's own ontological elucidation of the 'inoperative community,' by rendering the face to face secondary, obliterates alterity" (Bernasconi 1993). Christopher Watkin (2009) usefully summarizes and problematizes the various objections to Nancy's being singular plural.

12. Nancy (2000, 13). "Touching" is a central concept in Nancy's thought and recurs throughout his work, most prominently in *Corpus*; but the short section "Touching" in *The Sense of the World* gives a useful introduction to the concept (Nancy 1997, 59–63). In the context of reading another text written by Nancy, Derrida writes: "But I self-touches spacing itself out, losing contact with itself, precisely in touching itself. It switches off the contact, it abstains from touching, so as to touch itself" (Derrida 2005b, 34).

Nancy's appropriation of the term *curiosity* is an explicit rejection of Heidegger's criticism of curiosity as seeing "just in order to see," as opposed to seeing something to understand it (Heidegger 1962, 216).

CHAPTER 4

1. A thorough collection of the main philosophical essays on violence in the analytic philosophical tradition can be found in Buffachi (2009).

2. Referring precisely to this worry as a result of a reading of Levinas, Hent de Vries argues that one can see the extension of the concept of violence—which in Levinas becomes almost total—as both trivialization and intensification where "the distinction between them marks all that matters (ethically, politically, and otherwise)" (de Vries 1997, 17). However, it is not only in the work of some philosophers that violence is extended so far as to be coincident with experience itself. Anthropologist Arthur Kleinman writes that "wheresoever power orients practices—and that is everywhere—there is violence … Violence, in this perspective, is the vector of cultural processes that work through the salient images, structures, and engagements of everyday life to shape local worlds" (Kleinman 2000, 238). This violence includes, among other things, the "stress" of middle-class bourgeois life, life under the Communist Party in China, the status of hemophiliacs who suffered from AIDS after blood transfusions, and the violence of images of violence that circulate in the contemporary media. Kleinman's essay is an example of the benefits and conceptual difficulties of such an extension of the concept of violence.

3. A similar problem can be found in Nancy. In "Image and Violence" Nancy defines violence as follows: "Violence can be defined *a minima* as the application of a force that remains foreign to the dynamic or energetic system into which it intervenes" (Nancy 2005, 16). Now this definition is rich in philosophical allusion: first, "application of force" translates *mise en ouvre*, which in addition to *dynamique* and *energetique* suggests an entire Aristotelian tradition of thinking about possibility and actuality and actualization. Furthermore, as we learn later in the text, force itself is defined as "nothing other than the unity woven from a sensory diversity" (Nancy 2005, 22), which, I take it, is an allusion to Hegel's definition of Force in *The Phenomenology of Spirit*:

> In other words, the "matters" posited as independent directly pass over into their unity, and their unity directly unfolds its diversity, and this once again reduces itself to unity. But this movement is what is called Force. One of its moments, the dispersal of the independent "matters" in their [immediate] being, is the expression

of Force; but Force, taken as that in which they have disappeared, is Force *proper*, Force which has been *driven back* into itself from its expression. (Hegel 1977, §136; emphasis in original)

Force is the weaving of unity, the movement in which we perceive the object as a thing with multiple properties that nonetheless is a singular object, one thing, a unity in diversity. Violence, then, is the work of unifying the diverse and the plural from the outside, working on and regulating what is possible and action from a "position" not just exterior to but importantly foreign to, estranged from, that diversity and plurality of the possible and the actual. It is, I take it, something like the appropriative act, but one that comes, as all appropriative acts do, from "outside."

Nancy's first example of violence is mundane (he calls it anodyne): a frustrated individual pulling a screw out with pliers, thus intervening in the "logic" of the threads of the screw and in the material of the wood (form and content, possibility and actuality, etc.). But Nancy's definition of violence is expansive, for we learn in this short text that violence is Truth (but the not the True Truth), and true Truth is violence; violence names what States do when they punish or intervene in other countries; that the Kantian schematism of the understanding is violence; that on Kantian grounds, Time is violence; and so on. My concern is not the philosophical cogency of Nancy's brief text—I find it an incredibly powerful work of philosophy—but its reliance on the figure of violence (which he calls a "figure without figure") to name a force that is at work everywhere and always. A "violence without violence consists in the revelation's not taking place, its remaining imminent. Or rather it is the revelation of this: that there is nothing to reveal" (Nancy 2005, 26). In other words, we still have violence even in a violence without violence, but the foreign force at work in the world in this "violence without violence" empties out its violence by not putting itself to work, by remaining on the cusp of ordering, systematizing, cognizing, regulating, and so on the singular plural of the world. We find this most prominently for Nancy in art. Even this violence without violence is still, for all that, violence. This is why I would not follow Nancy in using the term, for without a coherent account of that which connects internally the various violences (and "violences without violence") to which he refers, I have a hard time employing the term in a useful and coherent way to challenge the particular manifestation of violence at issue in this book. For a useful account of Nancy's "ontological" exposition of violence see Morin (2013).

4. Of course, the issue is far more complex, as anyone who has read *Discipline and Punish* (1995) is aware. The relation between discourse and "physical" practices is too intimate, too material, and significant on both sides to allow for a clear distinction between physical acts and conceptual determinations or discursive practices. Yet again, for political reasons, I would like to emphasize the materiality of practices of state violence keeping in mind that such materiality is far richer than the mere idea of the "physical."

5. The idea of injury as wrongness is more clearly present in Ted Honderich's definition of violence: "An act of violence, we may briefly say, is a use of considerable or destroying force against people or things, *a use of force that offends against a norm*" (Honderich 1989, 151, emphasis added). Yet Honderich's definition appears to imply physical violence (although it need not be construed solely in physical terms). If one emphasizes injuriousness, then one tends toward a "violation" account of violence (Buffachi 2005, 196), but such an account is, again, not necessarily a great extension of the concept of violence.

6. The problem here is not that the rose is not human, and thus can't be a "real" object of violence. It is just as unclear why telling my the reason she is beautiful and intelligent constitutes an act of violence.

7. It is, I would argue, also the case that avoiding, denying, or repressing singularity to justify "psychological" violence or to justify hate speech is violence. But I will not argue for that here because I want to remain focused on acts of state violence, most of which are physical in nature.

8. More precisely, within Kant's system the aspects of singularity described by Nancy are "split" between the phenomenal and noumenal being. Insofar as coming-to-be in a particular space time—being posited—is essential to being a singular being, then only in the phenomenal "world" can there be singular beings. On the other hand, insofar as the singular being resists any attempt to "know" it by always being in excess of any particular predicate, then the singular being would have to be noumenal, for only the thing-in-itself resists all empirical determination. This indecision—which, of course, is imposed on Kant here because he is not all that interested in singularity—is a consequence of Kant's desire both to secure scientific knowledge of the empirical world (at the cost of subjecting the human to necessary causal relations and denying phenomenal freedom) and his desire to recognize and ground human freedom (at the cost of denying the possibility of "experiencing" that freedom in any assured way).

9. As far as I can see, not much work since Walzer has substantially changed the terms within which the problem is discussed, although authors have explored various ways of responding to the problem of dirty hands. For just a few examples, see Lauritzen (2010), Digeser (1998), and Griffin (1989). One notable exception is Dennis Thompson's "The Problem of Many Hands" (1980). Thompson rightly points out that in the complex bureaucracies that exist within modern states, one cannot very easily impute responsibility to a single actor; nor can one, however, rely on a "hierarchical model" that puts responsibility on those who make decisions (rather than administer them), or on a collective responsibility model. He instead argues for a "personal responsibility" model, one that depends on the ideas of causation and volition, but a model that really requires casuistry rather than abstract theory: we must work case by case. See Thompson (1980).

10. Their responses mostly take the form of being unclear what Nagel is arguing for and, to the extent that he is arguing for the viability of both absolutist and utilitarian reasoning, that he fails to provide a way of reconciling the two, something rule-utilitarianism can and does.

CHAPTER 5

1. On a personal note, I can remember working at one of the truly great bookstores in the United States, Cody's Books in Berkeley as an undergraduate and looking, with some coworkers, at *Without Sanctuary* just after it came out. It remains the only time I have simply been unable to continue looking at images of violence. Even now, twelve years later, I still cannot quite explain what exactly forced me to stop looking.

2. Much of this discussion is influenced by Derrida's seminar.

3. I have debated including the photo in this book, or a similar one, but decided against it. It is just too exploitative. In any case, a search will find images of a similar kind. An archived version of the original page, with the photographs, can be found by searching the original URL on the Internet Archive (http://archive.org/web).

4. The position I am arguing for—as I elaborate further in the next section—should not be confused with the various claims that human beings are genetically, or naturally, or "animalistically" violent, that is, that there is no difference between human and animal violence (save differences in degree and in technology). My claim is not that humans are naturally

violent or that human violence is "animalistic," hence beyond or before moral judgment or evaluation. My claim is that human beings are capable of but cannot succeed at morally justifying state violence, and this poses a threat to our identity as, our self-conceptions of being, human.

REFERENCES

Adorno, Theodor. 1973. *Negative Dialectics*. Translated by E. B. Ashton. New York: Continuum.

———. 2005. *Minima Moralia*. Translated by E. F. N. Jephcott. London: Verso.

Agamben, Giorgio. 1998. *Homo Sacer*. Translated by Daniel Heller-Roazen. Palo Alto, CA: Stanford University Press.

Agné, Hans. 2010. "Why Democracy Must Be Global: Self-Founding and Democratic Intervention." *International Theory* 2: 381–409.

Apel, Dora. 2003. "On Looking: Lynching Photographs and Legacies of Lynching after 9/11." *American Quarterly* 55: 457–478.

Arendt, Hannah. 1965. *On Revolution*. New York: Viking Press.

———. 1972. *Crises of the Republic*. San Diego, CA: Harcourt, Brace.

———. 1978. *The Life of the Mind*. San Diego, CA: Harcourt, Brace.

———. 1998. *The Human Condition*. Chicago: University of Chicago Press.

———. 2003. *Responsibility and Judgment*. Edited by Jerome Kohn. New York: Schocken.

———. 2005. *The Promise of Politics*. Edited by Jerome Kohn. New York: Schocken.

Aristotle. 1992. *The Politics*. Translated by T. A. Sinclair. London: Penguin Books.

Arnold, Jeremy. 2009. "Oedipal Sovereignty and the War in Iraq." In *States of Violence*. Edited by Austin Sarat and Jennifer Culbert. Cambridge: Cambridge University Press, 51–82.

———. 2011. "Should Death Do Us Part?: Singular Bodies and Ethical Responsibilities." *Theory & Event* 14: 4.

Austin, J. L. 1961. *Philosophical Papers*. Oxford: Oxford University Press.

Bäck, Allan. 2004. "Thinking Clearly about Violence." *Philosophical Studies* 117: 219–230.

Beardsworth, Richard. 2005. "In Memorium Jacques Derrida: The Power of Reason." *Theory and Event* 8: 1.

Bekoff, Marc. 2004. "Wild Justice and Fair Play: Cooperation, Forgiveness, and Morality in Animals." *Biology and Philosophy* 19: 489–520.

Benjamin, Walter. 1978. *Reflections*. Edited by Peter Demetz. New York: Schocken Books.

Bergson, Henri. 1992. *The Creative Mind*. Translated by Mabelle L. Andison. New York: Citadel Press.

Bernasconi, Robert. 1993. "On Deconstructing Nostalgia for Community within the West." *Research in Phenomenology* 23: 3–21.

Bernstein, J. M. 2001. *Adorno: Disenchantment and Ethics*. Cambridge, MA: Cambridge University Press.

———. 2004. "Bare Life, Bearing Witness: Auschwitz and the Pornography of Horror." *Parallax* 10: 2–16.

———. 2006. "Intact and Fragmented Bodies: Versions of Ethics 'After Auschwitz.'" *New German Critique* 33: 31–52.

Bernstein, Richard J. 1997. "Provocation and Appropriation: Hannah Arendt's Response to Martin Heidegger." *Constellations* 4: 153–171.

Boedeker, Edgar C. 2001. "Individual and Community in Early Heidegger: Situating das Man, the Man-self, and Self-ownership in Dasein's Ontological Structure." *Inquiry* 44: 63–100.

Brandt, R. B. 1972. "Utilitarianism and the Rules of War." *Philosophy and Public Affairs* 1: 145–165.

Brogan, Walter. 2010. "The Parting of Being." *Research in Phenomenology* 40: 297–302

Buchanan, Allen. 2002. "Political Legitimacy and Democracy." *Ethics* 112: 689–719.

Buffachi, Vittorio. 2005. "Two Concepts of Violence." *Political Studies Review* 3: 193–204.

———. ed. 2009. *Violence: A Philosophical Anthology*. New York: Palgrave Macmillan.

Butler, Judith. 1997. *Excitable Speech*. New York: Routledge.

———. 2010. *Frames of War*. London: Verso.

Carroll, Noel. 1990. *The Philosophy of Horror; or Paradoxes of the Heart*. London: Routledge.

Cavarero, Adriana. 2009. *Horrorism*. New York: Columbia University Press.

Cavell, Stanley. 1976. *Must We Mean What We Say?* Cambridge: Cambridge University Press.

———. 1989. *This New yet Unapproachable America.* Albuquerque, NM: Living Batch Press.

———. 1999. *The Claim of Reason.* Oxford: Oxford University Press.

———. 2004. *Cities of Words.* Cambridge, MA: Harvard University Press.

Christiano, Thomas. 2008. *The Constitution of Equality.* Oxford: Oxford University Press.

Coady, C. A. J. 2008. *Morality and Political Violence.* Cambridge: Cambridge University Press.

Connolly, William E. 1995. *The Ethos of Pluralization.* Minneapolis: University of Minnesota Press.

———. 2003. *Neuropolitics.* Minneapolis: University of Minnesota Press.

———. 2005. *Pluralism.* Durham, NC: Duke University Press.

———. 2008. *Capitalism and Christianity, American Style.* Durham, NC: Duke University Press.

Copp, David. 1999. "The Idea of a Legitimate State." *Philosophy and Public Affairs* 28: 3–45.

Corson, Ben. 2001. "Transcending Violence in Derrida: A Reply to John McCormick." *Political Theory* 29: 866–875.

Cover, Robert. 1986. "Violence and the Word." *Yale Law Journal* 95: 1601–1629.

Critchley, Simon. 1999a. *The Ethics of Deconstruction.* West Lafayette, IN: Purdue University Press.

———. 1999b. *Ethics—Politics—Subjectivity.* London: Verso Press.

Dagger, Richard 2000. "Philosophical Anarchism and its Fallacies: A Review Essay." *Law and Philosophy* 19: 391–406.

Dallmayr, Fred. 1980. "Heidegger on Intersubjectivity." *Human Studies* 3: 221–246.

———. 1997. "An 'Inoperative' Global Community? Reflections on Nancy." *The Sense of Philosophy: On Jean-Luc Nancy.* Edited by Darren Sheppard, Simon Sparks, and Colin Thomas. London: Routledge, 174–196.

Das, Veena. 2007. *Life and Words: Violence and the Descent into the Ordinary.* Berkeley: University of California Press.

Dean, Carolyn J. 2003. "Empathy, Pornography, and Suffering." *differences* 14: 88–124.

Deleuze, Gilles. 1983. *Nietzsche and Philosophy*. Translated by Hugh Tomlinson. New York: Athlone Press.

Deleuze, Gilles, and Félix Guattari. 1987. *A Thousand Plateaus*. Translated by Brian Massumi. Minneapolis: University of Minnesota Press.

Derrida, Jacques. 1978. *Writing and Difference*. Translated by Alan Bass. Chicago: University of Chicago Press.

———. 1982. *Margins of Philosophy*. Translated by Alan Bass. Chicago: University of Chicago Press.

———. 1988. *Limited Inc*. Translated by Samuel Weber. Evanston, IL: Northwestern University Press.

———. 1994. *Specters of Marx*. Translated by Peggy Kamuf. London: Routledge Press.

———. 1995. *The Gift of Death*. Translated by David Wills. Chicago: University of Chicago Press.

———. 2001. *Cosmopolitanism and Forgiveness*. Translated by Mark Dooley and Michael Hughes. London: Routledge Press.

———. 2002. "Force of Law." *Acts of Religion*. Edited by Gil Anidjar. New York: Routledge, 228–298.

———. 2005a. *Rogues*. Translated by Pascale-Anne Brault and Michael Naas. Palo Alto, CA: Stanford University Press.

———. 2005b. *On Touching—Jean-Luc Nancy*. Translated by Christine Irizarry. Palo Alto, CA: Stanford University Press.

———. 2009. *The Beast and the Sovereign, Volume I*. Chicago: University of Chicago Press.

Devisch, Ignaas. 2002. "A Trembling Voice in the Desert. Jean-Luc Nancy's Rethinking of the Political." *Cultural Values* 4: 239–256.

de Vries, Hent. 1997. "Violence and Testimony: On Sacrificing Sacrifice." *Violence, Identity, and Self-Determination*. Edited by Hent de Vries and Samuel Weber. Palo Alto, CA: Stanford University Press, 14–43.

———. 2002. *Religion and Violence*. Baltimore, MD: Johns Hopkins University Press.

———. 2005. *Minimal Theologies*. Translated by Geoffrey Hale. Baltimore, MD: Johns Hopkins University Press.

Diamond, Cora. 1978. "Eating Meat and Eating People." *Philosophy* 53: 465–479.

———. 2003. "The Difficulty of Reality and the Difficulty of Philosophy." *Partial Answers* 1: 1–26.

Digeser, Peter. 1998. "Forgiveness and Politics: Dirty Hands and Imperfect Procedures." *Political Theory* 26: 700–724.

Dreyfus, Hubert L. 1991. *Being-in-the-World: A Commentary on Heidegger's Being and Time, Division 1*. Cambridge, MA: MIT Press.

———. 1995. "Interpreting Heidegger on Das Man." *Inquiry* 38: 423–430.

Edmundson, William A. 1998. *Three Anarchical Fallacies*. Cambridge: Cambridge University Press.

Figal, Günter. 2005. "Being-with, Dasein-with, and the 'They' as the Basic Concept of Unfreedom, from Martin Heidegger: Phänomenologie der Freiheit." *Heidegger's Being and Time: Critical Essays*. Edited by Richard Polt. Lanham, MD: Rowman & Littlefield, 105–116.

Flathman, Richard E. 1980. *The Practice of Political Authority*. Chicago: University of Chicago Press.

———. 1998. *Reflections of a Would-be Anarchist*. Minneapolis: University of Minnesota Press.

Foucault, Michel. 1978. *The History of Sexuality: An Introduction, Volume I*. Translated by Robert Hurley. New York: Vintage Books.

———. 1994. *The Order of Things*. New York: Vintage Books.

———. 1995. *Discipline and Punish*. Translated by Alan Sheridan. New York: Vintage Books.

Frank, Jason. 2010. *Constituent Moments*. Durham, NC: Duke University Press.

Fraser, Nancy. 1989. *Unruly Practices*. Minneapolis: University of Minnesota Press.

Friedlander, Saul, ed. 1992. *Probing the Limits of Representation*. Cambridge, MA: Harvard University Press.

Gans, Chaim. 1992. *Philosophical Anarchism and Political Disobedience*. Cambridge: Cambridge University Press.

Garthoff, John. 2010. "Legitimacy Is Not Authority." *Law and Philosophy* 29: 669–694.

Gerhardt, Christina. 2006. "The Ethics of Animals in Adorno and Kafka." *New German Critique* 33: 159–178.

Green, Leslie. 1988. *The Authority of the State*. Oxford: Oxford University Press.

Griffin, Leslie. 1989. "The Problem of Dirty Hands." *Journal of Religious Ethics* 17: 31–61.

Habermas, Jürgen. 1979. "Consciousness-Raising or Redemptive Criticism: The Contemporaneity of Walter Benjamin." *New German Critique* 17: 30–59.

———. 1984. *The Theory of Communicative Action: Volume One.* Translated by Thomas McCarthy. Boston: Beacon Press.

———. 1987. *The Theory of Communicative Action: Volume Two.* Translated by Thomas McCarthy. Boston: Beacon Press.

———. 1994. *Justification and Application.* Translated by Ciaran P. Cronin. Cambridge, MA: MIT Press.

———. 1998. *Between Facts and Norms.* Translated by William Rehg. Cambridge, MA: MIT Press.

Halttunen, Karen. 1995. "Humanitarianism and the Pornography of Pain in Anglo-American Culture." *American Historical Review* 100: 303–334.

Hanssen, Beatrice. 1997. "On the Politics of Pure Means: Benjamin, Arendt, Foucault." *Violence, Identity and Self-Determination.* Edited by Hent de Vries and Samuel Weber. Palo Alto, CA: Stanford University Press, 236–252.

Hare, R. M. 1972. "Rules of War and Moral Reasoning." *Philosophy and Public Affairs* 1: 166–181.

Hegel, G. W. F. 1977. *Phenomenology of Spirit.* Translated by A. V. Miller. Oxford: Oxford University Press.

Hart, H. L. A. 1961. *The Concept of Law.* Oxford: Oxford University Press.

Heidegger, Martin. 1962. *Being and Time.* Translated by John Macquarrie and Edward Robinson. New York: Harper & Row.

———. 1977. *The Question Concerning Technology and Other Essays.* Translated by William Lovitt. New York: Harper & Row.

———. 1995. *The Fundamental Concepts of Metaphysics.* Translated by William McNeill and Nicholas Walker. Bloomington: Indiana University Press.

Hirsch, Marianne. 2001. "Surviving Images: Holocaust Photographs and the Work of Postmemory." *Yale Journal of Criticism* 14: 5–37.

Hobbes, Thomas. 1991. *Man and Citizen.* Indianapolis, IN: Hackett.

———. 1997. *Leviathan.* New York: W.W. Norton.

———. 2005. *The English Works of Thomas Hobbes of Malmesbury, Volume I.* Elibron Classics.

Honderich, Ted. 1989. *Violence for Equality.* London: Routledge Press.

Honig, Bonnie. 1991. "Declarations of Independence: Arendt and Derrida on the Problem of Founding a Republic." *American Political Science Review* 85: 97–113.

———. 2007. "Between Decision and Deliberation: Political Paradox in Democratic Theory." *American Political Science Review* 101: 1–17.

———. 2009. *Emergency Politics: Paradox, Law, Democracy*. Princeton, NJ: Princeton University Press.

Horkheimer, Max, and Theodor Adorno. 2002. *Dialectic of Enlightenment*. Translated by Edmund Jephcott. Palo Alto, CA: Stanford University Press.

James, Ian. 2006. *The Fragmentary Demand*. Palo Alto, CA: Stanford University Press.

Jütten, Timo. 2012. "Adorno on Kant, Freedom and Determinism." *European Journal of Philosophy* 20: 548–574.

Kant, Immanuel. 1964. *Groundwork of the Metaphysic of Morals*. Translated by H. J. Paton. New York: Harper & Row.

———. 1996. *Practical Philosophy*. Edited by Mary J. Gregor. Cambridge: Cambridge University Press.

———. 1998. *Critique of Pure Reason*. Translated by Paul Guyer and Alan Wood. Cambridge: Cambridge University Press.

———. 2000. *Critique of the Power of Judgment*. Translated by Paul Guyer and Eric Matthews. Cambridge: Cambridge University Press.

Kateb, George. 1992. *The Inner Ocean*. Ithaca, NY: Cornell University Press.

———. 2007. "Punishment and the Spirit of Democracy." *Social Research* 74: 269–306.

Kleinman, Arthur. 2000. "The Violences of Everday Life." *Violence and Subjectivity*. Edited by Veena Das, Arthur Kleinman, Mamphela Ramphele, and Pamela Reynolds. Berkeley: University of California Press, 226–241.

Klosko, George. 2004. "Multiple Principles of Political Obligation." *Political Theory* 32: 801–824.

Kripke, Saul. 1980. *Naming and Necessity*. London: Basil Blackwell.

Kropotkin, Peter. 2002. *Anarchism: A Collection of Revolutionary Writings*. Mineola, NY: Dover Publications.

Lauritzen, Paul. 2010. "Torture Warrants and Democratic States: Dirty Hands in an Age of Terror." *Journal of Religious Ethics* 38: 93–112.

Levinas, Emmanuel. 1969. *Totality and Infinity*. Translated by Alphonso Lingis. Pittsburgh, PA: Duquesne University Press.

———. 1998. *Otherwise than Being, or Beyond Essence*. Translated by Alphonso Lingis. Pittsburgh, PA: Duquesne University Press.

———. 2000. *God, Death, and Time*. Translated by Bettina Bergo. Palo Alto, CA: Stanford University Press.

Locke, John. 1988. *Two Treatises of Government*. Cambridge: Cambridge University Press.

Lyotard, Jean-François. 1988. *The Differend*. Translated by Georges Van Den Abbeele. Minneapolis: University of Minnesota Press.

Marrati, Paola. *Genesis and Trace*. Translated by Simon Sparks. Palo Alto, CA: Stanford University Press, 2005.

McCormick, John. 2001. "Derrida on Law; or Poststructuralism Gets Serious." *Political Theory* 29: 395–423.

Morin, Marie-Eve. 2013. "Nancy, Violence and the World." *Parrhesia* 16: 61–70.

Mouffe, Chantal. 2009. *The Democratic Paradox*. London: Verso Press.

Nagel, Thomas. 1972. "War and Massacre." *Philosophy and Public Affairs* 1: 123–144.

Nancy, Jean-Luc. 1991. *The Inoperative Community*. Edited by Peter Connor. Minneapolis: University of Minnesota Press.

———. 1993a. *The Birth to Presence*. Translated by Brian Holmes and others. Palo Alto, CA: Stanford University Press.

———. 1993b. *The Experience of Freedom*. Translated by Bridget McDonald. Palo Alto, CA: Stanford University Press.

———. 1997. *The Sense of the World*. Translated by Jeffrey S. Librett. Minneapolis: University of Minnesota Press.

———. 2000. *Being Singular Plural*. Translated by Robert D. Richardson and Anne E. O'Byrne. Palo Alto, CA: Stanford University Press.

———. 2003. *A Finite Thinking*. Edited by Simon Sparks. Palo Alto, CA: Stanford University Press.

———. 2005. *The Ground of the Image*. Translated by Jeff Fort. New York: Fordham University Press.

———. 2008. "The Being-With of Being-There." Translated by Marie-Eve Morin. *Continental Philosophy Review* 41: 1–15.

Näsström, Sofia. 2007. "The Legitimacy of the People." *Political Theory* 35: 624–658.

Nietzsche, Friedrich. 1954. *Thus Spoke Zarathrustra*. Translatd by Walter Kaufmann. New York: Penguin Books.

———. 1974. *The Gay Science*. Translated by Walter Kaufmann. New York: Vintage Books.

Norris, Andrew. 2000. "Jean-Luc Nancy and the Myth of the Common." *Constellations* 7: 272–295.

Oakeshott, Michael. 1991. *Rationalism in Politics and Other Essays*. Indianapolis, IN: Liberty Fund.

Olafson, Frederick A. 1987. *Heidegger and the Philosophy of Mind*. New Haven, CT: Yale University Press.

———. 1994. "Heidegger a la Wittgenstein or 'Coping' with Professor Dreyfus." *Inquiry* 37: 45–64.

———. 1998. *Heidegger and the Ground of Ethics: A Study of Mitsein*. Cambridge: Cambridge University Press.

Oosterling, Henk. 2005. "From Interest to 'Inter-esse': Jean-Luc Nancy on Deglobalization and Sovereignty." *SubStance* 34: 81–103.

Pitkin, Hannah. 1965. "Obligation and Consent—I." *American Political Science Review* 59: 990–999.

———. 1966. "Obligation and Consent—II." *American Political Science Review* 60: 39–52.

Raffoul, François. 1999. "The Logic of the With: On Nancy's Etre Singulier Pluriel." *Studies in Practical Philosophy* 1: 36–52.

Rawls, John. 1971. *A Theory of Justice*. Cambridge, MA: Harvard University Press.

Raz, Joseph. 1981. "Authority and Consent." *Virginia Law Review*, 67: 103–131.

———. 2009. *The Authority of Law*. Oxford: Oxford University Press.

Ricoeur, Paul. 1992. *History and Truth*. Evanston, IL: Northwestern University Press.

Rorty, Richard. 1998. *Truth and Progress: Philosophical Papers*. Cambridge: Cambridge University Press.

Rosenkrantz, Gary S. 1993. *Haecceity: An Ontological Essay*. Dordrect: Kluwer Academic.

Rousseau, Jean-Jacques. 1978. *On the Social Contract*. Translated by Judith R. Masters. Boston: Bedford/St. Martin's Press.

———. 1994. *The Collected Writings of Rousseau*. Edited by Roger D. Masters and Christopher Kelly. Lebanon, NH: University Press of New England.

Rubenstein, Mary-Jane. 2008. *Strange Wonder: The Closure of Metaphysics and the Opening of Awe*. New York: Columbia University Press.

Russell, Bertrand. 1993. *Introduction to Mathematical Philosophy*. Mineola, NY: Dover Press.

Sarat, Austin, ed. 1999. *The Killing State: Capital Punishment in Law, Politics, and Culture*. New York: Oxford University Press.

Sayre-McCord, Geoffrey, ed. 1988. *Essays on Moral Realism*. Ithaca, NY: Cornell University Press.

Scarre, Geoffrey. 2003. "Corporal Punishment". *Ethical Theory and Moral Practice* 6: 295-316.

Schmitt, Carl. 2005. *Political Theology*. Translated by George Schwab. Chicago: University of Chicago Press.

———. 2008a. *Constitutional Theory*. Translated by Jeffrey Seitzer. Durham, NC: Duke University Press.

———. 2008b. *The Leviathan in the State Theory of Thomas Hobbes*. Translated by George Schwab and Erna Hilfstein. Chicago: University of Chicago Press.

Schwarzmantel, John. 2007. "Community as Communication: Jean-Luc Nancy and 'Being-in-Common.'" *Political Studies* 55: 459–476.

Searle, John R. 1958. "Proper Names." *Mind* 67: 166–173.

Senor, Thomas. 1987. "What If There Are No Political Obligations? A Reply to A. John Simmons." *Philosophy and Public Affairs* 16: 260–268.

Simmons, A. John 1979. *Moral Principles and Political Obligations*. Princeton, NJ: Princeton University Press.

———. 1987. "The Anarchist Position: A Reply to Klosko and Senor." *Philosophy and Public Affairs* 16: 269–279.

———. 1992. *The Lockean Theory of Rights*. Princeton, NJ: Princeton University Press.

———. 1993. *On the Edge of Anarchy*. Princeton, NJ: Princeton University Press.

———. 2001. *Justification and Legitimacy*. Cambridge, MA: Cambridge University Press.

Smith, M. B. E. 1973. "Is There a Prima Facie Obligation to Obey the Law?." *Yale Law Journal* 82: 950–976.

Sontag, Susan. 2003. *Regarding the Pain of Others*. New York: Picador.

Sophocles. 1991. *Sophocles I*. Edited by David Grene and Richard Lattimore. Chicago: University of Chicago Press.

Sorel, George. 1999. *Reflections on Violence*. Edited by Jeremy Jennings. Cambridge, MA: Cambridge University Press.

Strawson, Peter. 1959. *Individuals*. Garden City, NY: Anchor Books.

Taminiaux, Jacques. 1997. *The Thracian Maid and the Professional Thinker*. Albany, NY: State University of New York Press.

Thompson, Dennis. 1980. "Moral Responsibility of Public Officials: The Problem of Many Hands." *American Political Science Review* 74: 905–916.

Thucydides. 1972. *History of the Peloponnesian War*. Translated by Rex Warner. London: Penguin Books.

Villa, Dana. 1996. *Arendt and Heidegger: The Fate of the Political*. Princeton, NJ: Princeton University Press.

Wagner, Andreas. 2006. "Jean-Luc Nancy: A Negative Politics?" *Philosophy and Social Criticism* 32: 89–109.

Walzer, Michael. 1973. "Political Action: The Problem of Dirty Hands." *Philosophy and Public Affairs* 2: 160–180.

———. 2006. *Just and Unjust Wars*. New York: Basic Books.

Watkin, Christopher. 2007. "A Different Alterity: Jean-Luc Nancy's 'Singular Plural.'" *Paragraph* 30: 50–64.

———. 2009. *Phenomenology or Deconstruction?* Edinburgh: Edinburgh University Press.

Weber, Max. 1946. *From Max Weber: Essays in Sociology*. Translated by H. H. Gerth and C. Wright Mills. New York: Oxford University Press.

Wolff, Robert Paul. 1969. "On Violence." *Journal of Philosophy* 66: 601–616

———. 1998. *In Defense of Anarchism*. Berkeley: University of California Press.

Žižek, Slavoj. 2008. *Violence*. London: Profile Books.

INDEX

www.ingramcontent.com/pod-product-compliance
Lightning Source LLC
Chambersburg PA
CBHW030331270326
41926CB00010B/1574